Preface

Aim

This book has been specifically written to meet the requirements of the GNVQ Advanced Business option on Business Law. It provides complete coverage of the BTEC and RSA unit specifications.

Need

GNVQ programmes require option units to be delivered in a relatively short period of time (30-60 hours).This book fulfils the need for course support material that is affordable, concise, straightforward and as jargon-free as possible. Students do not want to cover unnecessary material, so the text is tailored exactly to the course specification (the syllabus guides on page ix indicate which chapters are required by RSA or BTEC only), with each Part corresponding to an Element of the Unit. (For an explanation of the GNVQ structure see Introduction to GNVQ page vii.)

Approach

The book presents the subject in as clear and jargon-free way as possible, using examples that many students may recognise from their everyday lives. Each Part can be studied in any order, although the chapters within each Part are intended to be studied in sequence.

There are numerous activities throughout the text, many of which can be used for generating the necessary evidence for students' portfolios of evidence:

☐ *in-text tasks* that require students to apply the information in that chapter to a practical, business-related problem or question

☐ *group activities* that encourage students to work in groups and role play or represent various parties in legal situations

☐ *discussion topics* that allow students to debate and explore different legal issues, many of which will be directly relevant to their own experiences

☐ *review questions* at the end of each chapter, which allow students to check that they have absorbed and understood the key points of that chapter (answers in Appendix page 272)

☐ *end-of-element assignments* that together cover all the performance criteria of that element

Examples of forms and various types of contract are included in the Appendices for illustration purposes. These are referred to from the text as appropriate.

The BTEC and RSA guides to coverage of performance criteria on pages x to xvi indicates which performance criteria are covered by which of the tasks, activities or assignments.

Lecturers' supplement

A supplement, containing guidance as appropriate to tasks, group activities and assignments, is available free to those lecturers adopting the book as a course text (apply to the publishers on college-headed paper giving details of course and estimated student numbers).

He/She

For ease of expression, 'he' has been used throughout the text to mean both 'he' or 'she'.

Acknowledgements

I would like to thank the following for help in connection with the production of this book:

The Business and Technology Education Council and the Royal Society of Arts Examinations Board for permission to reproduce Business Law unit specifications.

The Controller of Her Majesty's Stationary Office for permission to reproduce tax, company and county court forms.

Perry Group plc for permission to reproduce their standard contract for the sale of second-hand cars.

A catalogue record for this book is available from the British Library

Copyright © Keith Abbott 1994

ISBN 1 85805 090 1

Typeset by Kai Typesetting, Nottingham

Printed by The Guernsey Press Company Ltd
Vale, Guernsey

Contents

Contents

Introduction to GNVQ

General National Vocational Qualifications (GNVQ) are designed to provide a broad foundation education. GNVQs in business are not specifically related to any particular job, industry or vocational area. They cover the full range of business and commercial activities carried on by different types of business organisations ranging from individual traders, such as your local newsagents shop, to multi-national companies, such as ICI.

The GNVQ Advanced Business programme consists of eight mandatory units, three core skill units and four option units (plus another six additional units if you wish to use your single GNVQ as entry to Higher education). Each unit is composed of elements. For BTEC Business Law, there are four elements:

☐ Investigate the legal forms of business organisations (covered in Part 1 Business Organisations of this textbook)

☐ Investigate the legal relationships in business (covered in Part 2 Business Relationships)

☐ Investigate contractual agreements made in business (covered in Part 3 Business Contracts)

☐ Investigate the rights of business customers and consumers (covered in Part 4 Business Consumers).

Each unit specification also describes for each element:

☐ *Performance criteria*

These explain what has to be done in order for a student to claim to be competent

☐ *Range*

This describes the spread of knowledge that must be covered

☐ *Evidence indicators*

These suggest the work that needs to be done to show that the necessary understanding, knowledge and skills have been achieved.

To pass the programme, students will have to show that they have achieved the performance criteria in each of the 15 (or 21) units. This will be done by compiling a portfolio of coursework which will be assessed by tutors as the course progresses. In addition there is an external test for each mandatory unit. Coursework will be graded as 'pass', 'merit' or 'distinction' depending on the degree of competence, initiative, planning and overall achievement.

Since GNVQs are both 'general' and 'vocational', successful students will:

a) Develop skills, knowledge and understanding that will be of real practical value to a wide variety of potential employers, and

b) Obtain a nationally recognised qualification that demonstrates academic achievement and provides an access route to higher education.

Syllabus guide

Range	BTEC	RSA	Chapter
Companies			
Legal status	Y	Y	1
Formation	Y	Y	2
Liquidation	Y	Y	4
Rights and liabilities of shareholders	Y	Y	3, 11
Rights and liabilities of directors	Y	Y	3, 12, 16
Partnerships			
Legal status	Y	Y	1
Formation	Y	Y	5
Dissolution	Y	Y	7
Rights and liabilities of partners	Y	Y	6, 16
Comparison of companies and partnerships	Y	Y	8
Sole traders	Y	Y	1
Companies limited by guarantee	N	Y	10
Worker co-operatives	N	Y	10
Franchises	N	Y	10
Employees	Y	Y	3, 13, 14
Customers	Y	Y	3
Lenders	Y	Y	3, 15
Business liability	Y	Y	9, 16, 17
Business taxation	Y	N	8
Contract			
Formation	Y	N	8, 19, 24
Contract terms	Y	N	21
Mistake, Misrepresentation, Illegality	Y	N	20
Termination of contract	Y	N	22
Remedies for breach	Y	N	23
Sale and supply of goods	Y	Y	25
Trade descriptions	N	Y	25
Consumer credit	Y	Y	26
Consumer protection	Y	Y	25
Data protection	Y	Y	27
Fair trading	N	Y	28
Consumer organisations			
(including pressure groups)	N	Y	28
Regulatory bodies	N	Y	28
Citizens charter	N	Y	28
Competition policy (United Kingdom)	Y	Y	29
Competition policy			
(European Union)	Y	Y	30
Resolution of disputes	Y	Y	31

[Y indicates topic is required for particular board, N that topic is not part of that board's syllabus]

BTEC and RSA guides to coverage of performance criteria

The following tables indicate how the assignments, tasks and group activities cover the performance criteria and evidence indicators for the BTEC and RSA syllabuses.

The performance criteria and evidence indicators are listed in the left-hand column. The Assignment column contains the number of the assignment which covers the criteria indicated.

The Task and Group Activity columns indicate the chapter numbers as well as task or group activity numbers. For example '2.1' in the Task column indicates Chapter 2 Task 1 covers that particular performance criteria. '2.1' in the Group Activity column would indicate Chapter 2 Group Activity 1 covers the criteria in question.

BTEC guide to coverage of performance criteria

9.1 Investigate the legal forms of business organisations

Performance Criteria and Evidence Indicators	Assignment	Task	Group activity
9.1.1 Legal characteristics of business organisations are compared	1	1.2, 11.1	
9.1.2 Legal process of formation and dissolution is outlined	2	2.1	2.1, 7.1
9.1.3 Reasons for choice of legal status by a business organisation are explained	1	8.1, 9.2	
Evidence indicator. A case study of business organisations which compares the legal characteristics of types of business organisations, identifies the legal structures and suggests reasons for the choice of that structure.	1, 2		

9.2 Investigate the legal relationships in business

Performance Criteria and Evidence Indicators	Assignment	Task	Group activity
9.2.1 Rights and duties of key parties are identified	3, 4	3.1, 3.2, 12.1 14.1, 15.1	3.1, 4.1, 13.1 14.1, 16.1
9.2.2 The inter-relationship between stakeholders is explained	3, 4	3.2, 5.1, 6.1 12.1, 13.1 16.1, 17.1	3.1, 4.1, 13.1 16.1
9.2.3 The nature of liability to others for wrongful acts is described	3, 4	6.1, 12.1 13.1, 16.1	3.1, 4.1, 14.1 16.1
Evidence indicator. An investigation and explanation of the implications for those involved, of a range of wrongful acts carried out by a business.	3, 4		

9.3 Investigate contractual arrangements made in business

Performance Criteria and Evidence Indicators	Assignment	Task	Group activity
9.3.1 The nature and scope of contractual agreements are described		21.1, 24.1	9.1, 10.1 21.1, 21.2 22.1
9.3.2 The legal requirements of a valid contract are identified	5, 6	19.1	
9.3.3 The effects and implications of defects in contractual agreements are explained		20.1, 20.2 22.1, 23.1 23.2, 24.2	
Evidence indicator. An analysis of one example of a standard form contract and one negotiated agreement used in business. The examples will have been chosen by the student and used to demonstrate their ability to identify and illustrate the legal requirements of a valid contract.	5, 6		25.1

9.4 Investigate the rights of business customers and consumers

Performance Criteria and Evidence Indicators	Assignment	Task	Group activity
9.4.1 The nature and scope of consumer protection is investigated	8	25.1, 28.1 30.1, 31.1	
9.4.2 Key rights of consumers are identified	7, 8	26.1, 28.1 31.1	26.1, 27.1 28.1, 28.2
9.4.3 Procedures for dispute settlement between customer and business are described	7, 8	28.1, 31.1	
Evidence indicator. A case study containing consumer problems which the student will identify, suggest solutions to and explain the procedure to be followed to attain a successful outcome	7, 8		

RSA guide to coverage of performance criteria

10.1 Investigate the implications of different legal status for business organisations

Performance Criteria and Evidence Indicators	Assign-ment	Task	Group activity
10.1.1 Alternative forms of legal status for business organisa-tions are explained		1.2	
10.1.2 The process by which legal status is established is described			2.1
10.1.3 The purpose of relevant forms of business documen-tation is explained		2.1, 9.1	
10.1.4 The differing rights and responsibilities of key players in business organisa-tions with different legal status are compared		3.1, 3.2 5.1, 6.1 8.1, 15.1 16.1, 17.1	3.1, 13.1 14.1 16.1
10.1.5 The ways in which liability is affected by differing legal status is explained		3.2, 5.1 9.2, 12.1 13.1, 16.1	4.1, 14.1 16.1
10.1.6 The process of dissolution of business with different legal status is explained			7.1
10.1.7 Recommendations for the legal status of a given busi-ness are proposed	1	9.1	
Evidence indicator. A review of the implications of different legal status of business organisations, leading to recommendations for the legal status for a business in a given case study. The recommendations should be justified.	1		

10.2 Investigate legislation protecting customers and consumers

Performance Criteria and Evidence Indicators	Assign-ment	Task	Group activity
10.2.1 The main features of key legislation are described and their impact on business practice is assessed		25.1, 28.1	27.1
10.2.2 Factors encouraging competition and benefits to customers and consumers are assessed		30.1	
10.2.3 The role of organisations protecting and representing customers is explained		31.1	28.1 28.2
10.2.4 Examples of customer and consumer rights in given business situations are provided	5	31.1	25.1 26.1 27.1 28.2
Evidence indicator. A survey of the legislation protecting customers and consumers supported by two case studies explaining customer and consumer rights in given situations.	7, 8		

Table of cases

Part 1
Business organisations

Element 9.1 Investigate the legal forms of business organisations

This part of the book introduces and describes the main features of companies, partnerships and sole traders. It looks at how these business organisations are formed, and how and why the life of the business might come to an end. It outlines the main consequences that follow from choosing to trade as a company or a partnership, both for the owner and other people, such as lenders and suppliers, who have an interest in the success or failure of the business. Finally it contains some practical advice on the alternatives to starting a new business from scratch, for example purchasing an existing business or entering into a franchise agreement.

On successful completion of Part 1 Activities and review questions, students will appreciate the main implications of the different legal structures for businesses (performance criteria 1), know how the different business types are formed and dissolved (performance criteria 2) and be able to recommend the structure best suited to the requirements of a particular business (performance criteria 3). The end of part assignments will generate the evidence required for your portfolio of coursework.

BTEC guide to coverage of performance criteria

The performance criteria and evidence indicators are listed in the left-hand column. The Assignment column contains the number of the assignment which covers the criteria indicated.

The Task and Group Activity columns indicate the chapter numbers as well as task or group activity numbers. For example '2.1' in the Task column indicates Chapter 2 Task 1 covers that particular performance criteria. '2.1' in the Group Activity column would indicate Chapter 2 Group Activity 1 covers the criteria in question.

9.1 Investigate the legal forms of business organisations

Performance Criteria and Evidence Indicators	Assignment	Task	Group activity
9.1.1 Legal characteristics of business organisations are compared	1	1.2, 11.1	
9.1.2 Legal process of formation and dissolution is outlined	2	2.1	2.1, 7.1
9.1.3 Reasons for choice of legal status by a business organisation are explained	1	8.1, 9.2	
Evidence indicator. A case study of business organisations which compares the legal characteristics of types of business organisations, identifies the legal structures and suggests reasons for the choice of that structure.	1, 2		

1

Types of business structure

For many people setting up and developing their own business is the most rewarding way of earning a living. Running any business is complex and time consuming and new owners often find it difficult to carry out all the management roles. For example, the owner may be experienced in production and sales, but have little knowledge of business administration, financial control, employment law and so on. Before considering the legal framework for a new business the entrepreneur must carefully consider whether he or she has the energy, self-confidence and all round ability to manage a business. Only then should time and money be spent on the technical aspects of starting a business.

This chapter gives a brief introduction to the different legal frameworks for business.

1 Business structures

Having decided to start a business the entrepreneur must decide on a structure for that business. The main possibilities are:

1. *Sole trader*

   This is the simplest form of business and there are few formalities to be complied with. The individual has the full responsibility for running the business and takes any profits. He will also be personally liable for income tax, value added tax, capital gains tax and for all the debts incurred in running the business. If these debts cannot be paid one or more of the creditors may seek to have him declared bankrupt. Sole traders often trade under their own name, with their own money or with relatively small sums borrowed from banks or other lenders. The fact that the business is a 'sole trader' does not mean that the trader cannot employ other people, it means that it is structured as a business with only one owner.

   Since there is no requirement for registration by sole traders and many do not have sufficient turnover to necessitate registration for VAT (the 1994/95 VAT threshold is £45,000 sales), it is difficult to obtain accurate statistics on the numbers of, and business activities of, sole traders. There was a major government report (The Bolton Report 1971) which found that very few manufacturing firms are run by sole traders, since the capital needed for such firms is usually beyond the reach of one individual. Outside the manufacturing sector sole traders accounted for 46% of the firms with fewer than 200 employees. When companies and partnerships were also considered the Bolton Report concluded that approximately 85% of businesses were controlled and owned by one or two people.

2. *Partnership*

This is a business with two or more owners (usually up to 20, except for certain professional partnerships such as accountants and solicitors where there is no limit), who share in the management, profits and losses. Like a sole trader, a partnership does not have a legal existence separate from the partners. Even if the partnership operates under a business name which is different from the names of the partners, this is only a convenient way of collectively describing the individuals, since all rights and liabilities attach to individual partners.

No formalities are required to create a partnership. In fact when two or more people carry on a business together the law will regard them as a partnership, even if there is no apparent agreement between them. Of course in most cases where people take a conscious decision to set up as partners, they will enter into a written agreement dealing with, for example, provision of capital, division of profits and losses, pension arrangements and so on.

If all small businesses are taken into account partnerships are much less common than sole traders or limited companies. However, in the financial services sector and the professions, for example solicitors, accountants, auctioneers and estate agents, partnership is the usual form of business structure.

3. *Limited company*

The main feature of limited companies that distinguishes them from sole traders and partnerships is that they have a legal existence completely separate from that of their owners (also known as shareholders or members). Since 1992 it has been possible to have a company with only one member. Previously the minimum number was two.

The law relating to limited companies is mainly contained in Acts of Parliament (statutes). The main statutes are the Companies Acts of 1985 and 1989. There are many other relevant statutes, for example the Insolvency Act 1986, the Company Securities (Insider Dealing) Act 1985 and the Company Directors Disqualification Act 1986, but you are not required to be familiar with them.

Despite the recession of the early 1990s new company registrations have continued to increase. Liquidations have also risen sharply. The figures in the following table relate to the 12 month period from 1st April until 31st March in each case.

Date	New registrations	Liquidations
1987/88	71,169	13,809
1988/89	78,006	13,863
1989/90	79,632	15,707
1990/91	89,823	21,825
1991/92	106,548	27,322
1992/93	108,800	28,744

 Task 1

As a student you will carry out some activities in groups and others as an individual. You will have noticed advantages and disadvantages of each method of working. Imagine that you are starting a small business. You will be coaching tennis and restringing tennis and squash racquets. What are the advantages and disadvantages of working with someone else? For the purpose of this task set out only the practical and personal issues, not the legal consequences of working together or on your own.

2 The consequences of incorporation as a limited company

Once a company has come into existence by registration under the Companies Acts it is regarded by the law as a legal person with rights and liabilities very similar to those of any natural person. The process of becoming a limited company is called incorporation.

The case that established that companies are legally separate from their owners was SALOMON v SALOMON LIMITED (1897). In this case Salomon formed a limited company with the other members of his family. He then sold his business to the company for £39,000. The company paid him by giving him 20,001 shares and £10,000 of debentures (documents acknowledging that Salomon had lent the company money and was entitled to repayment of that money prior to the creditors if the company went into liquidation). The balance was payable in cash. In total the company issued 20,007 shares, six other members of Salomon's family held one share each. About a year after its formation the company went into liquidation. The assets were worth about £10,000, but there were creditors with debts of about £7,500. The issue was whether Salomon, in his capacity as debenture holder, should have the £7,500, or whether it should go to the creditors. The creditors claimed that they should have priority because Salomon and the company were basically the same person. The House of Lords (the final court of appeal) held that Salomon and his company were separate legal persons, the company had been validly formed and that there had been no fraud on the creditors. Salomon was therefore entitled to the remaining assets.

The main rights and liabilities of companies that follow from the fact that companies are separate legal persons are set out below:

a) *Property.* A company can own property, land, motor vehicles, bank accounts and so on. These will be held in the company's own name, with no reference to the names of any members. Even though the members can be said to own the company they do not own the company's property, nor are they regarded as having any share in the ownership of its property.

b) *Contracts.* Since a company is a legal person, contracts will be made in the company's name, for example contracts to buy or sell goods, employ staff, or almost anything else that a natural person could contract to do. If there is a dispute the company can sue or be sued on the contract. Any damages (ie. compensation for breach of contract) will be paid out of or into the company's funds. Damages are not paid by or to the members, since they are not party to any company contracts. Similarly company debts are owed by the company not by the members.

c) *Continuity.* Members of companies own shares. They may sell their shares (either privately or through the Stock Exchange)to other persons without affecting the continuity of the existence of the company as a legal person. Even if all of a company's members were to be killed in a car accident the company would still be alive. In this case the shares of the deceased would pass to their personal representatives, then in due course to the people specified in their wills.

d) *Liability for negligence and other wrongful acts.* If an officer or employee of a company injures another person through negligence while acting in the course of his employment, the company will be vicariously liable for the employee's wrongful act. This means that although the injured person can sue the employee to seek compensation for their loss, they may also sue the company, since although the company, its managers, or its members are not at fault, the law tries to ensure that persons who are injured by employees have access to compensation.

3 Limited liability

a) *The company's liability.* All companies are liable without limit for their own debts and must pay their debts as long as they have assets to do so. If the company cannot pay its debts its creditors may commence proceedings to wind up the company.

b) *The members' liability.* The terms 'limited company' and 'limited liability' refer to the fact that members' liability is limited. The creditors cannot look to the private wealth of the members to satisfy claims against the company, even if the company is being wound up and there are no company assets from which they can be paid.

c) The vast majority of companies are *'companies limited by shares'*. This means that the liability of each member is limited to the amount he has paid or agreed to pay for his shares. If the shares are fully paid for (which will usually be the case) the member will lose all of the money paid for the shares if the company goes into insolvent liquidation, ie. if, on winding up, its liabilities exceed its assets. If the shares have been partly paid for, the member can be called upon to pay the balance of the agreed price, but no more.

d) Once a person becomes a member he will not normally be able to get his money back from the company, because the money paid constitutes the capital of the company. It acts both as a base from which the company builds its business and as a guarantee fund to which the creditors can look for payment of their debts. Members can however sell their shares, either privately or on the Stock Exchange. When they do so the shares are unlikely to have the same market price as at the time of purchase. The member will therefore make a profit or loss on the transaction.

4 The veil of incorporation

The fact that the separate corporate personality of the company prevents outsiders from taking action against the members (even though outsiders can find out who the members are and how many shares they hold) has led to comparison with a veil. The corporate personality is the veil and the members are shielded behind this *'veil of incorporation'*. There are however a number of situations when the law will lift the veil of incorporation either to allow an outsider to proceed against an individual member, or to regard several companies in the same group as one legal person for a particular purpose. Some examples are:

a) *Fraudulent trading.* If in the course of a winding up it appears that the business has been carried on with intent to defraud creditors, the court may order the persons responsible (who may be members i.e. share owners, directors or employees) to make a contribution to the company's assets. These assets will then be distributed to creditors in accordance with rules set out in the Companies Acts.

b) *Abuse of corporate personality.* This would occur if, for example, a person formed a company specifically to avoid obligations entered into as an individual. For example, in GILFORD MOTOR COMPANY v HORNE (1933) an employee promised that after the termination of his employment he would not solicit his former employer's customers. Soon after the termination of his employment he formed a company, which then sent out circulars to the customers of his former employer. The court lifted the veil of incorporation, granting an injunction which prevented both the former employee and his company from distributing the circulars, even though the company was not party to the original promise.

c) *Holding and subsidiary companies.* Modern business organisations are rarely constituted as one single limited company. Usually there will be a number of companies organised as a group consisting of a holding company and several subsidiaries. In order that the financial position of the group can be properly assessed from its financial statements, for certain purposes in relation to the accounts, the companies in a group must be treated as one.

5 Public and private companies

a) A company registered under the Companies Act may either be a public company or a private company. In mid-1992 there were approximately 13,300 public companies registered in the UK and 1,100,000 private companies.

b) *Private companies*

i) These are often small family businesses set up with a few thousand pounds of capital. Private companies are prohibited from issuing shares to the public and must therefore obtain their funds directly from their members, other individual lenders, banks or other financial institutions. Persons who lend to private companies will usually require security for their loan, for example a charge on the owner's house. The advantage of limited liability will not really help the owner, since if the company cannot pay its debts the lenders will enforce their security by selling the house to satisfy their debts. Small new companies may also encounter trading difficulties. They will need time to establish that they are credit worthy, they may not have the buying power to benefit from volume discounts and if debtors (often larger companies) are slow to pay, the adverse effect on cash flow may seriously damage the company.

ii) The advantage of private companies is that they are able to retain their private nature by refusing to allow a sale of shares, for instance when the purchaser is thought by the company to be suitable (this can be a disadvantage for a member who wishes to sell shares if there is not a buyer who is acceptable to the directors). This restriction on the right to transfer shares ensures that the original members are protected from take-over attempts. Private companies do not have to publish their accounts in as much detail as public companies. This slightly reduces the administrative burden and the extent to which they are subject to scrutiny from competitors.

iii) Private company status is suitable for most types of business, whether manufacturing, trading, retail, transport and so on. However, it will not be appropriate where the nature of the business inevitably requires large sums of capital, for example oil companies, banks, airlines, chemicals and pharmaceuticals.

c) *Public companies*

i) The main reason for becoming a public company rather than a private company is that a public company can raise money by issuing shares to the public, thus enabling it to access an almost unlimited supply of funds. From the members' point of view the advantage of holding shares in a public company is that the shares may always be sold or purchased on the Stock Exchange or Unlisted Securities Market. A disadvantage, certainly for the individual investor as opposed to an institutional shareholder, is that he will have virtually no influence on any of the decisions taken by that public company. A disadvantage for the directors is that because they lose the power to determine who shall be members, there is a risk that they will lose their jobs if there is a successful take-over bid.

ii) The large size of most public companies gives them a competitive advantage in the marketplace. They can benefit from economies of scale in the purchasing, production and distribution of goods. They are also more likely to have the funds for new product development or expansion into new markets. Public companies will be organised as groups with holding and subsidiary companies. Many will have overseas subsidiaries. Large multi-nationals such as British Petroleum have hundreds of subsidiaries operating throughout the world. Almost all 'household name' companies will be public companies, for example Boots, Tesco, Imperial Chemical Industries and British Airways. Hundreds of public companies are listed on the financial pages of the national daily newspapers.

d) There are well over 50 legal differences between public and private companies. They relate to constitutional documents, share capital, payment of dividends to members, proceedings at meetings, publicity and accounts and so on. The most important are as follows:

   i) A public company must have an authorised capital of at least £50,000. There is no minimum for a private company.

   ii) A public company's name must end with the words 'public limited company' which can be abbreviated to 'plc'. A private company's name must end with 'limited' which can be abbreviated to 'Ltd'.

   iii) A public company must have at least two members (in practice most public companies have thousands of members) whereas a private company need only have one member. Until 1992 private companies also had to have two members, but this was changed by the Companies (Single Member Private Limited Companies) Regulations 1992 which were passed to implement the European Community Twelfth Directive.

   iv) A public company must have at least two directors. A private company need only have one.

   v) To retain the private nature of a private company its articles (one of the constitutional documents of the company) will restrict the right to transfer the company's shares. Usually the restriction will be an absolute right given to the directors to refuse to register any transfer of the company's shares.

   vi) A private company may start trading as soon as it has been incorporated. A public company must first obtain from the Registrar a Certificate of Compliance that proves the company has met the capital requirements of public companies. This is known as a *trading certificate*.

Task 2

Carry out the necessary research in your college library and list ten further differences between public and private companies.

 Discussion topic

What practical and legal problems and challenges will be faced by a company as it grows in size? What will the directors have to consider if they want to convert to public company status?

 Review questions *(answers page 272)*

1. If a company shareholder dies how does this affect the existence of the company?
2. What is meant by 'limited liability'?
3. What is meant by 'vicarious liability'?
4. In what way is liability limited in respect of the debts of a company?
5. What is the legal effect of the Certificate of Incorporation?
6. Give one example of a situation when the court will lift the veil of incorporation.
7. What is the usual method by which a private company will restrict the right to transfer its shares?

2
Forming a company

Persons who wish to go into business will not necessarily start a new company from scratch. They may prefer to buy an existing company or unincorporated business, or they may decide to buy a 'ready-made company'. These possibilities are considered in Chapter 9. This Chapter explains the basic procedure for the formation of a new limited company and deals with some of the legal issues faced by new companies.

1 Forming a new company

Forming a new company completely from scratch is quite a complex operation and the persons concerned will need the help of solicitors or company formation agents. The basic procedure involves sending the following documents to the Registrar of Companies:

a) *Memorandum of Association.* This document sets out:

    i)   the company's name

    ii) intended address of its registered office

    iii) its objects (the objects clause sets out the activities that the company may engage in)

    iv) a statement that the liability of the members is limited

    v)   the amount of share capital registered on incorporation

    vi) witnessed signatures of the first members (known as subscribers), and

    vii) the number of shares taken by each subscriber.

    The Memorandum is one of the company's constitutional documents. Its basic purpose is to present the company to the outside world.

b) *Articles of Association.* These are the internal regulations of the company. There are usually about 110 articles dealing with, for example, the issue and transfer of shares, directors' powers, proceedings at meetings and the payment of dividends. The articles must be signed by the subscribers to the memorandum. A company may adopt Table A, which is a 'model' set of articles contained in regulations published in 1985. Table A will automatically apply to a company if its own articles do not exclude or modify Table A.

c) *Form 10* (see Appendix A). This gives details of the first directors and company secretary, i.e. their names, addresses, dates of birth, nationalities, occupations and details of other directorships held within the last five years. It will also give the address of the registered office.

d) *A statutory declaration* (i.e. a formal statement required by the Companies Act) made by the solicitor engaged in the formation of the company or by one of the first directors or secretary, stating that all the legal requirements relating to incorporation have been complied with.

e) *A statement of capital.* Tax known as capital duty is charged at 1% on the issued capital of a new company.

f) *Registration fee* of £50.

2 Choosing a company name

a) Persons forming a company may not be able to have the name they want for the company. It is therefore very important to ensure that the name is acceptable before printing the new company's notepaper, order forms and so on.

b) The Registrar may reject a proposed name for the following reasons:

   i) It is the same as (or very similar to) the name of an existing company.

   ii) It wrongfully gives the impression that the company is connected with Her Majesty's Government or a local authority.

   iii) It wrongfully uses one of a large number of sensitive words or expressions, for example 'international', 'insurance', 'co-operative', 'chartered' or 'trust'.

3 Business names

a) A company may chose to use a business name that is not the same as its registered name, for example *'Arthur Brown Cars Limited'* may prefer to use *'AB Cars'* as a business name. A notice must be prominently displayed at all locations to which customers or suppliers have access showing the exact name of the limited company and the address to which any legal documents may be sent.

b) Partnerships and sole traders often trade under their own names, for example this firm of estate agents trades in Dartmouth, Devon

c) A partnership or sole trader may also trade under a business name rather than the actual names of the individuals. If they do, a notice must be displayed at all locations to which customers or suppliers have access showing the names and addresses of all the proprietors of the business.

d) It is illegal to *'pass off'* your business as someone elses, whether intentionally or otherwise. For example, even if your name is 'Sainsbury' you will be likely to attract a passing off action from

15

the well known supermarket chain if you opened a supermarket and called it 'Sainsburys'.

4 Stationery

a) A company's letter heading, written orders for goods and services, and other documents must include:

   i)   Its business name (if it uses one).

   ii) The full name of the company including 'limited', 'Ltd', 'public limited company', or 'plc' as appropriate.

   iii) The business address in Great Britain where any documents relating to the company may be served.

   iv) All the directors' names or none of them.

   v) The address of the registered office, its registered number and place of registration.

b) If the business is registered for value added tax it must show the VAT number on invoices and credit notes. It is optional on other stationery.

c) Other information is normally included but is not compulsory, for example telephone and fax numbers.

 Task 1

Design a company letter-heading for Arthur Brown Cars Limited, trading as 'AB Cars', VAT registration number 12345678. The company's business is second-hand car sales.

5 Trading

a) A private company may start trading as soon as it receives its Certificate of Incorporation. The issue of a *Certificate of Incorporation* is *'conclusive evidence'* that the formalities of registration have been complied with. 'Conclusive evidence' means that even if it is subsequently discovered that the formalities of registration were not in fact complied with the registration will not be invalidated. The reason for this is that once a company has started business and entered into contracts, it would be unreasonable for either side to avoid the contract because of a procedural defect in registration.

b) A public company cannot commence business until it has obtained a Certificate of Compliance with the capital requirements of public companies, known as a trading certificate.

c) If, during the setting up of a company, any person makes a contract *'on behalf of'* the proposed company then, subject to any agreement to the contrary, he will be personally liable on the contract. It is not possible for the company to sue or be sued on the contract since it did not exist when the contract was made.

d) A document or contract will be executed (ie. signed) by a company if it is signed by two directors or a director and the company secretary, provided it is expressed to be executed by the company.

6 The first meeting

Soon after the formation of a new company, the company will need to meet to:

a) appoint additional or new directors and the company secretary

b) appoint auditors

c) decide the date for the financial year end

d) determine the banking arrangements

e) allot shares and approve transfers of subscribers' shares as appropriate

f) decide the address of the registered office

g) make arrangements for keeping the statutory books (ie. the company records required by the law) such as the register of members, register of directors, and the minute book of company general meetings.

 Group activity 1

Prepare an agenda for the first meeting of 'College Business Ltd'. This new company has been set up by four college students. Their business idea is to provide a consultancy service to college managers, who they believe are sometimes out of touch with the needs, views and feelings of 16 to 20 year olds. They believe that if colleges take their advice they will provide a better, more student-centred service.

Your agenda will probably include the above formal matters, but you may also wish to include some practical matters that will need to be dealt with by the new business.

 **Review questions** *(answers page 273)*

1. What are the main changes that would need to be made to the Memorandum and Articles of a company that changes from private to public?

2. Where must a company publish its name?

3. What is meant by 'passing off'?

4. Who is liable to pay for goods that are ordered 'on behalf of' a company that is about to be formed?

5. What is the difference between a business name and a company name?

6. Which documents need to be sent to the Registrar of Companies before a new company can be formed from scratch?

7. Explain the main purposes of:

    a)   The Memorandum of Association.

    b)   The Articles of Association.

8. What important procedures must be completed at the first meeting after a company has been formed?

9. Must a company list the names of its directors on its notepaper?

3

Who are the key players?

The relationship of a company to the local community, its members, directors, employees, financiers and creditors is discussed in more detail in Part 2 *Business Relationships*. This chapter gives a broad overview of the key people involved with companies.

1 Members

a) A company's membership will consist of individuals and other companies. If a company is a member of another company it will appoint a natural person to represent it at company meetings. A person may become a member by subscribing to the company for shares when it makes a new issue or by purchasing existing shares from a member who wishes to sell.

b) Every company must keep a *register of members* at its registered office. (Often the registered office is the office of its accountants or solicitors, rather than its main place of business). The register of members contains basic information about each member, in particular the name and address and the number of shares held. Company members and the public are entitled to inspect the register of members.

c) There are many different types of member, for example small private shareholders, large institutional shareholders and holding companies. A holding company is one which normally holds the majority of shares in another company (its subsidiary). It can therefore control the composition of the board of directors of the subsidiary and proceedings at its meetings.

d) People also have different motives for becoming members, especially of public companies. Some people purchase shares to make a quick speculative profit and sell again within a few days (or even hours) if their objective has been achieved. Other investors will look to hold shares for a long period of time, hoping to receive regular dividend income (ie. distributions of the company's profits) and a capital profit as the share price rises.

e) Every member is entitled to vote at company meetings, the number of votes being the same as the number of shares held. By passing resolutions at meetings the members can, at least in theory, make key decisions, for example who shall be the directors of the company, whether to change the company's constitution, and whether to commence winding up. In practice so few members attend meetings, especially meetings of public companies, that a block of as little as 5% of the shares can be sufficient to control the company.

2 Directors

a) Since a company is not a natural person it can only act through human agents. The persons who manage the company are called directors. The powers given to them will be set out in the company's Articles of Association, and will usually include a power to delegate any of their powers to a managing director.

b) Directors may be appointed and removed by a simple majority vote of the members, known as an ordinary resolution. Since they are in a position of trust where they control large sums of other peoples' money, and in a position where it is relatively easy to abuse this trust, directors are subject to a wide variety of statutory and non-statutory rules which try to ensure that they do not abuse their position. For example, directors must not normally accept a loan from the company.

c) When they are appointed, directors do not automatically become employees of the company, although it is usual for full-time directors, such as the managing director, to be given service contracts. Many large companies have part-time directors, known as non-executive directors, who act as advisers rather than full-time managers.

d) A private company need only have one director, but a public company must have at least two. In practice public companies usually have boards of 15 to 25 directors.

3 The secretary

a) Every company must have a secretary. In small private companies this will often be the company's solicitor or accountant acting on an occasional basis. In large companies the secretary is likely to be a full-time employee, possibly supported by several assistants.

b) The secretary is the chief administrative officer of the company and on matters of administration has authority to make contracts on behalf of the company, for example purchasing office furniture and hiring office staff. The secretary cannot, however, bind the company on a trading contract.

 Task 1

Make a list of the things that you think would be part of the day-to-day work of a company secretary. What sort of contracts do you think the secretary should have authority to make? What contracts should be beyond the secretary's powers?

4 Employees

a) There is a massive quantity of legislation concerned with employment law, dealing with, for example, the contract of employment, dismissal and redundancy, sex and race discrimination, maternity rights, trade unions, health and safety at work and so on.

b) Although most employees are far more dependent on the company than its members, they are not part of the company in the same way as the members or officers (ie. directors and secretary). Company law is almost completely silent on the rights and interests of employees, preferring to regard them basically as outsiders with whom the company has a contract. This is not the case throughout Europe. Germany, for example, has long had representation of employees at board level. There is also a draft European Community Directive, the Fifth Directive, which when implemented will require public companies employing more than 1,000 people to have some form of employee participation in company decision making. Companies are likely to have a choice between employee representation at board level or by means of a Works Council. The draft Fifth Directive was published in 1972 and has been revised several times. It is opposed by the current Conservative Government and by many trade unions who prefer to trust existing trade union machinery. Change is therefore unlikely in the near future.

c) Some of the main company law provisions relating to employees are as follows:

   i)   The directors have a duty to have regard to the interests of employees as well as the interests of members.

   ii) In a winding up, employees rank before trade creditors for arrears of wages up to a maximum of £800. Together with several other types of creditor, for example the Customs and Excise for VAT, they are 'preferential creditors'.

   iii) The company may lend money to employees to enable them to purchase company shares as part of an employees' share scheme. There are a number of exceptions, but the general rule is that a company may not lend money to anyone to enable them to purchase its own shares.

 Discussion topic

Why is it normally undesirable to allow a company to:

   i)   buy back its own shares from members, or

   ii) lend money to a person to buy the company's shares?

5 Auditors

a) Every company must have an auditor or auditors. The first auditors are appointed by the directors, thereafter the *auditors are normally appointed by the company at its Annual General Meeting.*

b) Auditors check that the company has kept proper accounting records and whether the accounts comply with the requirements of the Companies Acts and give a *true and fair* view of the company's affairs. Having done this the auditors report to the members on the accounts. If the auditors are of the opinion that proper accounting records have not been kept, or that proper assistance has not been given to them for the purposes of the audit, or that the accounts are not consistent with the accounting records from which they have been compiled, these facts will be stated in the report.

c) Many companies employ a firm of accountants both to advise and work for the company throughout the year and to act as the company's auditors. In theory the functions of company accountant and company auditor are quite different. The accountant is a contractor working for the company. The accountant's function is to do as asked, there is no right to make enquiries of the company. The auditor reports to the members, enabling them to judge how the company is being run by the directors. The auditor is independent of the directors, although initially chosen by them. Auditors must be members of a Recognised Supervisory Body, for example the Institute of Chartered Accountants, the Chartered Association of Certified Accountants or the Association of Authorised Public Accountants.

d) Auditors may be removed from office by the company (by a simple majority vote) but auditors are entitled to speak on a resolution to remove them. They may also make a written statement which the company must send to all members.

6 Liquidators, receivers and administrators

a) A *liquidator* is a person appointed either by the court (if it is a compulsory liquidation) or by the members or creditors (if it is a members' or creditors' voluntary liquidation). A liquidator is the person appointed to bring the company's life to an end, usually because it is unable to pay its debts. The liquidator's basic duty is to collect together all the assets of the company, convert them to cash, pay the creditors (so far as is possible) and distribute the remainder (if any) to the members. A liquidator must be a member of a recognised professional body, for example the Institute of Chartered Accountants.

b) A *receiver* is a person appointed by someone who has lent money to a company (usually a bank). They will be appointed when loan interest has not been paid or when some other key term of the loan agreement has been broken by the company. The loan agreement will have given the lender a mortgage (also known as a charge) over some or all of the company's assets (including the stock-in-trade). The receiver's basic task is to sell the assets subject to the charge and repay the lender out of the sale proceeds. Any surplus will be returned to the company. The appointment of a receiver does not necessarily mean the end of the company's life, but if the charge in question covers a substantial proportion of the company's assets the company will usually be forced into liquidation.

c) An *administrator* is a person appointed by the court, on the application of the company, its directors or its creditors. An appointment will be made when the company cannot pay its debts and the court considers that an administrator may be able to achieve the survival of the whole or part of the company (possibly by securing the agreement of creditors to take only a proportion of what is owed to them) or a more advantageous sale of the company's assets than in a liquidation. The administrator will take control of all of the company's property and manage its affairs with a view to achieving the purpose for which the administration order was made.

7 Lenders

a) Most businesses require more finance than their owners can afford or are prepared to provide. Even if equipment is leased or bought on hire purchase, new businesses are likely to need to borrow, both to start the business and to finance expansion.

b) Lenders will be very concerned with the quality of the managers, their motivation, their business skills, their track record and so on. They will look at the level of personal finance the owners are putting into the business, the viability of their business plan, and their proposals for repayment of the loan.

c) In particular they will be concerned to take security for their loan. This will be either a fixed charge (i.e. a mortgage) over the company's land, or a floating charge over the company's other assets or both. The meanings of fixed charge and floating charge are discussed in Chapter 15.

d) Since members have limited liability lenders cannot proceed against them if loans are not repaid. However in many cases this apparent advantage of limited liability does not really exist, because as a condition of granting the loan, the lender may insist on a personal guarantee by owner directors, secured by a mortgage on their houses.

 **Group activity 1**

The directors of College Business Ltd wish to borrow £10,000 to get the new business started. Split your group (ideally about six of you) into directors and bankers. Directors write a summary business plan and bankers write a list of lending criteria. Then role play the presentation of the business plan. The bankers should ask appropriate questions and at the end of the presentation they should decide how much to lend to College Business Ltd and subject to what conditions (if any).

8 Trade creditors

a) Since trade creditors have no access to the private assets of members, their protection is one of the main purposes of company law and there are many complex rules designed to protect them.

b) There are three main methods of creditor protection:

i) The *publicity* which accompanies registration enables potential creditors to find out basic information about the company before granting credit, although most creditors do not take advantage of this opportunity. A longstanding and simple example is the requirement that 'limited' or 'public limited company' is the last word of the name. This is to warn creditors of their lack of access to members' private assets. Recently the Government has been concerned that late payment by large companies is damaging Britain's small firms, because of the effect it has on their cash flow. The Department of Trade and Industry has therefore proposed a change in the law which will require large companies (defined as companies having sales in excess of £11.2m or more than 250 employees) to state in their accounts the average number of days taken to pay creditors.

ii) There are many rules which protect the *capital fund* of the company, since this is the fund on which creditors rely for payment. Capital may of course be lost in the ordinary course of business, but it must not, for example, be given back to members as dividends. The rule is that dividends can only be paid out of profits.

iii) The rules on *liquidation and receivership* allow creditors to have a more active say in the company's affairs if their debts have not been paid. However, unlike members, creditors are not part of the company and until times of difficulty they play no part in running the company.

 Task 2

You are a mail order supplier of office furniture. You have just received an order from a company called 'College Business Ltd' for £1,800 worth of desks, chairs, filing cabinets and so on. You have never heard of this company. Write back to the company informing them that either:

i) their order has been accepted,

ii) the order has been rejected, or

iii) asking for further information and/or imposing conditions for the sale.

If you wanted to find out about College Business Ltd without asking the company itself, how would you go about this?

 Review questions *(answers page 275)*

1. How are company directors appointed and removed?
2. What is the role of company auditors?
3. What information is recorded in the Register of Members?
4. Do employees have the right to insist that an employee representative is present at either meetings of shareholders (company meetings) or meetings of directors (board meetings)?
5. What are the differences between liquidation and receivership?
6. What sort of things will a lender look for in a company?
7. What are the three main methods of creditor protection?

4

Liquidation of companies

A company's life is ended by a process known as liquidation or winding-up (these two terms mean exactly the same thing). These terms do not, however, apply to partnerships. The end of a partnership is known as dissolution.

Any liquidation is likely to be a complex, lengthy and expensive process. There are over 200 sections dealing with liquidations in the Companies Acts of 1985 and 1989. It is far more difficult to end the life of a company than to start one up.

This chapter outlines the two types of liquidation, compulsory and voluntary. It also covers situations where companies have got into serious difficulties, but by appointing a receiver or an administrator, or by making a voluntary arrangement, the company may be saved.

1 Reasons for liquidation

There are a number of reasons why a company's life may come to an end. For example:

a) If business is poor and the company has no value as a going concern, the owners may cease trading and apply to the Registrar of Companies to have the company struck off the register without the need for a formal liquidation.

b) The business may be *insolvent* (ie. unable to pay its debts as they fall due) and the creditors or lenders may force the company into liquidation in an attempt to get at least some proportion of what is owed to them.

c) The business may be successful, but there is some reason for winding up the company, for example there may be a deadlock in the management, such that the owners cannot agree on vital matters or become personally antagonistic.

d) A successful company may have been merged with or taken over by another company. The new group structure may not require the continued existence of the target company(the company that has been taken over). It would therefore be wound up and its assets transferred to the acquiring company.

2 Compulsory liquidation

a) There are two basic types of liquidation, compulsory liquidation and voluntary liquidation. Compulsory liquidation occurs when the company is *ordered by the court* to be wound up.

b) The usual reason is that the company is *unable to pay its debts*. A company is regarded as unable to pay its debts if a creditor or creditors who are owed more than £750 (in total) present a written demand for payment and the company fails to pay the debt within 21 days.

c) On the making of a winding up order, a government official, the *Official Receiver*, becomes liquidator. The Official Receiver will investigate the company's affairs and the causes of its failure. He will summon meetings of creditors and members. These meetings will appoint a liquidator in place of the Official Receiver.

d) The job of the liquidator is to collect all the assets and use them to pay the debts in the following order of priority:

i) his own fees;

ii) preferential creditors (this includes some government tax, for example six months VAT and national insurance, and arrears of wages up to a maximum of £800 per employee);

iii) creditors secured by floating charges;

iv) unsecured trade creditors;

v) sums due to members.

Creditors secured by fixed charges may rely on the sale proceeds of their security for payment. If this does not cover what they are owed they rank as unsecured trade creditors for the remainder.

3 Voluntary liquidation

a) There are two kinds of voluntary liquidation, members' voluntary liquidation and creditors' voluntary liquidation.

b) A *members' voluntary liquidation* is commenced by a special resolution of the company (ie a 75% majority vote of the members).

The directors must then make a *'declaration of solvency'* ie a declaration that, having made a full enquiry into the company's affairs, they believe the company will be able to pay its debts in full within 12 months of the date of the resolution. In a members' voluntary liquidation the members appoint the liquidator.

c) A *creditors' voluntary liquidation* is commenced by an extraordinary resolution of the company (also a 75% majority vote of the members, but with only 14 days notice rather than 21 for a special resolution). It will be a creditors' voluntary liquidation if the directors are unable to make a declaration of solvency. In a creditors' voluntary liquidation the creditors appoint the liquidator. The creditors may also appoint a *'committee of inspection'* to advise and supervise the liquidator.

4 Main consequences of liquidation

a) The company will cease business, except so far as is necessary for its winding up.

b) The directors' powers cease.

c) Share transfers are void.

d) The liquidation is widely publicised.

e) A liquidator will conduct a detailed investigation of the company's affairs. Such an investigation may reveal, for example, fraudulent of wrongful trading. *Wrongful trading* occurs when a director of a company that has gone into insolvent liquidation carries on the business when he knows, or should have known, that the company could not avoid liquidation. In such a case the court may order that person to make a contribution to the company's assets. This is an example of lifting the veil of incorporation.

For example, in Re: PRODUCE MARKETING CONSORTIUM (1989) the two directors of the company were aware of a serious drop in sales and profits. They knew that insolvency was inevitable at some time. They nevertheless continued to trade with the purpose of reducing their secured bank overdraft. They also ignored warnings by their auditor. The company was eventually wound up and the liquidator claimed £108,000 compensation from the directors for wrongful trading. The problem for the court was to decide when the directors knew or should have known that the company could not avoid liquidation. The court decided that this was approximately 14 months before the eventual winding up. The judge said that the directors should have been aware of the inevitable insolvency despite the fact that the bank had not withdrawn overdraft facilities and despite the fact that the auditor had accompanied the directors to the bank to seek an increase in the company's overdraft. Although the directors had not been fraudulent, they had not taken sufficient steps to minimise the total loss, because they had allowed the company to trade for over a year after they had become (or should have become) aware of insolvency. The court held that the directors must personally pay £75,000 to the company.

 Group activity 1

The class should be divided into about 6 groups. Each group represents one category of person who will be affected by the liquidation of a company that cannot pay its debts. For example, one group will represent creditors, one group members, one group employees and so on. Each group should consider how it will be affected by the liquidation and what action it may be able to take. Each group must present a short report to the rest of the class.

5 Receiverships

a) A receiver is a person appointed by lenders (known as *debenture holders*) secured by a charge over the whole, or substantially the whole of the company's assets. The receiver has the power to sell the charged assets and apply the proceeds to reduce the debt owed to the lender.

b) When a receiver is appointed the directors' powers are suspended and the receiver will run the business. The receiver's powers and duties are determined both by statute and by the terms of the document under which he was appointed. Like liquidation, receivership is accompanied by detailed publicity requirements, for example all letterheads, order forms and so on must show the appointment of a receiver.

c) The appointment of a receiver does not necessarily mean the end of the life of the company. It may be possible to sell the assets subject to the charge, repay the lender and hand control of the company back to the directors. However, this is most unlikely. Usually the trade creditors will seek to protect their position by securing the appointment of a liquidator, since a liquidator must have regard for the the interests of all stakeholders, not just the interests of secured lenders. If both a liquidator and a receiver have been appointed the liquidator occupies the premier position.

6 Administration orders

a) An administration order is made by the court on the application of the company, its directors, or one or more of its creditors, when it appears that the company is, or is likely to become, unable to pay its debts and that such an order may achieve the survival of the company, or a voluntary arrangement (see below) or a more advantageous sale of its assets than in a winding up.

b) When an administration order is in force the company cannot be wound up and a receiver cannot be appointed. The making of an administration order is also accompanied by publicity, for example it will be advertised in a newspaper in the area where the company has its main place of business.

c) The administrator will take control of the company's property and prepare a proposal for achieving the objectives of the administration. If the proposal is approved at the meeting of the creditors, the administrator will manage the company in accordance with the proposal.

7 Voluntary arrangements

a) A voluntary arrangement is an arrangement in which the company comes to terms with its creditors, usually that they all receive an equal proportion of what is owed to them.

b) A voluntary arrangement may be proposed by a liquidator, administrator or the directors. If it is a directors' proposal a 'nominee' (who must be a qualified insolvency practitioner) will summon a meeting of creditors. If 75% of the creditors agree to the proposal, all creditors who had notice of the meeting are bound by the terms of the arrangement.

8 Numbers of liquidations, receiverships, administrations and voluntary arrangements

The following figures cover the period 1st April until 31st March in each case.

	87/88	88/89	89/90	90/91	91/92	92/93
Compulsory Liquidation	3911	3789	4511	7043	9210	9861
Creditors' Voluntary Liquidation	7064	6011	6981	10610	14124	15164
Total Insolvencies	10975	9800	11492	17653	23334	25025
Members' Voluntary Liquidation	2834	4063	4215	4172	3985	3719
Total Liquidations	13809	13863	15707	21825	27319	28744
Receiverships	1384	1252	2423	5580	8756	7815
Administrations	196	187	160	237	176	123
Voluntary Arrangements	27	52	49	75	129	67

 **Review questions** *(answers page 276)*

1. What is the main reason for company liquidation?

2. What is the role of the Official Receiver in a compulsory Liquidation?

3. What is the difference between a members' voluntary liquidation and a creditors' voluntary liquidation?

4. What is meant by wrongful trading?

5. What is a voluntary arrangement?

6. In what circumstances might a successful company be wound up?

7. List the main consequences of liquidation.

5

Partnerships

A partnership is a means by which two or more persons can join in business, each providing capital, labour and skills and each sharing in the profits or losses. In many cases the partners bring different skills to the business. For example one partner may specialise in sales, another in production and another in financial management. Clearly this type of division of labour is not available to sole traders or one-member companies. In these cases the owner will either need to possess the skills or buy them in.

Partnership law was developed through cases in the last century. The case law was then set out in the Partnership Act 1890, which is still the governing statute. To determine whether a partnership exists it is necessary to apply the definition in the Partnership Act, since there is no registration requirement (as with companies) which conclusively proves whether or not a partnership exists.

This chapter looks at the reasons for carrying on business as a partnership. It then explains the definition in the Partnership Act and finally it sets out some of the matters which should be included in a partnership agreement.

1 Choice of partnership

a) A partnership is appropriate for a relatively small number of persons who have each other's trust and confidence and who are able to provide adequate funds for the business from their own resources. Such partnerships are not suitable for development of large scale enterprises since they do not enable business people to limit their liabilities, nor do they enable them to gain access to sufficient capital. These are some of the reasons that many sole traders and partnerships have converted their business into limited companies.

b) Any type of business, for example retail, manufacturing, consultancy, can be run as a partnership, but partnerships are most common where mutual trust and confidence (both between partners themselves and between partners and clients) are more highly regarded than the benefits of incorporation. Thus, subject to a few exceptions, partnership is the compulsory form of business for many professional persons such as solicitors and accountants. This makes clients feel that they have a close personal relationship with the firm and that the partner has an individual professional responsibility towards them.

2 Definition

a) The Partnership Act 1890 defines a partnership as *'the relation that subsists between persons carrying on business in common with a view to profit'*.

    i) A partnership is described as a *'relation'* because, unlike a company, it is not a legal entity separate from the partners.

    ii) The partners must carry on a *'business'*, ie a trade, profession or vocation over a period of time. If they merely co-own property this does not create a partnership.

    iii) *'In common'* means that the business must be carried on for the joint benefit of the persons who are partners.

    iv) *'View to profit'* means that the partners must intend to make a profit. It does not mean that if the actual result is a loss there is no partnership.

b) Nothing in the definition obliges a partner to be active in the business. A partner who takes no part in the business is known as a *'sleeping partner'*.

c) Some people who are actively engaged in the business may be given a fixed annual salary, and in their dealings with outsiders, may be held out as partners, for example by adding their names to the letter-heading. Such people are known as salaried partners. They may either be full partners, or (so far as the internal organisation of the firm is concerned) employees.

d) In general the maximum number of partners is 20, except for certain professional partnerships such as solicitors and accountants, where there is no maximum.

e) The partners may trade under any name they wish, except that the word 'limited' must not be the last word of the name.

3 Creation of a partnership

a) A partnership is formed when the partners begin to carry on business in common with a view to profit. It does not matter if they have made no partnership agreement (written or otherwise). The sharing of net profits is evidence of the existence of a partnership. However, it is not conclusive and if there is a contrary intention, for example that the share of profits is merely the repayment of a debt by instalments, then no partnership will exist.

b) It therefore follows that no formalities are necessary to form a partnership. It is however convenient, but not legally necessary, to regulate the affairs of a partnership by agreement in writing. This makes it clear what has been agreed between the partners.

c) Questions relating to the existence of a partnership are most likely to arise when goods are purchased from a person who subsequently does not pay for them. If a seller can prove that the buyer was in partnership with someone else, then the seller can seek to recover the price from the other person. For example in KEITH SPICER LTD v MANSELL (1970) Mansell and a Mr. Bishop decided to form a limited company to run Mansell's restaurant. Bishop purchased goods from Keith Spicer Ltd, but they were never paid for. The plaintiff sought payment from Mansell on the grounds that he was in partnership with Bishop. However, the court held that there was no partnership because Bishop and Mansell were not carrying on a business. The goods had been ordered in preparation for the formation of a company and this did not amount to carrying on a business. Bishop was therefore the only person liable to pay for the goods.

 Task 1

Arthur wishes to help his friends Brian and Charles, who are antique dealers carrying on business in partnership. They have asked Arthur to lend them £25,000 and have offered him one third of the profits of the business instead of a fixed rate of interest on the loan. Arthur has asked you whether there are any dangers if he enters into this type of agreement, and if so how he may protect himself. Write a letter to Arthur dealing with his concerns and advising him what to do.

4 Contents of a partnership agreement

Partnership agreements vary according to the wishes of the partners and the nature of the business. Most partnership agreements will usually deal with the following matters:

a) The firm's name.

b) The place and nature of the business.

c) The date on which the partnership is to commence and it duration. If there is no fixed period then it is known as a partnership at will.

d) The proportions in which capital is to be provided, and whether interest is to be paid on capital before profits are divided.

e) Details of the firm's bank account, including who is allowed to sign cheques.

f) Whether all or only some of the partners shall manage the business and whether all partners shall give their whole time to the business.

g) How profits are to be shared and provisions for drawings.

h) Provisions for keeping regular accounts and the preparation of an annual profit and loss account and balance sheet.

i) What shall happen on the death or retirement of a partner. In the absence of an agreement to the contrary the death of a partner automatically dissolves the partnership.

j) Whether a retired partner is allowed (within limits) to compete with the firm.

k) Any limits on the business interests of the partners outside the firm.

l) A list or description of what is agreed to be partnership property.

m) Insurance against death or sickness of a partner and for the business generally.

n) An arbitration clause. This means that if there is a dispute between the partners they must seek to resolve it in private in the presence of an arbitrator, before any partner takes it to court. Such a procedure will probably be cheaper and quicker than court action. It also has the advantage of privacy and is therefore less likely to generate publicity which may be harmful to the firm.

 **Review questions** *(answers page 278)*

1. What is the maximum and minimum number of:
   a) Members of a company?
   b) Partners?
2. What is the definition of a partnership?
3. What formalities are necessary to create a partnership?
4. What is the purpose of an arbitration clause in a partnership agreement?
5. What is a 'sleeping partner'?
6. How does the death of a partner affect the existence of the partnership?

6
Partners' rights and liabilities

This Chapter is concerned with the rights and liabilities of partners between themselves. Their position in relation to persons who do business with the partnership is explained in Chapter 16.

1 General principles

The relationship between the partners in a firm is governed by two general principles:

a) That the partners are free to make their own rules. Therefore if there is a question concerning relations between the partners the first place to look is the partnership agreement. If this does not resolve the question it will be necessary to look at the Partnership Act.

b) The second principle is that a partnership contract is a contract of utmost good faith (known as a contract *'uberrimae fidei'*). Utmost good faith exists because each partner entrusts the other partners with all of their assets, because (as we shall see later) all partners are liable without limit for the liabilities of a partnership, whether or not they specifically agree to the particular transaction. Utmost good faith requires partners to be totally honest with each other. They should volunteer information about matters relevant to the partnership even if they are not asked for it. They must also seek no unfair advantage over their partners and account to the firm for any benefits that they obtain as a result of being partners. Three applications of this duty are covered by the Partnership Act which states:

i) partners are bound to render true accounts and full information on all matters affecting the partnership;

ii) partners must account for any profits made without the consent of the others from using the firm's property, name, or trade connections;

iii) partners may have a separate account unless they have agreed to the contrary, but partners must account for any profit made in a business of the same kind as, and competing with, the firm.

 Discussion topic

What would you want to know about a potential business partner?

2 Internal regulations

a) *Management.*

i) Subject to contrary agreement every partner is entitled to access to partnership books and may take part in the management of the business.

ii) Decisions on ordinary matters connected with the partnership business are by majority of the general partners. If there is a deadlock the views of those opposing any change will prevail, but unanimity is required for matters relating to the constitution of the firm, for example to change the nature of the partnership business or to admit a new partner.

b) *Capital, profits and losses.*

   i) Profits and losses are shared equally in the absence of contrary agreement. However, if the partnership agreement states that profits are to be shared in certain proportions, then losses are assumed to be shared in the same proportions.

   ii) No interest is paid on capital except by agreement. However, partners are entitled to 5% interest on advances beyond their original capital.

c) *Indemnity.* The firm must indemnify (i.e. compensate) any partner for liabilities incurred in the ordinary and proper conduct of the partnership business, or if a partner does anything essential to preserve the partnership property or business.

d) *Partnership property.*

   i) The initial property of the partnership is that which the partners, expressly or impliedly agree shall be partnership property. It is quite possible that property used in the business should not be partnership property, but should, for example, be the sole property of one of the partners. It depends entirely on the intention of the partners.

   ii) Property acquired afterwards is governed by the same principle, but clearly it will be partnership property if it is bought with partnership money.

e) *Retirement.* If a partner retires his capital will continue to be used by the firm until it is repaid. Until that time the retired partner has the option of:

   i) a share of profits, reflecting the firm's continued use of his share of the assets. This can be difficult to work out in practice, or

   ii) 5% interest per annum on his share of the partnership assets.

3 Liability of partners

a) *Liability for negligence.* All partners are liable for negligence committed by a partner in the ordinary course of business or with the authority of the other partners.

b) *Liability in contract.*

   i) Every partner is liable jointly with the other partners for all debts and obligations of the firm incurred while he was a partner.

   ii) This means that a creditor may sue any partner for the full amount of any debt owed by the firm. It is then left to the individual partner to obtain a contribution from the others. In practice it is possible to bring proceedings against the partnership as a whole, using the partnership name. Creditors are not therefore affected by, or concerned with the internal arrangements which have been agreed by the partners.

c) *Liability of a retired partner.* A retired partner does not cease to be liable for partnership debts incurred before retirement, unless the creditors agree to release him. A retired partner may be liable on contracts made after his retirement if he continues to be an *'apparent partner'* by for example allowing his name to remain on the firm's notepaper.

d) *Liability of a new partner.* A person admitted as a partner does not incur liability for debts incurred before joining the partnership.

 Task 1

A friend of your family, Bobby Hope, has just retired as a partner with the firm of Hope and Glory. Write a letter to him explaining how he should protect himself from any further liability.

 **Review questions** *(answers page 278)*

1. What is a contract *uberrimae fidei*?

2. What proportion of the existing partners of a firm must agree to the admission of a new partner?

3. April and June go into partnership as gardeners. April provides £10,000 capital to purchase a van and equipment. June is only able to provide £1,000. Since they are good friends they do not think they need to have a written partnership agreement. At the end of the first year the partnership accounts show a profit of £5,500. April claims entitlement to £5,000 profits, since she

provided £10,000 capital. June is claiming half of the profits, since she worked just as hard as April. In the absence of any prior agreement, how will profits be divided?

4. Is a partner allowed to carry on a business which competes with the partnership business?

5. To what extent is one partner liable for the negligence of another partner?

6. What is the effect of partners' joint liability for the firm's debts?

7

Dissolving a partnership

Dissolution means termination of the partnership. It may occur:

a) *Out of court* (i.e. without any involvement by the court) if:
   i) The partners agree to dissolve the partnership.
   ii) Any partner serves notice terminating the partnership; or
   iii) An event occurs and the Partnership Act or the partnership agreement states that this event terminates the partnership. This is known as automatic dissolution.

b) *By order of the court* in any of the circumstances set out in 4. below

1 Dissolution by agreement

A partnership agreement is a contract. Like any contract it may be terminated by agreement between the parties at any time. Dissolution by agreement requires the agreement of *all the partners*. The dissolution is effective from the moment of the agreement to dissolve. The form of the original agreement is irrelevant, thus a written partnership can be terminated by oral agreement.

2 Automatic dissolution

This occurs:

a) By expiration of time, if the partnership was entered into for a fixed time period.

b) By completion of the project, if the partnership was entered into for a specific project.

c) By the death or bankruptcy of a partner, unless the partnership agreement otherwise states. It would be usual for the partnership agreement to treat the death or bankruptcy of a partner as retirement. The firm would therefore continue in existence.

d) By a change in the law that would make it illegal for the partnership to continue.

e) By the happening of any event which is stated in the partnership agreement to end the partnership.

3 Dissolution by notice

If a partnership is entered into for an unspecified time (known as a *'partnership at will'*) any partner may dissolve the partnership at any time by serving notice on the others. The dissolution takes effect from the date specified in the notice, or if no date is specified as soon as the notice has been communicated. The notice may be in any form unless the partnership was set up by deed (a special type of formal written contract) in which case written notice is necessary. Once it has been given, notice of dissolution cannot be withdrawn.

4 Dissolution by order of the court

The grounds are as follows:

a) Where a partner, because of mental disorder or permanent physical illness, is incapable of managing his property or affairs.

b) Where a partner's conduct is damaging to the business.

c) Where a partner has been guilty of wilful or persistent breaches of the partnership agreement.

d) Where the business can only be carried on at a loss.

e) Where the court considers that it is *'just and equitable'* to order dissolution. This ground is also relevant to the compulsory liquidation of small private companies.

The best examples are from company law.

i) In RE YENIDJE TOBACCO CO (1916) the company had two shareholders who were both directors. Although the company was successful the directors failed to agree on many important matters, for example the appointment of senior employees. They would not speak to each other and all communication was via the company secretary. It was held that it would be just and equitable to wind up the company.

ii) In RE WESTBOURNE GALLERIES (1973) E and N had been business partners since 1945, taking an equal share in management and profit. In 1958 a private company was formed, E and N, each holding one half of the shares (500 shares each). They were also the company's directors. Later it was agreed to admit N's son, G, to the business. E and N each transferred 100 shares to him and he was appointed a director. The company made good profits, but no dividends were paid, all the profit being distributed as directors' remuneration. Following a disagreement between E and N a general meeting was called and N and G removed E as a director and excluded him from management. E petitioned for an order that the company be wound up on the just and equitable ground. It was held that the company must be wound up because when E and N formed the company it was clear that the basic nature of their personal business relationship would remain the same. Therefore N and G were not entitled to use their statutory power to remove E as a director and exclude him from management.

5 Rescission of the partnership agreement

If a person has been induced to enter into a partnership by fraud or misrepresentation they are entitled to rescind or end the partnership contract. This means that the court will order that they be restored to the position they were in before the agreement was made.

6 The effect of dissolution

a) A decision to dissolve a partnership will be implemented by collecting together and selling the firm's assets, paying its creditors, repaying loans and capital to the partners (if the assets are sufficient) and distributing surplus assets (if any) to them.

b) It is important to make a public announcement that the firm has been dissolved and write to persons who have dealt with the firm. This will ensure that the apparent authority of partners to contract on behalf of the firm has ended.

c) After dissolution the authority of each partner is limited to actions necessary to wind up the partnership and complete contracts entered into before dissolution, but unfinished when dissolution began.

d) The *goodwill* of the partnership is the value of its reputation and trade connections. This is likely to be linked with the name of the firm. The goodwill is an asset which belongs to the firm and can be sold on dissolution. On dissolution the partners are not allowed to try to exploit the firm's goodwill for their own benefit. When the goodwill is sold the purchaser buys the exclusive right:

   i) To use the name of the firm;

   ii) To represent himself as successor to the firm in carrying on the business;

   iii) To solicit business from the firm's former customers or clients.

The sale of goodwill will usually be accompanied by a restraint of trade clause which will prevent the partners from approaching and doing business with the firm's customers or clients.

 Group activity 1

Andy, Ben and Craig are in partnership as car dealers. Andy and Ben have decided to dissolve the partnership because Craig keeps exceeding internally agreed limits on the amount any one partner can spend on a second-hand car without the agreement of the others. Who should Andy and Ben inform of the dissolution? How will they get their message across and what will it say? What other practical steps should they take?

Review questions *(answers page 279)*

1. What is a partnership at will?

2. What is goodwill?

3. What proportion of the partners are entitled to decide that a partnership shall be dissolved by agreement?

4. What is a restraint of trade clause?

5. How is a decision to dissolve a partnership implemented?

6. What is the extent of a partner's authority after dissolution?

8

Company versus partnership

When choosing a business structure most people will make a rational choice between company, partnership or sole trader, taking into consideration most of the important issues. A minority of people will be influenced by less rational feelings. They may believe that the word 'limited' at the end of the name persuades customers or suppliers that they are dealing with an organisation of size and resources. Alternatively they may simply prefer to describe themselves as 'company directors' rather than partners. In most cases, where logic prevails, people start as partnerships and convert to limited company status at a later date when the business has been established.

This Chapter looks at the advantages and disadvantages of operating as a company or a partnership. Many of the differences follow from the fact that a company is a separate legal person, whereas others are unrelated to this. The Chapter also gives a brief insight into the complex taxation issues which are likely to affect the choice.

1 Advantages of companies arising from the fact that a company is a separate legal person

Company	*Partnership*
a) The company owns its property.	a) The partners jointly own partnership property.
b) The debts of the company belong to the company. The creditors therefore cannot sue the members.	b) Every partner is personally responsible for the debts of the partnership as long as he has any assets at all.
c) Members' liability is limited to the amount they put into the company.	c) Partners' liability cannot be limited (except in the case of a limited partnership).
d) The existence of a company is not affected by the death or retirement of its members.	d) Death or retirement of a partner causes dissolution, unless there is agreement to the contrary.
e) Shares can be easily transferred.	e) It is not possible for a partner to sell or assign (i.e. transfer)his position as a partner, although it is possible to assign his share of profits.
f) Owners and managers do not need to be the same people.	f) Every partner has the right to share in the management of a partnership (subject to contrary agreement).
g) Other businesses can be separated by setting up a different company for each business. If one business fails the others will not be directly affected.	g) It is not possible for a partnership to have legally separate businesses, since it is not a separate entity from the partners.

2 Advantages of companies that do not arise from the concept of separate legal personality

Company	*Partnership*
a) A company can create a floating charge over its assets.	a) A partnership can only grant a mortgage over the partnership's fixed assets.

A *floating charge* grants a lender security over all of the present and future assets of the company, for example its stock-in-trade. The company is still able to deal with the assets in the ordinary course of business. As assets are sold, they are automatically released from the charge, whilst assets purchased become subject to the charge.

b) There is no upper limit on the number of members.	b) Subject to certain exceptions, for example solicitors and accountants, the number of partners is limited to 20.
c) A member of a company is not an agent of the company and therefore cannot bind the company by his acts.	c) A partner is an agent of the firm, therefore it will be bound by his acts.

3 Disadvantages of companies

Company	*Partnership*
a) Formation requirements (although relatively simple) are more onerous than for a partnership.	a) It is very easy and inexpensive to form, since a written agreement is not legally necessary (although it is advisable). It is straightforward to transfer the business to a limited company at a later stage.

Company	Partnership
b) During its existence the company must comply with numerous formal requirements, for example accounts must be audited, an annual general meeting must be held, registers must be maintained and an annual return must be submitted to the Registrar of Companies.	b) There are no external controls while the partnership exists, although proper records will of course need to be kept for income tax, value added tax and other purposes.
c) Financial and other information is freely available to the public.	c) Confidentiality is maintained since the public has no access to partnership accounts.
d) A company's issued capital is protected by the rule that dividends (payments to shareholders) can only be declared out of profits.	d) Partners' drawings of profit and capital are a matter of agreement.
e) Lenders are likely to seek personal guarantees from directors, thus reducing the benefit of having limited liability.	

 Task 1

List five legal differences between partnerships and sole traders.

4 Taxation

a) Taxation is an important factor in the choice of business structure and in the continued operation of that business. It is very complex and professional advice will be needed if liability to taxation is to be minimised. Advisers will wish to consider, among other things:

i) When purchasing a company, whether the purchasers buy its assets rather than its shares.

ii) How can the long term effects of capital taxes such as capital gains tax and capital transfer tax be minimised? It may be possible to do this by giving part ownership of the business to members of the owner's family from the outset.

iii) Can a tax efficient remuneration package for the members or partners be planned, including shares, dividends, pensions and so on?

iv) Should profits be retained in the company (thus attracting corporation tax) or become part of directors' remuneration (which would then attract income tax)?

b) *The taxation of sole traders and partnerships.*

i) Sole traders and partnerships are taxed on their total income received from all sources whether earned or unearned. The rates applicable for the tax year 1994/95 are:

Taxable Income	Percentage Rate of Tax
£1.00 to £3,000	20%
£3,001 to £23,700	25%
Over £23,700	40%

ii) Example:

Total income for the year	£20,000
Less personal allowance (single person)	£3,445
Taxable income	£16,555
Tax payable at 20%	£600
Tax payable at 25%	£3,388.75
Total tax payable	£3,988.75

iii) The Inland Revenue will accept a simple summary of accounts for businesses with a turnover of up to £15,000. The owner should send form 41K to the Inland Revenue (see Appendix B). For example

Turnover	£12,500
Less business expenses	£4,500
Net profit	£8,000

Personal allowances will then be deducted and tax payable calculated as in the above example. If the business is a partnership, the net profit will be shared between the partners in accordance with the partnership agreement. Each partner's share is taxed at his or her own rate of tax. If one partner does not pay their share of tax the others are liable for payment under the general principle that each partner is responsible for the debts of the partnership.

iv) One advantage of trading as a sole trader or partnership is that business income is aggregated with other income or losses. Thus an individual's loss that is unrelated to the business will reduce that individual's liability to tax on income from the business.

v) The 1993 Autumn budget statement helped the self employed by replacing the *'preceding year'* basis for tax assessment with the simpler *'current year'* basis. The income tax year runs from 6th April until the following 5th April. The preceding year basis assesses profits on the twelve months trading period ending in the previous tax year. Thus if a partnership runs its trading period from 1st September to 31st August the tax liability for the tax year 1993/4 would be based on the twelve months ending 31st August 1992. Under new legislation the assessment will be based on the twelve months ending 31st August 1993. This will have immediate effect for new businesses formed after 5th April 1994, but existing businesses will move to the new basis for the tax year 1997/98.

c) *Companies.*

i) Companies are only liable for tax on their profits (whether retained in the company or distributed). A company is taxed on profits after all expenses, including directors' remuneration, have been deducted. The tax is payable by the company and not personally by the directors or shareholders. Directors will pay tax on their personal income, but are entitled to the normal personal allowances against such income.

ii) Companies pay corporation tax at 25% on profits up to £300,000, thereafter higher rates of corporation tax apply. The tax is payable either 9 months after the end of the chargeable accounting period or within one month from the date of the assessment, whichever is the later.

 **Review questions** *(answers page 280)*

1. Must company directors also be:
   a) Shareholders?
   b) Employees?
2. What are dividends?
3. What is a guarantee?
4. Who is liable to pay corporation tax, the company or the directors?
5. How much income tax will be paid by a single person (with no other allowances) who has an income of £30,000?

9

Further considerations when starting a business

About 10 years ago the accounting firm Peat Marwick estimated that a director of a new company would need 24 hours and 27 minutes to read all the relevant government regulations on VAT, pay as you earn (PAYE), national insurance, employment and health and safety (a total of about 270,000 words) and this ignores all the time spent gathering the information.

No-one will have all the skills and knowledge needed for every aspect of the business, but it is essential to have some skills and work experience relevant to the proposed venture. It is also vital to have the energy and determination to make the business work. Anyone who starts up half-heartedly will certainly fail. The first and most important thing any potential entrepreneur should assess is their own level of skill, experience and commitment. Only then should they consider the matters covered in this Chapter.

The Chapter looks at two alternatives to starting a business from scratch, namely buying an existing business and buying a 'ready-made' company. It then deals with some of the more important practical matters faced by new businesses.

1 Buying an existing business

a) The purchase of an existing business or company is an alternative to starting a new business from scratch. Complex legal, commercial and taxation problems will arise and the vendors will of course be looking after their own interests. Professional advice on such purchases is essential. It is particularly important to ensure that adequate finance can be raised to purchase and operate the business before a commitment to purchase is entered into.

b) The main questions to be considered in the purchase of a partnership or sole trader's business are:

   i) Are the accounts for previous years satisfactory and consistently prepared?

   ii) Is any valuation of stock and fixed assets accurate?

   iii) Will the vendors retain cash to pay existing liabilities and agree to collect their own debts?

   iv) Is any payment for goodwill fair and reasonable? *Goodwill* is basically a payment for the likely income and profitability of the business and for its name and reputation. If the business is not profitable a payment for goodwill should not be made.

   v) Has the vendor told the buyer as much as possible about customers, suppliers, employees and facilities?

   vi) What are the legal implications of the statutory automatic transfer of contracts of employment?

c) The purchase of an existing limited company is likely to be even more complex. Many of the above considerations will apply, concerning for example the value of the company's assets. The main difference (assuming the buyer purchases the company's shares, not just its assets) is that the buyer automatically purchases all of the company's liabilities.

 Group activity 1

For this activity students should work in groups of four. Two students should act as buyers and the other two as sellers. The business to be sold is an accountancy practice with two partners, Mr.

David Smith and Miss Sue Brown. They employ two assistant accountants, two secretaries and a receptionist. The firm's name is 'Arthur Smith & Co.'. The two potential buyers are newly qualified chartered accountants – Donald Smith (no relation to David Smith) and Peter Black. The two students acting as buyers should make a list of questions and issues for discussion at a meeting with David Smith and Sue Brown. The two sellers should consider what the buyers may wish to know and make up a suitable history for the firm.

The group should then role play a meeting between buyers and sellers where the main issues are discussed. The aim of the meeting is to reach a preliminary agreement for the sale (subject to formal contract).

2 Buying a 'ready-made' company

a) There are a number of companies that provide a range of services to other existing companies or to persons wishing to start a limited company. These services include for example, dealing with changes of name or objects, increasing share capital, carrying out company searches and providing standard forms, stationery or brass plates. They will also form new tailor-made companies from scratch or offer for sale ready-made companies.

b) A ready-made company is a registered company which has no assets or liabilities and which has never traded. It will have been formed for the specific purpose of being sold to a person who wishes to start their own business. The main advantage of purchasing a ready-made company is that is it quicker and cheaper than forming a company from scratch. It will be possible to complete the formalities within a few hours (one company vendor advertises '10 minutes' for buyers who call in at their offices) compared with 7 to 10 days for a new tailor-made company. The cost is likely to be about £150 (including the company registration fee of £50). The documents provided will vary depending on the vendor chosen, but are likely to include:

i) Certificate of incorporation (see Appendix A).

ii) Several bound copies of the memorandum and articles.

iii) Certificate of non-trading, confirming that the company has never traded.

iv) Minutes of the first meeting.

v) Looseleaf register of members.

The companies offering for sale ready-made companies will probably have a 'stock' of over 100 companies to chose from. Even so the buyer will probably wish to change the name. This will add about £75 to the cost (£50 being the Registrar of Companies' charge for change of name).

d) Once a buyer has decided to purchase a ready-made company a meeting of the company will be called at which:

i) The first directors and secretary (nominees of the vendor) will resign and new directors and secretary (the buyers or their representatives) will be appointed. This will be recorded on form 288 (Appendix A) and sent to the Registrar of Companies.

ii) The situation (i.e. the address) of the registered office will also be changed using form 287 in Appendix A. The Registrar of Companies will be notified.

iii) A resolution will be passed, changing the company name (if required by the buyer).

 Task 1

Refer back to the group activity in Chapter 2 page 17. This briefly described a new company 'College Business Ltd.' As a new director of College Business Ltd you are asked to complete forms 287 and 288 (Appendix A) ready to send to the Registrar of Companies.

3 Informing the authorities

The requirements will vary depending on the choice of business structure and the nature of the business. Since most small businesses are set up as sole traders or partnerships, the main requirements for such businesses are set out below.

a) *Inland Revenue.*

i) The local taxation office must be advised as soon as the business starts trading. This is done by sending them form 41G

(Appendix B). This puts the owner or partners on Schedule D taxation, which is a tax on profits.

ii) If the new owners have given up previous employment, they must send form P45 to their local tax office. This is given to a person leaving employment by the employer. It states the pay and tax deducted during the year to date.

b) *National Insurance Contributions.* The Department of Social Security must be advised of the business start-up date. Self employed people aged 16 to 65 (60 for women) pay flat rate contributions of £5.65 per week, provided annual income exceeds £3,140, but is less than £6,490. If income exceeds £6,490 the rate is 7.3% of profits.

c) *Value Added Tax.* The standard rate of VAT is 17.5%. The threshold for VAT registration for 1994/5 is £45,000 turnover (i.e. sales) per year. Businesses must monitor their turnover on a cumulative monthly basis and notify Customs and Excise within 30 days when this annual limit is exceeded for any 12 month period (or less). A business with a turnover of less than £45,000 may apply for registration if customers normally expect the business to be registered, or if it will affect the business if it is not registered.

4 Other important considerations

a) *Employing People.* Full time employees must have 'pay as you earn' (PAYE) tax and national insurance contribution deductions made from their wages or salaries. The employer also contributes national insurance. The standard rate employee contribution is 10% and the employer rate is 10.2%. There are reduced rates for both employees and employers where the employee is low paid.

b) *Health and Safety.* The Health and Safety at Work Act 1974 applies to all businesses, including sole traders. It covers safety of machines, processes, training, environment and so on.

c) *Licences.* Some businesses need a local authority licence, for example businesses that offer credit or hire facilities. Employment agencies require a licence from the Department of Employment.

d) *The Data Protection Act 1984.* If a computer is used in the business to hold personal data or to process such data for others, registration under the Data Protection Act may be necessary. Payroll, purchase or sales data used in the normal course of business does not require registration, but if personal data, sickness records or trade union deductions are included, registration is necessary.

e) *Planning Regulations.* If a person works from home and a part of the house is used exclusively for business and numbers of people may call in connection with the business, there may be a sufficient change of use to require planning permission. If in doubt the owner should contact the Planning Department at the Local Authority.

f) *Insurance.* There are various classes of insurance that the owner of a business may consider essential, for example insurance against fire, theft, loss of money, personal accident or sickness. However there are only two classes of insurance required by law. These are motor insurance and employers' liability insurance.

  i) *Motor insurance.* It is an offence to use a motor vehicle without having insurance cover in respect of legal liability for causing death of injury to third parties arising out of the use of the motor vehicle. This is known as *'third party insurance'*. This is usually extended to include loss or damage to the insured vehicle by fire or theft. The fullest form of cover available is *'comprehensive'* which will include accidental damage to the vehicle, however caused. When using a vehicle in connection with a business it is essential to ensure that the policy covers the use of the vehicle for business purposes.

  ii) *Employers' liability insurance.* The Employers' Liability (Compulsory Insurance) Act 1969 obliges every employer carrying on a business in Great Britain to maintain insurance against liability for injury or disease sustained by employees and arising out of and in the course of their employment in Great Britain. An employer is not obliged to insure members of his or her family. The insurance company will issue an annual certificate which must be displayed at every place where the employer carries on business so that it can be seen and read by everyone employed there.

g) *Pensions.* A self employed person or partner will need to provide for their own pension. A sole trader or partner may get tax relief on up to $17\frac{1}{2}$% of taxable earnings paid into an approved pension arrangement. It is advisable for sole traders or partners to take professional advice on pension arrangements.

h) In addition to the above main points there are potentially hundreds of other personal, practical and legal matters which will need to be considered. A few are listed below.

i) Has the owner got enough energy, skills and knowledge to run a business?

ii) Has the product and market been adequately tested and researched?

iii) What advantages, for example price, speed or quality, does the business have over existing competitors?

iv) Has enough capital been arranged?

v) Are budgeted costs, sales and profits realistic?

vi) How will the product or service be advertised?

vii) Have space requirements been calculated and suitable accommodation arranged?

viii) Have reliable suppliers been organised?

ix) Can purchases be stored securely?

x) Has an adequate book-keeping and record system been set up?

xi) Have telephone and fax services been arranged?

xii) If people are being employed, is an adequate skilled labour force available?

 Task 2

Write a letter to your local Training and Enterprise Council (TEC). Ask them to send you any literature they publish giving advice on how to start a new business. Based on this literature and on your coursework to date, identify what you consider to be the ten factors most vital to the success of a new business (for example 'experienced managers,' 'adequate finance,' 'quality product'). Write a brief report explaining why each of these ten factors is so important.

Review questions *(answers page 281)*

1. What is the cost of registering a limited company?
2. What is a ready-made company?
3. What two types of insurance must a business take out?
4. What type of resolution is necessary to change the name of a company?
5. What does PAYE stand for?
6. Is it essential for every new business to charge its customers value added tax?

10

Other ways of being in business

There are three basic reasons for forming a company.

a) To enable the public to invest in an enterprise and share in its profits without taking part in the management. These are public companies. They are far less numerous than private companies, but economically they are much more important.

b) To enable a sole trader or small group of people to make a profit by running a business. For these private companies incorporation is a way of giving the business a legal personality and separating its liability from that of its members, despite the fact that those members share the profits and control the company.

c) For purposes other than profit for the members. These companies are set up for social, economic or charitable purposes and are usually structured as a company limited by guarantee.

This Chapter briefly describes guarantee companies and also looks at two other ways of being in business, namely franchising and workers co-operatives. It is important to realise that a franchise or workers co-operative could be carried on under any appropriate business structure i.e. company or partnership. They are therefore ways of being in business, not different legal structures. In contrast a guarantee company (although subject to the Companies Acts) will have a quite different structure and constitution.

1 Franchising

a) The term franchising is used to describe a business arrangement in which one party (the franchisor) allows others (the franchisees) to use a particular name or trade secret, or to sell products, in such a way that the franchisees can operate their own legally separate businesses. Franchising is a different method of being in business – it does not involve a different legal structure, since either the franchisor of franchisee (or both) may be either a limited company, a partnership of a sole trader. In the USA franchises take about 30% of the retail market. In the UK it is 2-3%, but the sector is growing. Some of the best known high street stores are franchises, for example The Body Shop, Wimpey, Clarkes Shoes, Benetton, Prontoprint and Budget Rent a Car.

Franchising is not limited to retailing. For example in the USA the National American Football League (the NFL) is a franchise. The NFL is the franchisor and each team owner is a franchisee. These franchises are extremely valuable. For example early in 1994 the Miami Dolphins changed hands for £160,000,000.

b) The usual form of franchising is known as *'format franchising'*, in which the franchisor offers a complete business format including:

i) trade name

ii) the right to produce or sell goods or services

iii) business style and/or logo

iv) detailed product or service specification

v) operating systems and manuals

vi) accounting and financial systems

vii) training and help to establish the business

viii) continued assistance and back-up

ix) marketing, public relations and advertising support

c) The franchisee will pay a fee to the franchisor to purchase this complete package, enabling the franchisee to set up and operate the business to a proven format, governed by a contract between the franchisor and the franchisee.

d) For a person wishing to start a business the advantage of a franchise (provided it is a good, proven franchise) is that it is likely to be a less risky and more straightforward method of going into business than starting up independently from scratch. This is because:

i) the business idea and operating methods have been proven, and

ii) the franchisee has start-up help, training and continuing support.

Franchising will also provide individuals with access to types of business which would not have been open to them if they had sought to establish an independent business based on their existing skills and experience.

e) The disadvantages of franchising are:

i) lack of independence, since the franchisor will determine the basic method of running the business.

ii) cost, since the initial franchise fee will need to be paid in addition to the normal cost of establishing the business. The franchisee will also have to pay continuing management fees, usually based on a percentage of sales.

iii) the success of the franchisee is linked to that of the franchisor, thus a successful franchisee can be ruined if the franchisor's business gets into difficulty.

f) Before signing a franchise contract a potential franchisee should thoroughly research what is available and take professional advice. The following matters should be carefully considered:

i) Is there a strong market for the product or service offered?

ii) Does the franchise grant exclusive rights over a particular geographic area?

iii) What degree of control is exercised by the franchisor?

iv) What level of assistance is provided by the franchisor?

v) Is the franchisor financially sound?

vi) What is the duration of the franchise contract and how may it be terminated by each side?

vii) Is the franchise fee reasonable and what other set-up costs and ongoing fees and costs are involved?

viii) What is the overall level of risk involved in investing in the franchise?

Group activity 1

For this activity a group of four or six should split into two teams of two or three. One team will be franchisors and the other team franchisees. The whole group should select a well-known franchise and each team should find out as much as they can about it in preparation for the activity.

The group will then role-play a meeting at which the possible sale of a new franchise is considered. Each side should come to the meeting with some factual information about the chosen franchise. At the meeting the parties should try to find out as much as possible about each other, the contract terms and the business in general, with a view to deciding whether they wish negotiations to continue.

 Discussion topic

Do you think that franchising will continue to grow for the foreseeable future?

2 Workers co-operatives

a) A workers co-operative is a business owned and democratically controlled by the members. The members will normally be all of the employees of the co-operative. Co-operative businesses differ from other kinds of business because they operate under different principles.

   i) Membership is open to all employees.

   ii) Members have one vote each, irrespective of their financial commitment or seniority.

   iii) The return on any investment in the co-operative is limited to a reasonable rate.

   iv) Profits are not distributed according to money invested, but according to work put in.

b) The main benefits claimed for co-operatives are increased job satisfaction and reduced conflict, since the workers and owners are the same people. This may also help motivation and lead to higher quality products or services. Members must, however, be prepared to take responsibility and participate in the running of the business.

c) Most co-operatives are registered as companies under the Companies Acts, since co-operative principles can easily be incorporated into the memorandum and articles of limited companies, for example by entrusting control of the company to trustees for the benefit of employees. Employees as members would then share in any distributed profit after the payment of interest on loans and any provision for re-investment. The John Lewis Partnership is organised in this way.

d) Very few (approximately 50) wholesale and productive businesses adopt co-operative principles. There are over 100 retail co-operatives societies, but most co-operative bodies are either housing associations, social and recreational clubs, or agricultural societies.

3 Guarantee companies

a) Guarantee companies are usually formed for charitable, social or other non-trading purposes. They are used by schools, colleges, professional and trade associations, 'friends' of museums and art gallaries, clubs supported by subscriptions and management companies for blocks of flats in which all the tenants are members.

b) These organisations do not have an objective of distributing profits to members. Members will not therefore wish to invest capital in the company, nor would it be appropriate to divide the company into shares. The organisation may however need the other benefits of corporate status, in particular the ability to operate as a legal person separate from its members.

c) The Companies Acts do not allow companies to be created with members who have no liability whatsoever. However instead of limiting liability to the amount payable for their shares, the Act does enable members of a guarantee company to agree an amount (usually £1 or £5) that will be paid if the company goes into liquidation. While the company is a going concern the member is under no liability to pay any money, it is only if the company is wound up and a contribution is needed to enable the debts to be met that any liability on the guarantee arises.

Review questions *(answers page 282)*

1. What is a franchise agreement?
2. What is a workers co-operative?
3. How does a company limited by guarantee differ from a company limited by shares?
4. Why may franchising be less risky than starting a business from scratch?
5. What are the main advantages claimed by supporters of workers co-operatives?
6. What are the main disadvantages of purchasing a franchise?

 Part 1 assignments

Assignment 1

Two groups of friends have recently approached you for advice in connection with business ideas.

a) Andrew Bates and Jeremy Castle are excellent young tennis players. They had both represented their county and Andrew has just qualified as a full LTA registered professional coach. Like Andrew, Jeremy is 23, he has just passed part 2 of the LTA professional coaches examinations and hopes to get the full LTA qualifications within the next 12 months. Andrew works as the club coach at South Herts Tennis Club, one of the largest clubs in England with 800 members, including 300 junior members. The demand for coaching exceeds what Andrew can provide by himself and he has invited Jeremy to join him at South Herts.

Coaches provide both individual and group coaching. Andrew's individual price as a fully qualified professional is £12 per hour. Jeremy as a part qualified coach charges £10 per hour. The income from group coaching depends on the size of the group. Usually one coach teaches 8 to 12 children, who each pay £1.50 per hour.

b) Aleem, Asif, Munir and Pratap left college at the end of 1992. They have relatives in India and decided to build on these contacts by starting a business. They intend to import a wide range of Indian goods, particularly clothing and food. They will then sell direct to the public from a warehouse type premises situated in North London. They can each contribute £4,000 to the business. In addition Aleem's father is willing to invest £20,000 and Pratap's brother will lend him £10,000. In total they have calculated that they will need £90,000 to start the business.

Your assignment is to:

1. To write a report suitable for both groups of friends comparing the legal characteristics of different types of business organisations.

2. Write a letter to Andrew and Jeremy, enclosing your report and recommending a structure for their business, giving full reasons for your recommendation.

3. Write a similar letter to Aleem, Asif, Munir and Pratap.

Assignment 2

On the basis of your report Andrew and Jeremy have decided that they ought to form a partnership and they have arranged to meet you to discuss the matter in detail.

Your assignment is to:

1. Write out a list of the main questions you will ask Andrew and Jeremy.

2. Write down the answers that Andrew and Jeremy might realistically give.

3. Draw up a partnership agreement for them that reflects their wishes as expressed in the answers to 2. above.

Part 2

Business relationships

Element 9.2 Investigate the legal relationships in business

This part builds on the introduction to business organisations set out in Part 1. It describes in more detail the legal consequences of particular business relationships. It sets out the rights and liabilities of company shareholders (ie members), company directors, employees of companies and partnerships, banks and others who finance (ie lend to) business organisations, and suppliers who grant them credit. It also briefly outlines the liability of businesses for negligence and criminal acts, and considers the extent to which businesses owe a duty to the community as a whole.

On successful completion of Part 2 activities and review questions, students will understand the rights and duties of key parties in business organisations and appreciate the inter-relationship between them (performance criteria 1 and 2). Students will be able to identify the consequences for these key individuals of a range of acts, both wrongful and legitimate, carried out by businesses. The end of part assignments will generate the evidence required for your portfolio of coursework.

BTEC guide to coverage of performance criteria

The performance criteria and evidence indicators are listed in the left-hand column. The Assignment column contains the number of the assignment which covers the criteria indicated.

The Task and Group Activity columns indicate the chapter numbers as well as task or group activity numbers. For example '2.1' in the Task column indicates Chapter 2 Task 1 covers that particular performance criteria. '2.1' in the Group Activity column would indicate Chapter 2 Group Activity 1 covers the criteria in question.

9.2 Investigate the legal relationships in business

Performance Criteria and Evidence Indicators	*Assignment*	*Task*	*Group activity*
9.2.1 Rights and duties of key parties are identified	3, 4	3.1, 3.2, 12.1 14.1, 15.1	3.1, 4.1, 13.1 14.1, 16.1
9.2.2 The inter-relationship between stakeholders is explained	3, 4	3.2, 5.1, 6.1 12.1, 13.1 16.1, 17.1	3.1, 4.1, 13.1 16.1
9.2.3 The nature of liability to others for wrongful acts is described	3, 4	6.1, 12.1 13.1, 16.1	3.1, 4.1, 14.1 16.1
Evidence indicator. An investigation and explanation of the implications for those involved, of a range of wrongful acts carried out by a business.	3, 4		

11

Company shareholders

Company members or shareholders were identified as 'key players' in Chapter 3.1. where it was explained that:

a) Company members may be either invididuals or other companies.

b) That persons become members by subscribing to the company for shares when a company makes a new issue or by purchasing existing shares from a member who wishes to sell.

c) That companies keep a register of members containing basic information about each member.

d) That there are different motives for owning shares, including short term speculative profit, long term dividend income or active participation in the business.

e) That the main membership rights are the right to vote at company meetings and the right to share in company profits.

1 Capital

a) The word *'capital'* is generally used to describe the amount by which the assets of a business exceed its liabilities. This implies that the amount of capital and the value of the business changes as the company trades. For company law purposes the capital of a company is its issued share capital. This is the amount that the members have given for their shares. They may give cash or transfer an asset with an agreed value. The amount of issued capital does not change as the value of the business fluctuates as a result of trading.

b) The money received by the company when shares are issued must be retained, so far as possible, in the business, because it provides a guarantee fund from which creditors can expect to be paid. Capital cannot be used to pay dividends to shareholders or to buy back their shares from them (unless strict and complex conditions are complied with).

2 Buying and selling shares

a) *Buying new shares.* A public company that wants its shares to be traded on the Stock Exchange must set out the details of the sale in a prospectus and advertise it in at least one daily newspaper. This method has also been used to sell government privatisation issues to the public for example British Telecom, British Gas and the Regional Electricity and Water companies. Anyone who wants to buy the shares fills in the application form and sends it (with a cheque) to the address given in the prospectus. This is the offer. The company will then accept the offer in whole or in part (having reserved the right to make a partial acceptance in the prospectus). The company needs to reserve this right since the total number of shares applied for will, inevitably, not equal the total number of shares available.

b) *Buying existing shares.* Investors are not limited to buying new shares. The main function of the Stock Exchange is to allow existing shares to be bought and sold at any time. Stockbrokers, banks and building societies buy and sell shares on behalf of their clients, both private individuals and large institutions. In addition most stockbrokers will advise clients on the merits of buying and selling shares in particular companies.

c) *Private companies.* These companies are prohibited from issuing shares to the public and must therefore obtain their share capital directly from their members. In addition, to retain the private nature of the company, the articles will give the directors the power to refuse to register any share transfer.

3 The share certificate

Once a person has purchased shares, a share certificate must be made out by the company and delivered to the member within two months (14 days for companies quoted on the Stock Exchange). An example of a share certificate is in Appendix D page 265.

4 Ordinary shares and preference shares

a) *Ordinary shares.* Most shares are ordinary shares. Holders of these shares control resolutions at general meetings and receive payments of dividends, provided the company has made a profit. The level of dividend will vary depending on the company's profitability and in good years ordinary shareholders will do much better than other classes of shareholder. The disadvantage is that ordinary shareholders take most of the risk of failure. Thus if the company becomes insolvent and is wound up, ordinary shareholders will not receive any money at all. An advantage for holders of ordinary shares is that when new shares are issued they are offered to ordinary shareholders (in proportion to their existing shareholding) before they are offered to anyone else.

b) *Preference shares.* Preference shares are designed to appeal to investors who want a steady return on capital combined with a higher level of safety. They carry a fixed rate of dividend, for example 8%. This must be paid before the ordinary shareholders receive anything. Usually preference shareholders do not have the same voting rights as ordinary shareholders, but in the event of liquidation they normally have a prior right to the return of their capital.

5 The payment of dividends

a) Dividends are payments made out of profits to the members of a company. Members do not have an automatic right to dividends even if profits are available, since directors may consider it more prudent to retain profits within the company. Dividends must be distinguished from interest. Interest is paid to lenders. It is a debt of the company and must be paid whether or not profits have been earned.

b) The rules for calculating the profits available for distribution are very complicated. Basically dividends cannot be paid if this would result in the company being unable to pay its debts as they fall due. The dividends may then be paid out of the surplus of accumulated realised profits over accumulated realised losses. This means that profits of previous years may be used to pay dividends, but unrealised profits (for example created by the revaluation of an area of land) may not be used.

6 **Company meetings**

a) *The annual general meeting.* The general rule is that every company must hold an AGM every calendar year with not more than 15 months between each AGM. Certain standard matters will be dealt with, for example:

   i) Consideration of the accounts, the directors' report and the auditor's report.

   ii) Declaration of a dividend.

   iii) Election of directors in place of those retiring.

   iv) The appointment and remuneration of auditors.

b) *Extraordinary general meetings.* Any meeting which is not an AGM is an EGM. An EGM may be called by the directors, by members holding at least 10% of the shares or by a resigning auditor.

c) *Notice of meetings.* Every member is entitled to 21 days written notice of an AGM and 14 days written notice of an EGM. The notice will specify the date, place and time of the meeting, together with the full text of any special or extraordinary resolutions. It will also set out the members' rights to appoint proxies to attend and vote on their behalf.

d) *Conduct of meetings.*

   i) A *quorum* is the minimum number of persons who must be present to conduct a meeting. The quorum for company meetings is generally two members personally present.

   ii) There must be a *Chairman* to preside over the meeting. The Chairman must:

   ❏ ensure that business is conducted in an orderly manner in the order set out in the agenda

   ❏ allow all points of view to be adequately expressed and then put the resolution to the vote and declare the result

   ❏ decide whether amendments to resolutions are acceptable

   ❏ sign the minutes of the meeting.

   iii) *Voting* is usually by a show of hands i.e. each member present has one vote regardless of the number of shares held. If a *poll* is demanded then a member's votes will depend on the number of voting shares held. Usually this will be one vote for each ordinary share. A *proxy* is a person appointed by an absent member to attend a meeting and vote on the member's behalf.

e) *The Cadbury Report.* Company meetings have been criticised as being ineffective since agendas consist mainly of standard business on which there is minimal discussion, consequently very few members attend. The Cadbury Report on Financial Aspects of Corporate Governance (1992) made several suggestions to increase the effectiveness of company meetings, for example:

i) That members should be able to send in written questions in advance of the AGM, so that prepared answers could be given.

ii) That chairmen of audit and remuneration committees (recommended by the Report, but not law at present) will be responsible for answering questions at the AGM.

iii) A brief summary of points raised at the AGM should be sent to all members after the event.

7 Resolutions

a) *Ordinary resolutions.*

i) This is a *simple majority* of members present in person or by proxy entitled to vote and voting. For example a company has 10 members holding an equal number of shares. Four do not attend the meeting (or appoint proxies), three abstain, two vote for the resolution and one votes against it. The resolution has been passed.

ii) An ordinary resolution is used whenever the law or the company's articles do not require a special or extraordinary resolution. In some cases the law specifies an ordinary resolution, for example to remove directors or to remove auditors.

b) *Special resolutions.*

i) These require a 75% majority of members present in person or by proxy entitled to vote and voting. A period of *21 days notice* is generally required. A copy of every special resolution which is passed must be filed with the Registrar of Companies within 15 days.

   ii) Special resolutions are required for a number of important company decisions for example:

       ☐ To alter the objects clause (this sets out the activities that the company may engage in) of the memorandum of association

       ☐ To alter the articles

       ☐ To commence winding up proceedings

       ☐ To re-register a private company as a public company

       ☐ To re-register an unlimited company as limited.

c) *Extraordinary resolutions.* An extraordinary resolution is similar to a special resolution, except that only 14 days notice is required. The main use of an extraordinary resolution is to commence the voluntary winding up of an insolvent company.

d) *Written resolutions.* Since 1989 a private company can substitute the unanimous written agreement of its shareholders for any resolution passed at a general meeting (except a resolution to remove a director or auditor before their period of office has expired).

8 The protection of minority shareholders

a) The basic principle of company law is majority rule. A simple majority of votes is sufficient to control the composition of the Board of Directors and take most of the decisions at company meetings. A company is however a democracy, not a dictatorship and 51% do not have absolute power over 49%. Company law must find a balance between the principle of majority rule and the protection of the rest of the shareholders from abuse of power by the majority. Problems of this nature are most likely to occur in relatively small companies.

b) The main statutory protection for shareholders is S.459 Companies Act 1985 which states that a member may petition the court for an order on the ground that the affairs of the company are being, or have been, conducted in a manner which is unfairly prejudicial to the interests of its members generally or some part of the members (including at least himself) or that any proposed act or omission of the company is or would be unfairly prejudicial.

c) The Section is very widely drafted in order to cover any potential abuse of power. Typical examples from past cases are as follows:

   i) The directors, whilst negotiating a contract on behalf of the company, made the contract in their own names. At the AGM they used their votes to pass a resolution declaring that the company had no interest in the contract. The resolution was declared void.

   ii) The controlling directors and shareholders (Mr. and Mrs. D) caused the company to sell a piece of land to Mrs. D for much less than it was worth. A minority shareholder was able to succeed in an action requiring Mrs. D to pay her profit to the company.

   iii) The controlling directors and shareholders made an issue of new shares which was specifically designed to reduce a minority shareholder's holding from 45% to just under 25%, thus removing the power to defeat a special resolution. The issue of shares was declared void.

   iv) The 89 year-old controlling shareholder of a family company ran the company in an irrational and dictatorial manner. The minority shareholders (his sons) obtained an order removing him from the Board of Directors, together with a court order that he should not interfere with the affairs of the company.

   v) The directors of a company made incorrect statements (i.e. lied) to their shareholders in an attempt to persuade them to accept an offer for their shares made by another company which was owned by those directors.

 Task 1

Carry out research and then list the different ways by which the affairs of companies are subject to public scrutiny.

 Discussion topic

Do you consider that sufficient Company information is publicly available to members, creditors, lenders and employees?

 **Review questions** (answers page 283)

1. What does 'simple majority' mean?
2. What is a prospectus?
3. What are preference shares?
4. What are the two types of company meetings?
5. Summarise the main section of the Companies Act 1985 which is intended to protect minority shareholders.
6. What are the various types of company resolution?

12

Company directors

Directors are the persons to whom management of a company is entrusted. Their position is similar to that of agents, in that they can bind the principal (i.e. the company) without incurring personal liability. Every public company must have at least two directors and every private company must have at least one.

The object of this Chapter is to introduce the main powers and duties of directors and briefly describe the role of the company secretary.

1 Appointment and removal

a) The usual method of appointment is by the company in general meeting i.e. by *ordinary resolution*. Certain people may not act as company directors, for example undischarged bankrupts (that is people declared bankrupt who have not repaid their debts) and persons disqualified by the court because of their previous conduct as a company director.

b) The office of director is usually vacated either by retirement or removal. Normally directors retire after three years, but are eligible for re-election. Directors may also be removed at any time by *ordinary resolution*.

c) *Directors' remuneration.* Directors cannot vote pay to themselves, it is fixed by the company in general meeting. However the directors may fix the remuneration of a managing director appointed by them.

d) Directors will not necessarily devote their whole time to the company's business. Many companies appoint *non-executive directors* who act in an advisory capacity. Executive directors (i.e. directors who manage an area of the company's business) are normally given service contracts. They will therefore also have the status of company employees.

2 Powers of directors

a) The company's articles will provide that 'the business of the company shall be managed by the directors who may exercise all the powers of the company'. If the shareholders do not approve of the directors' acts they must either remove them or alter the articles to regulate their future conduct. They cannot simply take over the functions of the directors. For example in SCOTT v SCOTT (1943) the members passed a resolution that the affairs of the company should be investigated by a firm of accountants. It was held that the resolution was invalid as it took away powers which the articles had given to the directors.

b) If the directors exceed their powers, or exercise them improperly, their acts can be ratified by an ordinary resolution of the company. For example in BAMFORD v BAMFORD (1970) in order to prevent a take-over bid, the directors issued 5,000 new shares to another company. This diluted the percentage share-holding of the take-over bidder. Two shareholders sought a declaration that the issue was void because it was made for an improper purpose i.e. to block a take-over bid rather than to raise capital. One of the duties of directors is to use their powers for a proper purpose. The directors were therefore in breach of this duty, however the company then passed an ordinary resolution approving the issue of shares and waiving the directors' breach of duty.

Cases such as BAMFORD v BAMFORD illustrate the need to strike a balance between the principle of majority rule and the protection of minority shareholders. In many cases the directors and the majority shareholders will be the same people. In such a situation if the company ratifies a breach of duty by the directors, the reality is that individuals will be ratifying their own breach of duty. In the absence of such ratification, the company could bring an action against the wrongdoers for their breach of duty and obtain compensation. The ratification would therefore have an adverse affect on the company and almost certainly be against the interests of minority shareholders. Their remedy would be to bring an action under S.459 Companies Act 1985 on the ground that the majority shareholders' action is unfairly prejudicial (see Chapter 11.8 page 72).

c) *The managing director.* The articles of the company will state that the directors may appoint one of their number as managing director. The person will receive a service contract and will not be subject to the usual rules for retirement of directors. However if the managing director is removed as a director, the appointment as managing director will automatically cease. If this happens the individual will be entitled to damages for breach of contract, unless the removal is justified because of, for example, misconduct or negligence.

d) *The power of directors to bind the company.* Until 1989 any act outside the objects clause of the memorandum was *ultra vires* (beyond the powers) and therefore void. Now, if a person deals with a company in good faith, the power of the directors to bind the company, or authorise others to do so, is free of any limitation under the company's constitution. Thus a completed act or contract will have protection from the ultra vires rule and will be enforceable by both the company and the outsider. However this does not prevent members bringing proceedings to restrain an intended act or contract which would be beyond the capacity of the company (for example to prevent the payment of a bribe to obtain business) nor from suing directors in respect of liability incurred in relation to a contract beyond the capacity of the company.

3 Fair dealing by directors

a) The Companies Act 1985 contains over 30 sections of great complexity dealing with situations where the interests of a director and the company may conflict, concerning, for example, service contracts, property transactions and loans.

b) Briefly the main general rules are:

i) Any payment as compensation for loss of office (golden handshakes) must be approved by the members. This is done by passing a ordinary resolution at a general meeting.

ii) If a director might benefit (directly or indirectly) from a contract made by the company, the director must disclose his interest in the contract at a board meeting. An example would be a sale of land from X Ltd to Y Ltd. If A is a director of both companies he must declare his interest in the contract at a board meeting of Y Ltd.

iii) Certain property transactions between a director and the company must have the prior approval of the members.

iv) A company may not make a loan to its directors or enter into any guarantee or provide any security in connection with a loan to its directors.

v) If the company is insolvent, a director has a duty to discontinue trading. In such situations directors must not use company funds to make payments to some creditors in preference to other creditors.

4 Fiduciary duties and duties of care and skill

a) The law imposes *fiduciary duties* when a person is in a position of trust and the persons who gave that trust are not in a position to ensure that it has not been misplaced. The law is again complex. Briefly summarised, directors' fiduciary duties are:

i) To have regard to the interests of the company's employees as well as the interests of members.

ii) To act for the benefit of the company as a whole.

iii) To use their powers for a proper purpose.

iv) To observe limitations on their powers.

v) To retain freedom of action i.e. they must not enter into contracts determining how they will vote at future board meetings.

vi) To avoid a conflict of duty to the company and personal interest. Thus if they make a profit as a result of their directorship this must be revealed to the company, which will then decide whether the director should be allowed to retain it.

b) *Duties of care and skill.*

   i) In contrast to onerous duties of good faith and loyalty, there is very little obligation on directors to display any care and skill. Directors are not required to have any formal qualifications nor undertake any training. They must however exhibit the degree of skill which may reasonably be expected from a person of their knowledge and experience. Thus in financial matters more would be expected of a director who is a qualified accountant than a director who has no accountancy training.

   ii) Directors are not bound to give continuous attention to the company's affairs, nor will they be liable for the acts of co-directors or other officers unless they participate in the wrongdoing, for example by signing a cheque for an unauthorised payment.

 Discussion topic

It is already difficult for directors to balance the interests of members and creditors. Is it impossible to have regard to the interests of employees as well?

 Discussion topic

In most large companies ownership is quite separate from control, because the directors only hold a tiny proportion of the company's shares and most shareholders never attend company meetings or participate in any way in company decisions. Do you think that this is a cause for concern in a society dominated by large companies? In particular do you think that there is any difference in the motives of directors as managers and shareholders as owners?

5 The secretary

a) Every company must have a secretary. Usually the secretary will be *appointed by the directors* on such terms as they think fit. Often one of the directors will also act as the secretary. In a small company the secretary may only be needed for a few hours each month, but in large public companies the secretary will be a full time officer, supported by several staff.

b) The secretary is the chief administrative officer of the company and on matters of administration has authority to make contracts on behalf of the company, for example contracts to hire office staff or purchase office equipment. The secretary cannot however:

i)   bind the company on a trading contract

ii) borrow money on behalf of the company

iii) issue a writ in the company's name, or

iv) register a transfer of shares.

c) The secretary's duties include:

i)   Ensuring that the company's documentation is in order and that the required returns are made to the Registrar of Companies.

ii) Taking minutes of meetings.

iii) Sending notices to members.

 Task 1

A friend of yours, Dennis, is a director of Agrifood Ltd and he holds 10% of the shares. There are three other directors, Alan, Barry and Charles. They are also the only members and they hold 40%, 30% and 20% respectively of the company's shares. Dennis is very unhappy about the following events which he has just found out about.

a) Agrifood Ltd is being sued by Executive Car Rentals Ltd. It seems that Charles hired a Rolls Royce car for the day. He told the rental company that he was going to use it to collect an important customer from Heathrow Airport, but in fact he used it to impress his friends. Dennis is worried that the company's reputation will suffer if it does not pay the hire charges.

b) Last year Alan's wife sold some land to the company for £120,000. Last month she bought it back from the company for £35,000.

c) Barry, who works in the company's research lab, has discovered a process which doubles the protein content in any given weight of chicken food. He has privately signed a £3m contract selling the process to ICI plc.

The task is to draft a letter in Dennis' name to Alan, Barry and Charles, explaining the legal position in each case, telling them what must be done, and advising them of the consequences of failure to carry out the required action.

 **Review questions** *(answers page 284)*

1. What should be considered if some of the members wish to remove the managing director?

2. What is the ultra vires rule? Does it have any real importance?

3. Is it necessary to pass any examinations to become a company director?

4. What are the main duties of the company secretary?

5. Who normally appoints the managing director?

6. What is the extent of the company secretary's authority to make contracts on behalf of the company?

13

Employers and employees: main rights and duties

Every business will either need to employ people to carry out work or engage contractors to fulfil particular tasks. In recent years the use of contractors has expanded. For example many companies do not directly employ people to clean their offices or run the staff canteen. They make a contract with a company that can provide a complete service. The rights and duties of employees are covered by a combination of statute law, common law and contract terms which may have been individually agreed or collectively negotiated by a trade union.

This Chapter explains the differences between employees and independent contractors and describes the main legal provisions relating to contacts of employment.

1 Employees and independent contractors

a) Assume you are the premises manager for a large company called Data Administration plc. It has several office blocks all of which have numerous windows. One of your jobs is to ensure that the windows are kept clean and your annual budget is £24,000. You have two basic options:

    i) Employ two, three or four staff on a full time or part time basis to clean the windows throughout the year.

    ii) Make a contract with a window cleaning company or firm under which they will clean all windows on a regular basis, for example once a month.

b) If you choose option i. above the staff will be employees of Data Administration plc and a relationship will exist which imposes certain rights and duties on both the company and the employees. If you choose ii. above the company or person doing the job will be an independent contractor and different rights and liabilities will exist.

c) Sometimes it can be difficult to distinguish between employees and independent contractors. The courts will look at what the contract says, the extent to which the employer controls the way in which the person does the job and whether or not the work is an integral part of the business or merely an addition to it. The following factors would also tend to indicate a contract of employment:

    i) Remuneration by way of payment of wages or salary, net of tax.

    ii) Membership of a company pension scheme.

    iii) Holiday pay.

iv) Payment when absent for illness.

v) A prohibition on working for competitors.

vi) Control by the employer's disciplinary code.

vii) Supply of uniform and/or equipment.

viii) Work done on the employer's premises rather than at home.

ix) Lack of personal business risk on the part of the worker.

 Group activity 1

Refer back to Assignment 1 at the end of Part 1 of the book (Aleem, Asif, Munir and Pratap). Assume their business has now raised its start-up capital and has acquired suitable premises. Working in small groups, each group should make a list of all the things that will need to be done to run an import/retail business of the type described. For example purchasing, selling, advertising, asset management, book-keeping, cleaning, security, window cleaning and so on. You should be able to think of 40 or 50 different things that are essential for the business.

Having made your list decide which jobs will be done by employees and which will be contracted out to independent contractors. Give brief reasons in each case.

2 The contract of employment

a) To be legally binding a contract of employment must fulfil all the normal contractual requirements.

i) *Offer and acceptance.* The offer must contain the terms of the contract or indicate where they may be found. No particular form is required, the contract may be oral or in writing.

ii) *Consideration.* The consideration is the employer's promise to pay the agreed wages in return for the employee's promise to perform particular tasks.

iii) *Capacity.* There is some restriction on the contractual capacity of minors (persons under the age of 18). There are also special rules relating to women, disabled persons and ethnic minorities.

iv) *Legality.* A contract of employment must not involve anything illegal, for example a deliberate attempt to defraud the Inland Revenue.

b) The contract will contain terms expressly agreed between the parties and implied terms, which are discussed below. It may also incorporate the terms of a collective agreement negotiated between a trade union and the employer.

c) Once the contract has been agreed the Trade Union Reform and Employment Rights Act 1993 requires the employer to provide the employee with a written statement of the terms of employment not later than two months after starting work. The statement is not the contract, but may be taken into account by a court or industrial tribunal. Employees are not required by the Act to sign anything in connection with these written particulars. The main matters to be included in the particulars are:

i) Names of employer and employee.

ii) Date when the employment began.

iii) Scale or rate of remuneration or the method of calculating it.

iv) Intervals at which remuneration is paid.

v) Terms and conditions relating to hours of work.

vi) Terms and conditions relating to entitlement to holidays, including public holidays and holiday pay.

vii) Terms and conditions relating to incapacity for work due to sickness or injury, including any provision for sick pay.

viii) Pensions and pension scheme.

ix) Length of notice to terminate employment.

x) Job title.

xi) Place of work, or an indication of the fact that the employee is expected to work at various places.

xii) Any collective agreements directly affecting the terms and conditions of employment.

3 The duties of an employee

These are governed by the express and implied terms of the contract. In addition there are further duties implied by the law. Contravention of any of these duties may give an employer the right to dismiss the employee. The main duties implied by the courts are as follows:

a) *Indemnity.* Where the employer suffers loss because of the wrongful act of an employee, the employee may be liable to indemnify (compensate) the employer. For example in LISTER v ROMFORD ICE (1957) Lister was a driver employed by the company. His father assisted Lister and due to Lister's negligence his father was injured and claimed damages from the company. The company in turn was able to successfully claim an indemnity from Lister to compensate for its loss.

b) *Misconduct.* This includes, for example, insolence, persistent laziness, immorality, dishonesty and drunkeness. It will justify dismissal if it directly interferes with the employer's business or the employee's ability to perform his job.

c) *Personal service.* The employee must not allow people outside the employer's control to perform his tasks.

d) *Loyalty and good faith.* The employee must not accept bribes or make a profit from the employment of which the employer is unaware.

e) *Interests of the employer.* The employee must do nothing to harm the employer's interests, even in his spare time. Nor should an employee do anything to cause the employer to lose confidence. For example in SINCLAIR v NEIGHBOUR (1967) a betting shop manager 'borrowed' £15 from the till, intending to replace it the following day, although he knew his employer would not approve. The employer discovered the employee's act and dismissed him without notice. It was held that dismissal was justified.

f) *Careful service.* An employee must exercise care and skill in the performance in his duties. For example in SUPERLUX v PLAISTED (1958) a vacuum cleaner salesman left his van outside his house overnight. Several cleaners were stolen. It was held that this breach of duty of careful service justified dismissal.

g) *Trade secrecy.* An employee must maintain secrecy over the employer's affairs during the time of his employment. This can be extended beyond the period of employment if an appropriate restaint of trade clause has been inserted in the contract of employment.

h) *Inventions.* Employees have a duty to disclose all inventions made using the employer's facilities. In BRITISH SYPHON COMPANY v HOMEWOOD (1956) a technical adviser was asked to design a soda syphon. He then patented the syphon in his own name. It was held that the patent right belonged to the employer.

i) *Obedience.* An employee must obey all lawful and justifiable orders given by the employer in the ordinary course of business.

j) *Notice.* An employee must give proper notice of intention to terminate a contract of employment.

4 Duties of employers

a) *Provision of work.* The general rule is that the employer has no duty to provide work. However there are several exceptions, for example

   i) Where work is essential to provide a reputation for future employment. For example in CLAYTON AND WALLER v OLIVER (1930) an actor was engaged for the leading role in a show. The management then took on someone else but nevertheless paid the actor the agreed wages. The actor successfully obtained further damages for loss of reputation.

   ii) Where remuneration depends on the provision of work, for example sales commission.

b) *Pay.* The employer must pay the agreed remuneration, even if the employee cannot work because no work is available.

c) *Indemnity.* The employer must reimburse employees' expenses properly incurred in the performance of their duties.

d) *To provide a reasonably safe system of work.* This was originally a common law duty, but it is now contained in the Health and Safety at Work Act 1974. The law is complex, but the main features of a safe system are:

   i) Reasonably safe workfellows. Thus if an employer knows or should know that some employees are a danger to others, he is obliged to remove them.

   ii) Training of employees. Employees must be instructed in the proper use of equipment.

iii) Effective arrangements with regard to safety apparatus. Safety apparatus must be provided to reduce dangers to a minimum.

iv) Proper co-ordination. When safety depends on co-ordination of the work of a number of departments, the employer must ensure that such co-ordination exists.

v) Suitable working conditions. However the employer will not be liable if he does not control the premises.

 Task 1

Michael Frederick Inman (known as 'MF' to his friends) is employed by Kingsway Furniture Limited. The company's main business is to sell a wide range of furniture to the public from large warehouse style buildings. MF has worked for the company for 5 years. His basic salary is £10,000 per year for a $5\frac{1}{2}$ day (38 hour) week. He also has the opportunity for a regular 3 hours a week overtime at £6 per hour. He also receives commission of 1% of sales. This usually works out at about £300 per month.

Over the last 3 years company sales and profitability have been falling. In addition the law has been changed, allowing large stores to stay open to 6 hours every Sunday. All of Kingsway Furnture's employees have just received a letter explaining the worsening business environment, and the new policy for Sunday opening. It also encloses a new employee contract. This contract does not alter the basic salary, but it does increase the hours per week to 40 and it reduces the rate of commission to $\frac{1}{2}$%. It also entitles Kingsway Furniture Limited to require MF to work at least 3 hours every Sunday. The company have asked MF to sign and return the new contract within 10 days.

Your task in to advise MF as to the practical and legal considerations that he should take into account in responding to the company's letter and contract.

Review questions

1. What is an independent contractor?
2. Is it necessary for a contract of employment to be in writing?
3. What is the difference between an express term and an implied term?
4. What is the extent of the employer's duty to provide work.
5. Is an employee entitled to make a profit over and above the agreed pay?
6. What is the legal status of employees' written particulars provided within two months of starting work?

14
Ending a contract of employment

Every year thousands of employees leave their jobs. Many will retire, some will leave by mutual agreement, others will resign to start a new job and a few will be dismissed. This Chapter is mainly concerned with employees who have been dismissed and with the provisions in the Employment Protection (Consolidation) Act 1978 (as amended) which are intended to protect employees from hardship resulting from unfair dismissal.

1 Notice of termination

The usual way of terminating a contract of employment is for either the employer or employee to give notice. Under the 1978 Act both the employer and employee are entitled to minimum periods of notice or termination of employment, during which time the employee will be paid. An employer must give an employee a least one week's notice after one month's employment, two week's notice after two year's employment, three weeks after three years and so on, up to twelve weeks after employment lasting twelve years or more. If a contract of employment specifies a longer period, this longer period will apply. Either the employer or employee may waive their rights to notice or accept a payment in lieu of (instead of) notice. The notice provisions in the Act do not prevent either party terminating the contract without notice if the conduct of the other party justifies it.

2 Written reasons for dismissal

Employees who have been dismissed are entitled under the 1978 Act to receive from their employer (provided they make a verbal or written request) a written statement of the reasons for dismissal. The employer must comply with this request within 14 days. If the employer refuses to provide the statement, or provides one which the employee believes to be inadequate or untrue, the employee may take the matter to an industrial tribunal.

3 Industrial tribunals

Industrial tribunals are independent judicial bodies. They have permanent offices in large towns and cities and sit in most parts of the country. Each tribunal has a legally qualified Chairman, appointed by the Lord Chancellor. There are two other members drawn from two panels appointed by the Secretary of State for Employment, one after consultation with employees' organisations and one after consultation with employers' organisations. In addition to issues of unfair dismissal and redundancy, industrial tribunals will consider disputes concerning for example equal pay, maternity rights, race relations, sex discrimination, trade union membership rights and occupational pension schemes.

4 Unfair dismissal

a) *The meaning of 'dismissal'*. Before a claim for unfair dismissal can be heard by a tribunal, the employee must prove that dismissal took place. This occurs when:

   i)   the employer terminates the contract with or without notice,

   ii) a fixed term contract expires without being renewed or,

   iii) the employee resigns (with or without notice) because the employer is in breach of a fundamental term of the contract thereby entitling the employee to leave. This is known as constructive dismissal.

b) *Employees who may not claim unfair dismissal.* The main categories are:

   i) employees who have not completed two years continuous employment with their employer and,

   ii) employees who have reached the normal retirement age for their employment, or if there is no normal retirement age, have reached the age 65.

   However there is no qualifying period of employment or age limits for those complaining that they have been unfairly dismissed because of their trade union membership or activities or because of non-membership of a trade union. There is also no qualifying period or age limit for those complaining of unfair dismissal on the grounds of racial or sex discrimination.

c) *Reasons justifying dismissal.* Dismissal will normally only be fair if the employer can show that it was for one of the following reasons:

   i) *Lack of capability or qualifications* i.e. if the skill, aptitude, health or any other physical or mental quality falls below that which is required for the job, or if the employee lacks any technical, academic or professional qualification relevant to the position.

   ii) *The conduct of the employee.* Examples of misconduct which justify dismissal include dishonesty, breach of safety regulations, conviction for a criminal offence, fighting and disclosing information to competitors. Conduct outside working hours may amount to a valid reason for dismissal if it could affect the employer's business. In CREFFIELD v BBC(1975) a cameraman was dismissed following his conviction for indecent assault.

   iii) *Redundancy.* Redundancy occurs when an employee is dismissed because (a) the employer has ceased, or intends to cease, either to carry on the business, or to carry on the business in a place where the employee was employed or (b) the requirements of the employer's business for employees to carry out work of a particular kind have ceased or diminished, or are expected to cease or diminish.

iv) The employee could not continue without contravening a *statutory restriction*. For example in FEARN v TAYFIELD MOTORS (1975) the employee was a vehicle supervisor. His duties included driving vehicles. He was convicted of careless driving and failing to stop after an accident and was disqualified from driving for 12 months. His dismissal was held to be fair since he could no longer legally do the job he was employed to do.

v) *Some other substantial reason*. This would include for example (a) the employer carries out a genuine re-organisation to increase efficiency, and in doing so has to dismiss employees (b) where a person is taken on for a fixed short term contract to stand in for an employee away on secondment or long term sick leave, then the termination of employment upon the other person's return will not normally be unfair.

If pressure is brought on an employer by other workers or by their Union to sack a person, this would not amount to 'some other substantial reason'

Where the employer shows that the reason was one of the above, the tribunal will consider whether the employer was reasonable in the circumstances to treat it as sufficient for dismissing the employee.

d) *Dismissal in connection with illness.*

i) The inability of an employee to do a job, for whatever reason, is a valid reason for dismissal. However special consideration should be given to a person who becomes physically or mentally unable to do their job because of illness or who is persistently absent from work. Tribunals nevertheless recognise, particularly in small firms, that it will not be possible for the organisation to keep a job open indefinitely for somebody who is off sick.

ii) The employer should discuss the position with the employee to ascertain the facts about their state of health. The employer may need to take medical advice about the employee's condition by talking (with the employee's permission) with his or her doctor. If there is less demanding work available which, the employee would be capable of doing, the tribunal will normally expect the employer to offer it to the employee.

e) *Dismissal associated with maternity.*

    i)   A woman who is expecting a baby will be unfairly dismissed if her employer dismisses her because she is pregnant, or for a reason connected with her pregnancy, unless her condition makes it impossible for her to do her job, or it would be against the law for her to do that particular job while pregnant for example. In such cases the employer must offer a suitable alternative vacancy if one is available.

    ii) If a woman has been continuously employed for at least two years prior to the 11th week before her expected week of confinement (birth of her baby), and continues to be employed until that time she is entitled to return to her former job at any time up to 29 weeks after the birth. An employee who is not permitted to return would normally be unfairly dismissed.

f) *Dismissal on the transfer of an undertaking.* Where a business or part of a business is transferred from one employer to another (for example when a business is sold) if either the old or the new employer dismisses an employee solely because of the transfer, the dismissal will be unfair. However if the dismissal is necessary for economic, technical or organisational reasons, it may be considered fair if it is the main reason for the dismissal and the employer acted reasonably in treating this reason as sufficient to justify dismissal.

g) *Unfair dismissal on grounds of redundancy.* Redundancy is a valid reason for dismissal, but an employee dismissed for redundancy may be found to have been unfairly dismissed if:

    i)   The employee was chosen for redundancy by reason of his or her trade union membership or activities, or non-membership of a union or,

    ii) Because the employer disregarded any customary arrangements or agreed procedure relating to the selection of employees for redundancy.

h) *Unfair dismissal in connection with trade union activities.* Employees have the right not to be dismissed, or chosen for redundancy, for being members of a trade union or for not belonging to a trade union. They also have the right not to be dismissed for taking part at an appropriate time in the activities of a trade union.

Where dismissal is unfair because it infringes employees' rights in connection with trade unions any award of compensation will normally be paid at a substantially higher rate than in other unfair dismissal cases.

i) *Remedies for unfair dismissal.* There are three possible remedies:

   i) *Reinstatement* i.e. the employee is treated in all respects as if the dismissal had not occurred.

   ii) *Re-engagement* i.e. the employee is re-employed, but not necessarily in the same job or on the same terms and conditions of employment.

   iii) *Compensation.*

j) *Calculation of the amount of compensation.*

   i) The employee will receive a *basic award* calculated by reference to the period of continuous employment, the age of the employee and their weekly pay:

   ☐ for each complete year of employment when the employee was 41 to 65 – one and a half week's pay

   ☐ for each complete year of employment when the employee was 22 to 40 – one week's pay

   ☐ for each complete year of employment when the employee was 18 to 21 – half a week's pay.

   There is a limit of £205 on the amount of a week's pay and a limit of 20 years. The maximum payment is therefore £205 x 20 x 1 1/2 = £6,150.

   ii) An employee will also receive a *compensatory award* based on the loss arising from the dismissal. The maximum compensatory award is currently £11,000. This would only be awarded in exceptional cases. The usual compensatory award would be £2,000 – £4,000.

   iii) If an employer fails to comply with an order for reinstatement or re-engagement they may be required to pay an *additional award* of compensation, up to a maximum of £5,330 (£10,660 in sex and race discrimination cases).

   iv) A *special award* may be made when employees who have been unfairly dismissed because of their membership or non-membership of a trade union ask to be re-employed by their employer. If the tribunal does not order re-employment, the special award will be 104 week's pay, with a maximum amount of £26,800. If the tribunal does order re-employment but the employer does not comply the special award will be 156 week's pay, with no maximum figure specified.

5 Constructive dismissal

A tribunal may decide that an employee who resigns because of the conduct of the employer has been 'constructively dismissed'. For a tribunal to make this ruling the employer's action has to be a substantial breach of the employment contract, indicating that the employer no longer intends to be bound by the contract. An example would be if the employer demotes the employee to a lower rank or a less well paid position. For example in COLEMAN v BALDWIN (1977) the buyer in a greengrocery business had the most interesting part of his work removed from him, which left only repetitive and boring duties. This was done without any agreement. It was held that there was a sufficiently substantial breach of contract that he could resign and successfully claim that he had been unfairly dismissed.

6 Redundancy

a) *Consultation.* Employers who recognise an appropriate trade union have a statutory duty, under the Employment Protection Act 1975, to consult its representative in advance about any redundancy, whether the employee to be made redundant is a member of the union or not. When 10 or more employees are to be made redundant, there is a minimum time for advance consultation with unions.

b) *Redundancy pay.* Under the Employment Protection (Consolidation) Act 1978 employers are required to make a lump sum compensation payment called a '*redundancy payment*' to employees dismissed because of redundancy. The amount of the payment is related to the employee's age, length of continuous service and weekly pay. It is calculated in the same way as the basic award for unfair dismissal. The maximum amount is therefore £6,150. The employer must give the employee a written statement showing how the payment has been calculated at or before the time the payment is made.

c) *Employees qualifying for payments.* This is also the same as in unfair dismissal i.e. employees who have not completed two years employment, or who have reached 65 have no entitlement to a payment. Service under the age of 18 does not count and the maximum length of service used to calculate redundancy payments is 20 years.

d) *The effect of an offer of a new job.* A redundant employee will not be entitled to a payment if a new job is offered with the same employer, provided the new job is offered before the old employment contract expires and starts within four weeks after the end of the old contract. In such cases the employee can put off the decision whether to accept the new job for a four week trial period. If at the end of this period the employee is still in the job, he will be regarded as having accepted it.

7 What happens when an employee makes a complaint of unfair dismissal?

a) Many disputes about dismissals are settled through voluntary procedures without the need for the employee to complain to an industrial tribunal. An employee can make an application to an industrial tribunal as soon as he has received notice of dismissal. The application will give the grounds for the complaint and must be submitted within three months of the date of termination.

b) The tribunal office dealing with the application will send the employer a copy of the application and a form called a Notice of Appearance. The employer will fill in this form indicating whether or not the case will be contested, and if so, the grounds for doing so. The employer and employee may request further particulars from each other.

c) Before the hearing takes place the parties will be given an opportunity to settle the case by conciliation. Copies of the application and the Notice of Appearance will be sent to the *Advisory, Conciliation and Arbitration Service (ACAS)*, which is an independent service separate from the industrial tribunal. Conciliation is carried out by an ACAS officer, who will try to help the parties make a voluntary agreement without having to go before a tribunal.

d) The conciliation officer will talk to both parties separately, encouraging them to use any agreed voluntary appeals procedure, if this has not already been done. He will help them to understand points of law and draw their attention to previous cases which may be similar. However the conciliation officer will not offer any opinion on the merits of either side's case or take sides in any way. Where the parties are willing the conciliation officer will explore the possibility of reinstatement or re-engagement. If the employee unreasonably refuses such an offer any eventual award of compensation made by a tribunal may be reduced. The result of most conciliation settlements is the payment of an agreed sum to the employee. Even if conciliation is unsuccessful the officer will not normally attend the tribunal hearing nor will he give the tribunal any report on the conciliation action.

 Group activity 1

For this activity you should work in groups of three or four. Each group is the Personnel Sub-Committee of the Board of Governors of a large college, operating on four sites. The Principal has asked your advice on two recent incidents.

a) Mr. Brown, an economics lecturer, recently awarded a student a fail grade in an important assignment. There was a heated argument which ended when Mr. Brown grabbed the assignment out of the student's hand, said that it was 'absolute rubbish' and tore it into tiny pieces.

b) One of the caretakers has 'resigned' and said that he is going to take the college to an industrial tribunal and claim constructive dismissal. He resigned because all of the other caretakers have totally ignored him for the last six weeks because he won £25,000 on the football pools and has not bought any of them a drink.

8 Advisory, Conciliation and Arbitration Service (ACAS)

a) ACAS has the general duty of promoting the improvement of industrial relations. It gives advice to employers on a wide range of industrial relations and employment matters. Employers may also request the assistance of its conciliation officers in helping to settle disputes. In most cases where employees or trade unions complain to an industrial tribunal, employers may seek the assistance of ACAS conciliation officers who will try to obtain an agreement between the parties without the need for a tribunal hearing.

b) ACAS publish a code of practice called '*Disciplinary Practice and Procedures in Employment*'. Failure to observe any provision of this code does not render an employer liable to any proceedings, but if there are proceedings before an industrial tribunal the code of practice is admissible in evidence and if any provision of the code appears to be relevant, the tribunal may take it into account. The code gives practical advice on how to draw up disciplinary rules and procedures and how to operate them effectively. It contains a number of guidelines, in particular it lists the main features of a disciplinary procedure, for example that such procedures should:

i) Be in writing.

ii) Specify to whom they apply.

iii) Provide for matters to be dealt with quickly.

iv) Indicate the disciplinary actions which may be taken.

v) Specify the levels of management which have the authority to take various forms of disciplinary action.

vi) Provide for individuals to be informed of the complaints against them and to be given an opportunity to state their case.

vii) Give individuals the right to be accompanied by a trade union representative or by a fellow employee of their choice.

viii) Ensure that, except for gross misconduct, no employees are dismissed for a first breach of discipline.

ix) Ensure that disciplinary action is not taken until the case has been carefully investigated.

x) Ensure that individuals are given an explanation for any penalty imposed.

xi) Provide a right of appeal and specify the procedures to be followed.

 ## Task 1

You have recently started work in the personnel section of a large company. The managing director has asked you to write a report:

a) Summarising the reasons for which an employee may be dismissed, and

b) Explaining the differences between unfair dismissal and redundancy.

 ## Discussion topic

1. Do you consider that industrial relations would be improved if employees were represented on the boards of directors of companies? (This has been the situation in Germany for many years.)

2. Do you think that the law 'interferes' too much in the law relating to contracts of employment? Is it really necessary to have so many rules on, for example, trade unions, sex discrimination, maternity rights, redundancy and so on?

 ## Review questions *(answers page 286)*

1. What are the remedies for unfair dismissal?

2. What is the definition of redundancy?

3. How much notice must be given to an employee whose contract is to be terminated?

4. What is the role of industrial tribunals?

5. What is meant by constructive dismissal?

6. What is the role of ACAS in promoting good industrial relations?

15

What is the relationship of a business to its financiers?

Most businesses require more finance than their owners can afford or are prepared to provide. The arrangements for finance will have a direct effect on the success of the business. For example, if a new business has substantial borrowing, its future could be at risk if interest rates are increasing or if cash flow becomes tight. It is therefore important to arrange finance so as to minimise the costs in the early years. Before approaching financiers, such as banks, it will be necessary to prepare a proposal or business plan even if only a small loan is required. No financier will lend to a person who approaches them with no plan, no written evidence, and no clear trading idea.

1 The proposal

This should be in two parts:

a) A one or two page summary indicating
   i) the background to the venture,
   ii) brief details of the produce and the market,
   iii) brief details of the management and organisation structure,
   iv) what the finance will be used for,
   v) the amount required,
   vi) summaries of projected profits, for at least one, but preferably three years.

b) More detailed information on the above and on other areas of the business, for example
   i) detailed product information,
   ii) qualifications, skills and experience of the management team,
   iii) how projected sales will be achieved,
   iv) information on competitors,
   v) details of past performance and accounts,

vi) a detailed monthly cash flow projection, together with underlying assumptions,

vii) sensitivity analysis i.e. an assessment of the situation if the main assumptions prove to be optimistic or pessimistic,

viii) details of the owner's personal financial stake in the business.

2 Sources of finance

Having used the projections to assess the level of finance required, the owners will need to consider the available alternatives. The main ones are:

a) Personal finance, raised from savings or from family and friends.

b) Borrowing from banks and lending institutions.

c) Venture capital borrowed from institutions specifically geared to start-up companies, who will take a percentage of the company's share capital to cover their risk and required rate of return.

d) Government and local authority grants.

e) Leasing and hire purchase for the acquisition of assets. The choice between leasing and hire purchase will involve a consideration of the tax position. When an asset, such as a vehicle, is purchased outright or leased the business can claim a capital allowance against taxable profits. If a vehicle is bought on hire purchase, only the rental is allowable for tax purposes, since the asset remains the property of the finance company.

f) Finance from customers and suppliers, by way of loans or credit. For example if a business collects its debts in 30 days on average, but pays its creditors in 50 days on average, it is in effect obtaining 20 days 'free' finance from its creditors. The amount of free finance will depend upon the sums involved as well as the time taken to pay.

3 Borrowing from banks

a) Most small and medium size businesses will obtain their finance from banks. In addition to their assessment of the business plan, the bank will be very concerned to assess the character and competence of the management team during one or more meetings with them. Normally banks will seek to secure their loans on the assets of the business. When lending to limited companies they will often take *personal guarantees* from the directors, secured on the directors' private assets, in particular their houses. The borrowing may be on an overdraft or a fixed term loan. Banks are likely to charge higher interest rates in start-up situations since the risk of failure is high.

b) The main reasons why a new venture may fail to attract finance are:

   i) Inadequacies in the management team, such as lack of motivation, financial skills, marketing ability, or the lack of an impressive track record.

   ii) Inadequate personal finance provided by owners, since this can often indicate a lack of commitment.

   iii) A poorly presented business plan.

   iv) Inadequate security available.

   v) Lack of detail as to how the loan will be repaid.

   vi) The venture as a whole is too risky, possibly because it is over ambitious, or because the product or service is weak.

 Discussion topic

As a condition of granting a loan to a company, a bank may require that one of its own representatives be appointed as a director of the borrowing company, in order to protect the bank's interests. Is such an arrangement inconsistent with the normal duties and responsibilities of a company director?

4 The difference between lending to companies and partnerships

a) Persons who lend to limited companies risk losing their money if the company goes in liquidation, since they will not have access to the private funds of members or directors. Persons who lend to partnerships can demand repayment from the partners' private assets and will only lose their money if the partners are forced into personal bankruptcy.

b) Companies must observe any borrowing limits in their memorandum. Partnerships are not be subject to such limits.

c) Public companies may issue debentures to the public. Private companies and partnerships cannot make a public issue of debentures.

d) A company may give a lender a floating charge over its assets as security for the loan. Partnerships can only give fixed charges.

5 Debentures

a) A debenture is a document issued by a company acknowledging its indebtedness under a loan. Debentures usually give a fixed or floating charge over the company's assets (or both) as security. A debenture may be an individual debenture evidencing a large sum lent by one person, or the company may issue debenture stock to a number of persons, each of whom is given a debenture stock certificate, which is similar to a share certificate.

b) *The differences between shares and debentures.*

   i) The legal position of shareholders and debenture holders is quite different. Shareholders are the owners of the business, they have provided share capital and they have a financial stake in the business. Debenture holders may well be dependent on the success of the business for repayment of capital and interest, but they are still outsiders who have a claim against the company rather than a stake in it.

   ii) Shares carry a greater degree of risk than debentures, and ordinary shareholders may get a variable return on their investment. If profits are good this will probably exceed the fixed rate of interest paid to debenture holders. Debentures carry less risk, since debenture interest is a contract debt and must be paid whether or not profits have been earned. In addition debentures will be secured by fixed and/or floating charges on the company's assets.

6 Fixed and floating charges

a) A *fixed charge* is a mortgage of land or fixed plant and machinery. It prevents the company selling the assets charged without the consent of the charge holder.

b) A *floating charge* is a charge on some or all of the present and future assets of the company. Provided the company carries on business in the ordinary way assets sold will automatically be released from the charge and assets purchased will automatically become subject to the charge.

c) A floating charge will convert to a fixed charge (thus allowing the debenture holders to enforce the security) if the company ceases business, or if a receiver or liquidator is appointed.

d) The ability to grant a floating charge is one advantage of choosing to conduct business as a limited company. It is particularly useful if the company has a small amount of land, but carries a large or valuable stock-in-trade, for example a jeweller's shop. From the lender's point of view a floating charge is not as good security as a fixed charge. In particular the value is uncertain, since the value of the assets subject to the charge will fluctuate. When the charge is most needed, i.e. when the company is in difficulty, the value of the assets is likely to be at its lowest level.

 Task 1

A friend of yours wishes to support one of his relatives by investing £25,000 in the relative's private limited company. Your friend has heard of ordinary shares, preference shares and debentures, but does not know the difference between them. Write a letter to your friend advising him of the differences and suggesting how he can best protect his investment.

7 Registration of charges

a) When a company creates a charge this must be registered with the Registrar of Companies within 21 days. This is important since it ensures that when other potential lenders search the company's file at the Companies Registry, they will find out whether the assets offered by the company as security are already subject to charges. It is pointless for a lender to take an asset as security if existing charges secured by that asset exceed its value.

b) Once a charge has been properly registered, everyone in the world is regarded as knowing that the charge exists. They are said to have *'constructive notice'* of the charge. This is important since it establishes the priority of the charge over any later charges created on the same property.

c) In addition to registration with the Registrar of Companies, the company must record all charges in its own register of charges. This will contain:

i) a short description of the property charged,

ii) the amount of the charge, and

iii) the names of the persons entitled to the charge.

8 Remedies of debenture holders

If the company fails to pay interest to debenture holders, or if the assets subject to the charge are threatened in any way, the debenture holders may wish to seek an appropriate remedy. They may:

a) Sue as creditors for arrears of interest.

b) Petition to wind up the company on the ground that it is unable to pay its debts, or

c) Apply to the court to appoint a receiver, or appoint a receiver themselves if they were given the right to do so when the debentures were created. The receiver's job is to sell the assets subject to the charge and repay the debenture holders out of the sale proceeds. Any surplus will be returned to the company (or the liquidator, if the company has subsequently gone into liquidation).

 Review questions *(answers page 287)*

1. Can either debenture interest or dividends be paid out of capital?

2. What is a floating charge?

3. When will a floating charge convert to a fixed charge?

4. Why is a floating charge an inferior form of security compared with a fixed charge?

5. What is meant by constructive notice?

6. What is the function of a receiver?

7. What are the main remedies of debenture holders?

8. Why is it important for a charge created by a company to be registered with the Registrar of Companies?

16

Doing business with companies and partnerships

This Chapter briefly introduces the concept of agency, since anyone who does business on behalf of a company or partnership is its agent. It then highlights the distinction between the capacity of a company to make a contract and the capacity of directors and employees to make contracts on behalf of a company. The same distinction is not necessary with partnerships, since the firm is not legally separate from the partners.

1 The law of agency

a) An important similarity in the position of persons dealing with companies and partnerships, arises as a result of law of agency. An agent is a person who is able to make a contract on behalf of someone else (called the principal). Company directors (and some company employees) are agents who can make binding contracts on behalf of the company. All partners are agents of the other partners.

b) The law is faced with an interesting dilemma when dealing with agents who make contracts which are beyond the authority given to them by the principal. Should the law protect the principal by holding that the contract is void, or should it protect the other party by holding that the contract is valid? The dilemma is resolved by saying that if the contract is within the apparent authority of the agent, the contract will bind the principal. This is the case whether the contract is made by a director, partner or employee.

2 Dealing with companies – the capacity of the company

a) Firstly it is necessary to decide whether the contract is within the capacity of the company.

b) One of the clauses in the memorandum of association is the *objects clause*. This sets out the activities that the company may engage in. Originally its main purpose was to tell prospective members the kind of business they were investing in. However both companies and persons dealing with them found this limit on the company's powers very inconvenient, since contracts entered into in good faith would be ultra vires (beyond its powers) and void if they fell outside the stated objects.

c) The law was fundamentally changed by the Companies Act 1989.

   i) The Act provides that it is sufficient for the memorandum to state that the object of the company is to carry on business as a general commercial company. This will allow it to carry on any trade or business whatsoever and do anything that is incidental to any trade or business carried on by it. This makes it almost impossible to enter into an ultra vires contract.

   ii) The Act also states that the validity of an act done by a company shall not be called into question on the ground of lack of capacity by reason of anything in the company's memorandum. In other words, even if it is outside the objects clause, the contract will still be valid. Consequently a completed act or contract will have total protection from what was known as the 'ultra vires rule' and will be enforceable by both the company and the outsider.

   iii) Members may still bring an action to restrain an intended act that is beyond the capacity of the company, but in all other respects the 1989 Act has effectively abolished the ultra vires rule.

3 Dealing with companies – the capacity of directors and employees

a) In this paragraph we are concerned with contracts which are within the capacity of the company, but beyond the powers of the person claiming to act on the company's behalf.

b) The outsider will be protected, i.e. the contract will be valid, if the company ratifies (i.e accepts) it. If it will not do so, the outsider must rely on another new provision in the 1989 Act (see c. below), or on the rules of agency.

c) The 1989 Act states that if a person deals with a company in good faith, the power of the directors to bind the company, or authorise others to do so, shall be free of any limitation under the company's constitution. This effectively means that no limits can be placed on the directors' powers.

d) The rules of agency allow an agent (for example a company employee) who has no actual authority, to bind the principal (the company) to a contract if the outsider:

   i) was induced to make the contract by the agent being represented as occupying a certain position in the company, and

   ii) the representation was made by persons with actual authority to manage the company, and

   iii) the contract was one which a person in the position which the agent was held out as occupying would usually have authority to make.

 Task 1

Refer back to Chapter 12, Task 1 (page 79). Your friend Dennis has made some further worrying discoveries on which he would like your advice:

a) In March 1993 (just prior to Agrifood Ltd's incorporation on 1st April 1993) one of the promoters (Alan) contracted in the name of the company for some machinery, paying 50% of the purchase price on placing the order and undertaking to pay the remaining 50% on delivery. The machinery was supplied in November 1993 and has been in continuous use by Agrifood Ltd since that date. However the 50% due on delivery has not been paid and Barry has written to the supplier denying that Agrifood Ltd is liable on the ground that it did not place the order.

b) Alan (who is Agrifood Ltd's managing director) has just signed a contract on behalf of Agrifood, giving an Exeter based company, sole distribution rights for the company's products in the West of England, despite the fact that the Company's Articles provide that no contract concerning the appointment of agents can be made by Agrifood Ltd without the unanimous resolution of the Board.

Write a letter to Dennis advising him of the legal position in each case.

4 Dealing with partnerships

a) Every partner is an agent of the firm and therefore has authority to bind the firm to transactions entered into in the *ordinary course of business*. Thus an outsider who contracts with a partner within what is apparently the ordinary course of business, may treat the firm as bound, despite any internal restriction on the authority of that partner, unless the outsider knew of the restriction.

In MERCANTILE CREDIT v GARROD (1962) A and B were partners in a firm which let garages and repaired cars. The partnership agreement expressly excluded buying and selling cars. Without B's knowledge A, acting without the owner's consent, sold a car to a finance company for £700, paying the proceeds into the partnership account. It was held that B was liable to repay the £700 to the finance company. The prohibition on buying and selling in the partnership agreement did not entitle B (or the firm) to avoid liability since A's conduct was of a kind normally undertaken by persons trading as a garage, i.e. they apparently had authority to sell cars.

b) In a trading partnership the following acts are within the implied authority of a partner.

i) Borrowing money in the name of the firm and giving security for a loan.

ii) Signing cheques.

iii) Employing a solicitor to defend an action against the firm. However it is doubtful if a partner would have authority to commence proceedings other than routine actions to recover trade debts.

iv) Receiving payment of debts and giving valid receipts.

v) Buying and selling goods on account of the firm.

vi) Engaging employees to work for the firm. A partner probably does not have implied authority to dismiss employees.

c) The following acts are outside a partner's implied authority.

i) Consenting to a judgment against the firm.

ii) Executing a deed.

iii) Giving a guarantee in the absence of a trade custom to do so.

iv) Referring a dispute to arbitration.

v) Accepting property other than money in payment of a debt.

5 Remedies for breach of contract

If a company or partnership breaks a contract, the innocent party has the usual contractual remedies described in Chapter 23. In addition a person who has not been paid by a company may petition to wind up the company if the debt exceeds £750.

 Group activity 1

One of the tasks in Chapter 1 (page 5) was based on a tennis coaching business. Imagine that this business has three partners, who have each contributed £5,000 to the new firm. The partners will coach tennis, re-string tennis, squash and badminton rackets and sell sports footware. They will work from home. Each person wants to be fully involved in every aspect of the business.

Working in groups of three write some rules defining what will be within the authority of any one of the partners, what will need the agreement of two partners and what will require the unanimous agreement of all three partners.

Review questions *(answers page 289)*

1. Who is able to make a binding contract on behalf of a company?

2. What is the purpose of the objects clause in a company's memo-randum?

3. Does the ultra vires rule apply to partnerships?

4. Give three examples of contracts that a partner in a trading part-nership would have implied authority to make.

17

Other liabilities that affect businesses

The previous Chapters have considered the relationship of companies to owners, directors, employees, customers and financiers. They also dealt with the relationship between partnerships and their customers and between the partners themselves. The vast majority of these relationships are based on the existence of a contract between the parties.

This Chapter considers other liabilities which may affect businesses, but which are not based on the law of contract.

a) *Vicarious liability* normally arises when an employee commits a negligent act in the course of his employment. The employer is liable merely because of the employment relationship, not because of any personal fault.

b) *Liability for torts* arises when a company has broken a general duty imposed by the law, for example the duty not to commit a nuisance.

c) *The criminal liability* of companies is a difficult area. The concept of vicarious liability does not apply to criminal law, so where a company is held to be guilty of a crime, it is primary liability that has been imposed.

d) *Liability to the community* exists through the tort of nuisance and through many statutory provisions. There is however no overall obligation to act in a socially responsible manner or for the benefit of the community as a whole.

1 Vicarious liability

a) Vicarious liability means liability for the conduct of someone else, for example liability for their negligence. An employer will be liable for the negligence of an employee if the negligent act is committed in the *'course of their employment'*.

b) The main difficulty that has surrounded this area of law is the definition of 'course of employment'. It has been held that if an employee is doing what he was employed to do he will be within the course of employment even if the conduct was negligent, fraudulent or even expressly forbidden by the employer. For example in ROSE v PLENTY (1976) Plenty was a milkman. His employer did everything possible to stop the common practice of taking young children on the van and paying them to help deliver the milk. A notice at the depot said 'children must not in any circumstances be employed by you in the performance of your duties'. Contrary to this instruction Plenty employed Rose. While Plenty was driving the van Rose left one leg dangling from the van so that he could jump off quickly. Plenty drove too close to the kerb and Rose's foot was crushed between the van and the kerb. It was held that Plenty's employers were liable because Plenty had been acting within the course of his employment, i.e. Rose was being used directly to enable Plenty to do his job of delivering milk.

This case also illustrates the rationale for vicarious liability. Employers will be aware of potential liability and can insure against it, thus providing injured parties with access to sufficient compensation. In the absence of such a provision it is unlikely that an employee such as Plenty would have sufficient money to compensate Rose.

c) A person will not be within the course of their employment if (even during working hours) they do something different from what they were employed to do. For example if a bus conductor drives a bus and causes an accident the bus company will not be liable since conductors are only employed to collect fares, not to drive buses.

d) Where the employer is held vicariously liable for the conduct of the employee, the employee will still be personally liable. If a blameless employer is held liable for an employee's conduct, the employer can seek indemnity (i.e. reimbursement) from the employee.

e) An employer will not be liable for the conduct of an independent contractor. An *independent contractor* is a person taken on to produce a specific result and who in the execution of their job is not under the direct control of the employer. For example if a building company instructs its own employees to install windows in a new building it will be liable if an employee's negligence causes injury. If, however, the company sub-contracts the whole job to a specialist firm of glaziers, it will not be liable for any negligence by that firm or their employees. Only the firm of glaziers (and their negligent employee) would be liable.

2 Liability for torts

a) If a person commits a tort they break a general duty imposed by the law.The law of tort deals with a wide variety of wrongs for example:

i) Intentionally or negligently causing physical injury to another person (trespass to the person and negligence).

ii) Interfering with the use or enjoyment of another person's land (nuisance and trespass to land).

iii) Publishing false statements that tend to injure a person's reputation or cause them to be shunned by ordinary members society. This is known as defamation. There are two forms of defamation, libel which is generally written statements and slander which is generally spoken.

b) The usual remedy for the injured party is *damages*. When fixing damages the court will aim to put the injured party in the position he would have been if the tort had not been committed. In some cases an injunction, for example a court order instructing a person to stop committing the tort of nuisance, would be the appropriate remedy.

c) In 1. above it was explained that an employer (whether a sole trader, company or partnership) will be vicariously liable for torts committed by employees in the course of their employment. If a tort is not committed by an employee, but by a partner in the ordinary course of business, or with the authority of the other partners, all the partners will be liable.

d) The situation with companies is more complex because although a company is a legal person, it can only act through human agents. The problem is to decide when an act such as negligence can be regarded as an act of the company itself, instead of merely an act of an employee for which the company is vicariously liable. There is no simple answer to this question and it will depend on the circumstances of each case. The court will take into account the influence and seniority of the person concerned. In most cases an act of a director or the company secretary would be regarded as the company's act.

3 Liability for crimes

a) *Partnerships.* A partner will not usually be liable for the criminal acts of co-partners. However some statutes, for example the Health and Safety at Work Act 1974, impose duties on all the partners. If such duties are broken it will be no defence for a partner to say that responsibility for complying with the Act had been delegated to one or more co-partners. Such criminal liability attaches to each partner personally and not the firm, since the firm has no legal personality.

b) *Companies.*

i) As an artificial person it is impossible for a company to commit certain crimes, such as murder. In some situations it will be difficult to decide whether the conduct of an officer or employee can be regarded as the company's conduct. For example in MOORE v BRESLER (1944) the company was convicted of making false tax returns as a result of the conduct of its secretary and a branch manager. In contrast in TESCO v NATRASS (1972) the company was held not guilty of an offence under the Trade Descriptions Act 1968 when a shop manager failed to ensure that goods advertised for sale at a particular price were in fact being offered for sale at that price. The court took the view that the shop manager could not be identified with the company, but was a separate person.

ii) In most cases where criminal liability is imposed by statute, the statute will make it clear that both the individual and the company commit the crime. For example the Companies Act 1989 states that if a company fails to submit an annual return both the company and the individual responsible are guilty of an offence and can be fined.

 Discussion topic

What is the difference between a crime and a civil wrong?

4 Companies and the community

a) Companies operate in a very complex environment. The other players and stakeholders are illustrated in the following diagram.

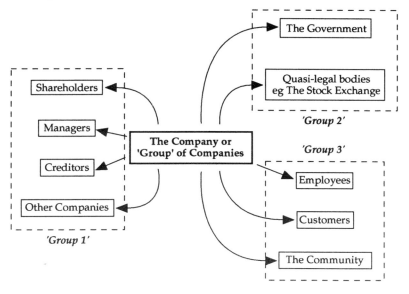

b) Company law is mainly concerned with the stakeholders in 'group 1'.

It seeks to ensure:

i) That the majority of shareholders do not abuse their power at the expense of the minority.

ii) That the directors do not abuse their position of trust and responsibility.

iii) That creditors (who do not have access to the private funds of members) are given some protection by rules to maintain the capital of the company and by the publicity requirements that accompany incorporation.

iv) That there is an effective formal legal structure that enables companies to exist, trade, merge with or acquire other companies and finally cease business.

c) The players in 'group 2' make the rules that govern companies. Companies are subject to numerous statutes, concerning for example health and safety at work, taxation and so on. The Companies Act 1985 is the most substantial Act ever passed, with 747 sections and 25 schedules. Companies must also be very aware of European regulations, and public companies must comply with Stock Exchange rules if they wish to keep their stock exchange listing.

d) Company law is less concerned with the stakeholders in group 3. Employees and customers are basically outsiders with whom the company has a contract. Of course a contract of employment is a special type of contract, which is also regulated by several Acts of Parliament.

e) Companies have very few formal responsibilities to the community as a whole. There are some common law and statutory duties concerning for example air and water pollution, but there is no overall requirement to act in a socially responsible way or do anything that confers benefit on the community. Many companies do however act for the benefit of the local or national community. Probably the main area of activity is in the field of education. For example thousands of companies each year offer work experience places to school and college students. Some larger companies run educational projects. For example each year British Telecom grants 30 fellowships to schoolteachers, enabling them to spend 10 days or more gaining industrial experience at one of BT's locations. Another example is Nuclear

Electric. In 1993 and 1994 they sponsored a competition called 'Science Challenge' which aimed to help classes of 9 to 13 year olds develop their understanding of the principles and application of science.

There have been some cases where shareholders have attempted to force their company to pursue policies with social objectives, even if this resulted in lower profits. For example the shareholders of the American company 'Dow Chemicals' tried to amend its constitution to prevent it selling napalm for use in the Vietnam war. In the UK the shareholders of Distillers Ltd. put pressure on the company to behave generously to the children born handicapped as a result of their mothers' use of the drug thalidomide during pregnancy. A more unusual situation occurred when a number of individuals purchased one share each in Tarmac, solely to enable them to have the right to attend company meetings, so that they could disrupt these meetings as a protest against Tarmac's involvement in the construction of the military facility at Greenham Common.

As long ago as 1973 the Confederation of British Industry (CBI) acknowledged that companies should accept social responsibility over and above that required by the law concerning such matters as pollution, conservation and local community affairs. However it is most unlikely that this will ever be introduced as a legal requirement since it would be extremely difficult to define the criteria to be applied and measure each company's performance.

 Task 1

Select a British 'household' name company. Find out the location of their head office. Write to their Public Relations Department and ask if they are engaged in any activities or projects which benefit the community as a whole. Try to find out why they are involved. For example is it for genuine reasons of social responsibility or do they regard it as another way of advertising?

Discussion topic

The world's largest companies are massive multi-national conglomerates. In 1991/2 the world's largest company (in terms of sales) was Itoh & Co. Ltd of Japan. Its annual sales were £86,616,000,000 i.e. about £237m per day. British Petroleum (twelfth on the world list) is just under half the size of Itoh, and Sainsburys (tenth on the UK list) is less than 1/10th its size.

Do you think that these companies are so large that in some respects they are 'above the law'?

 Review questions *(answers page 290)*

1. What is a tort?
2. What remedies are available for the victim of a tort?
3. Is it possible for a company to commit a crime?
4. Are companies legally obliged to act in a socially responsible way?
5. Briefly explain the tort of defamation.
6. If an employer has been held vicariously liable for the negligence of one of their employees, what action can the company take against the employee?

 Part 2 assignments

Assignment 3

Three years ago Harold, Ted, Margaret and Neil graduated from university with good degrees in computing and electronics. They decided to set up Videotron Limited to produce software for computer games and virtual reality applications. The business was an instant success. The company has grown and now has four directors, Harold, Ted, Margaret and Neil, who each hold 20% of the company's shares. Harold is also the managing director. They have a sales and marketing manager, Barbara who holds 10% of the shares.

Similarly their office manager and company secretary, Alec also holds 10% of the shares. They also have six other employees.

To date the success of the business has been due to the quality of the products, rather than the business skills of the directors. They are all well motivated, but very product centred. As a result a number of problems and disputes have arisen. Alec, who has some business experience, is very concerned and has asked your advice. The problems he has identified are as follows:

a) Neil and Alec feel that Harold is managing the business so inefficiently that, despite several new contracts, the company is on the verge of insolvency.

b) Barbara and Alec are most annoyed that the company has never declared any dividends, although good profits have been earned and directors' remuneration has been increased by 25% each year.

c) Ted wrote a new games programme called 'Ten Pin' simulating ten pin bowling. It took him 280 hours of company time. The New Product Appraisal Committee (Harold, Margaret and Barbara) rejected it. Ted has now sold it privately to Sega for £40,000. To date no-one other than Alec knows this.

d) Harold has just sent Ted a letter informing him that since he had wasted so much time on 'Ten Pin', he has been removed from his position on the Board of Directors.

e) A leading competitor has alleged that one of the company's most successful games is a copy of one of their games. Examination of the two games reveals so many similarities that it has to be accepted that the other company is correct. Videotron's game was developed by Margaret and no-one else in the company had any reason to suspect that it was not completely original.

f) Despite his business experience, Alec has just realised that the company has neither held an annual general meeting, nor submitted an annual return for 19 months.

Write a report for Alec advising him how to respond to the above situations.

Assignment 4

Andrew Bates and Jeremy Castle (see Assignments 1 and 2 pages 63 and 64) established their tennis coaching partnership about six months ago. Everything seemed to go well at first, but recently a number of problems have arisen. Earlier in the week Andrew came to see you with a number of problems and last night Jeremy also asked for your help.

Andrew's concerns are:

a) 400 tennis balls purchased by Jeremy five months ago have not been paid for. Andrew did not realise that Jeremy had purchased so many tennis balls and regards the purchase as very foolish since, even new tennis balls go soft after about eight weeks. Andrew has now received a letter from the supplier saying that if he does not receive Andrew's cheque within seven days he will issue a summons without further notice.

b) Last week, when demonstrating an overhead smash, Jeremy's racket slipped out of his hand and hit a young pupil who was standing nearby, breaking her cheekbone. Her parents have informed Andrew and Jeremy that they will be seeking compensation.

c) Andrew has just discovered that Jeremy has been coaching the county under-14 champion for one hour every day for the last four weeks for £1 per hour (instead of the usual £10 per hour) since the pupil's parents have said that they can only afford £1 per hour.

Jeremy's concerns are:

a) For three weeks Andrew had a trapped nerve in his back and was only able to work 14 hours per week, instead of the usual 38 hours. Now that Andrew's back is better he works a full day at the South Herts Club, but Jeremy has just discovered that for the last two weeks Andrew has been doing a further two hours coaching per night (9.00pm until 11.00pm) at the David Lloyd Centre in Watford.

b) Andrew failed to turn up for two lessons last Saturday morning. The first was a two hour individual lesson for one of the competitors in the club's under 18 final, due to be played the next day. The final went ahead and was a very close match, but Andrew's pupil lost and blames this on missing his lesson. The other lesson was a two hour group session. This was taken by Andrew's father, who is a good club player, but who has no coaching qualifications. Some of the parents, whose children were taught during this session have asked for their money back.

1. Write a report:

   a) Summarising the rights and liabilities of partners.

   b) Giving Andrew and Jeremy general advice on the future conduct and organisation of their business.

2. Write a letter to Andrew enclosing the above report and giving him specific advice on the matters about which he is concerned.

3. Write a similar letter to Jeremy.

Part 3

Business contracts

Element 9.3   Investigate contractual agreements made in business

Every business, whatever its size or legal structure, will have as its key activity the making of business contracts. These may be trading contracts for the purchase and sale of goods, or they may be contracts that enable the business to provide a service, for example as cleaning contractors or management consultants. Some business contracts will be for a few pence, for example the sale of a packet of sweets, others will be for millions of pounds.

The basic rules of the law of contract set out in this Part of the book apply to all contracts, whatever their value or nature. These rules deal with the requirements for the formation of a valid contract, the different types of contract term, the ways in which a contract may come to an end (for example because it has been performed or because one party is in breach) and the remedies available to a person who is the victim of a breach of contract. There is also a brief introduction to some special types of contract, for example cheques and contracts of insurance.

On successful completion of Part 3 activities and review questions, students will understand the nature and scope of different types of contract (performance criteria 2) and appreciate the main consequences of defects in either the formation or performance of a contract (performance criteria 3). The end of part assignments will generate the evidence required for your portfolio of coursework.

BTEC guide to coverage of performance criteria

The performance criteria and evidence indicators are listed in the left-hand column. The Assignment column contains the number of the assignment which covers the criteria indicated.

The Task and Group Activity columns indicate the chapter numbers as well as task or group activity numbers. For example '2.1' in the

Task column indicates Chapter 2 Task 1 covers that particular performance criteria. '2.1' in the Group Activity column would indicate Chapter 2 Group Activity 1 covers the criteria in question.

9.3 Investigate contractual arrangements made in business

Performance Criteria and Evidence Indicators	Assignment	Task	Group activity
9.3.1 The nature and scope of contractual agreements are described		21.1, 24.1	9.1, 10.1 21.1, 21.2 22.1
9.3.2 The legal requirements of a valid contract are identified	5,6	19.1	
9.3.3 The effects and implications of defects in contractual agreements are explained		20.1, 20.2 22.1, 23.1 23.2, 24.2	
Evidence indicator. An analysis of one example of a standard form contract and one negotiated agreement used in business. The examples will have been chosen by the student and used to demonstrate their ability to identify and illustrate the legal requirements of a valid contract.	5, 6		25.1

18

What is a contract?

Millions of contracts are made every day. They range from commercial contracts for millions of pounds, for example a contract to build a factory, to numerous small contracts made each day by individuals, for example the purchase of a cup of coffee for 30p in the college refectory. The commercial contract will probably have taken months to negotiate and could contain several hundred written terms and conditions. In contrast the purchase of a cup of coffee will be an instant decision and nothing will be written down. Even so it is a legal contract containing terms and conditions. Both of these contracts are governed by the same general principles, mainly contained in case law built up over the past hundred years. There are some Acts of Parliament relevant to contract, for example the Sale of Goods Act 1979, the Unfair Contract Terms Act 1977, the Misrepresentation Act 1967 and the Bills of Exchange Act 1882, but unlike company law there is no major Act of Parliament containing all, or most, of the relevant law.

This Chapter gives a brief introduction to the essential elements of a contract. These are discussed in more detail in the following Chapters.

1 The concept of a contract

a) The basic philosophy underlying the law of contract is that the parties have complete freedom to contract on whatever terms they wish and that the resulting contract is the outcome of a meeting of minds. In reality this is often not the case. For example:

   i) The growth of large-scale business has led to *standard form contracts*. An individual must usually enter into such a contract on a 'take it or leave it' basis. There will be no opportunity to negotiate special terms for, for example, the supply of electricity or water.

   ii) The law will *imply terms* into contracts to ensure that certain standards are maintained. A person will be bound by these terms even if they are never mentioned or even thought of.

For example, the sale of coffee referred to above will contain an implied term that the coffee is 'fit for its purpose'. This term is implied by the Sale of Goods Act 1979. If the cup contains some broken glass there would be a breach of this implied term.

iii) The *public interest* also sometimes requires that freedom to contract is modified. For example, the Unfair Contract Terms Act 1977 makes void any term in a consumer contract under which the consumer gives up rights given by the Sale of Goods Act.

b) Legal contracts are sometimes described as *'enforceable agreements'*. This is rather misleading since, if one person breaks a contract, the court will not normally insist that it is performed. Usually the remedy for breach of contract is damages, i.e. a payment of money by the person in breach to the other party. If the court does enforce the contract by ordering it to be carried out this is known as the remedy of *specific performance*.

 Discussion topic

If you decided to have a written contract for the sale of a cup of coffee what would you include?

2 The essential elements of a contract

A contract is an agreement that will be enforced by the law. The law will only enforce agreements if certain essential elements are present. These are as follows:

a) *Agreement.* To decide whether an agreement has been reached the court will ask whether one person has made an *offer* which the other person has *accepted*. The agreement must result from a genuine consent. There will be no contract if, for example, a person's agreement has been obtained by fraud, misrepresentation or threats. In some cases if the parties have made a mistake this will also mean that there is no agreement, for example if the vendor thought he was selling product X, but the buyer thought he was buying a completely different product, product Y.

b) *Intention to create a legal agreement.*

   i) Many agreements are not intended by the parties to be legal contracts, for example an arrangement to meet someone for lunch, or an agreement by parents to pay pocket money to their children. If the lunch arrangement is broken or the pocket money is not paid, no legal remedy exists because these were social or domestic arrangements, which were clearly not intended to have legal consequences. Of course this does not mean that someone can avoid a contract at a later date by saying that they never had any intention to create a legal agreement.

   ii) If the court has to decide whether someone intended to create a legal agreement they will judge intention by looking at what that person said, wrote or did. If their conduct would indicate to a reasonable person that they intended to make a contract, they will be regarded as having made a contract, whatever their actual intention. This is known as judging intention by an *objective test*.

c) *Value.* There must be an element of value in a contract. If someone gives you something and you give nothing in return you cannot sue them if the thing given turns out to be defective. It is not generally necessary for value to be represented by money given in return for goods or services. A contract may involve an exchange of goods or services. Furthermore the thing given does not have to be of similar value to the thing given in return. All that is required is that there is 'something for something' rather than 'something for nothing'. This element of value is known as *consideration*.

d) *Capacity.* Both parties must have capacity to contract i.e. be allowed by the law to make the contract.

   i) *Minors* (persons under 18) have restricted capacity. They will however be bound by contracts to purchase necessary goods and services (which are very widely defined) or by contracts of service (employment).

   ii) *Corporations* also have a limited capacity. In theory they can only make contracts which are within the objects clause of their memorandum. Until 1989 contracts outside their objects were *ultra vires* (beyond their powers) and void. However, since 1989, the validity of a contract made by a company cannot be called into question on the ground of lack of capacity. Thus although members may bring proceedings to restrain an intended act which is beyond the capacity of the company, once the contract has been made, the ultra vires rule does not apply and the contract can be enforced, both by the company and by the other party.

e) *Form.* The general rule is that the contract may be in writing, or made orally, or inferred from conduct, or a combination of any of these. There are three categories of exception:

   i)   Contracts which must be *by deed*. This includes a conveyance or transfer of a legal estate in land (including a mortgage) or the grant of a lease for three years or more.

   ii) Contracts which must be *in writing*. The main types are company share transfers, contracts promising to transfer title to land (as opposed to the actual transfer document which must be by deed), cheques, consumer credit contracts and policies of insurance.

   iii) Contracts which must be supported by *written evidence*. The courts will not enforce a contract of guarantee unless there is written evidence of all the material terms signed by the guarantor. For example Susan (aged 19) borrows £5,000 from Central Bank to start a business. Carol (Susan's mother) promises to re-pay the loan if Susan does not do so. Carol's guarantee of Susan's loan will not be enforceable unless there is written evidence of the main terms, signed by Carol.

f) *Legality.* The courts will obviously not enforce a contract to do an unlawful act, for example a contract to commit a crime. Nor will they enforce certain contracts which are regarded as contrary to public policy, for example a contract which restricts a person from freely exercising a trade or profession. There are exceptions to this, for example it is possible to prevent an ex-employee from competing with their former employer, provided the duration of the restraint and the area covered are not unreasonable. Similarly the vendor of a business can be prevented from competing with the new owner.

Discussion topic

When making contracts minors (persons under 18) must be protected from the consequences of their own inexperience. On the other hand the law needs to protect people who make contracts with persons who appear to be at least 18 years old. How can the law resolve this dilemma?

 Review questions *(answers page 292)*

1. Is it necessary for all contracts to be in writing?
2. What is an implied term?
3. What is the legal term for the element of value in a contract?
4. What categories of person have restrictions placed on their capacity to enter into contracts?
5. What is meant by an 'objective test'?
6. What are damages?

19

How contracts are made

This Chapter looks in more detail at the essential elements introduced in the previous chapter. The first requirement is that there must be an agreement. An agreement will exist when one party has accepted an offer made by the other. It was suggested some years ago by Lord Denning, who was then the Head of the Civil Division of the Court of Appeal, that in order to determine whether an agreement existed, the court should look at all of the relevant circumstances (i.e. what the parties had said, written or done). However Lord Denning's view did not prevail and the existence of an agreement is still determined by a rather artificial analysis based on offer and acceptance.

The Chapter also looks at the element of value (known as consideration) necessary for a valid contract, and the requirement that the parties must intend their agreement to be a legal contract as opposed to a social or domestic arrangement.

1 Offer

a) An offer is an expression of willingness to contract on specific terms. An offer may be made to a particular person, a class of persons or to the public at large.

b) It is important to distinguish an offer from an *invitation to treat*, which is an invitation made to another person to make an offer. There are several types of invitation to treat.

   i) *General advertising of goods.* Advertising goods, for example in a newspaper, is not an offer for sale even if a price is stated. Similarly the circulation of a price list to potential customers is only an invitation to treat. Even if words such as 'special offer' are used, no legal offer is being made by the person advertising the goods. However advertisements of reward for the return of lost or stolen property are offers since they clearly show an intention to be bound without the need for further negotiation.

   ii) *Exhibiting goods for sale.* Goods on display, even if priced, are not an offer to sell at that price. Thus if a person notices a television displayed for sale wrongly priced at £15 instead of £150, that person cannot claim to 'accept' at £15. The shop will be able to say that the television on display was an invitation to treat, and that they have decided not to accept the customer's offer of £15.

In the case which established that goods on display are an invitation to treat, the decision determined whether or not a crime had been committed. In PHARMACEUTICAL SOCIETY OF GREAT BRITAIN v BOOTS CHEMISTS (1953) an Act of Parliament required certain drugs to be sold in the presence of a qualified pharmacist. Boots operated a self-service shop, with a qualified pharmacist present at the checkout, but not at the shelves on which the drugs were displayed. The precise point of sale was therefore relevant to determine whether or not an offence had been committed. It was held that the display was an invitation to treat, the customer then made an offer to buy when the drugs were brought to the checkout, and the taking of the money by the pharmacist was the acceptance. The sale therefore took place at the checkout and Boots therefore did not commit an offence.

iii) *An auctioneer's request for bids.* The request for bids is an invitation to treat. The bid is the offer and the fall of the auctioneer's hammer is the acceptance. An auctioneer is not therefore compelled to sell to the highest bidder.

iv) *An invitation for tenders.* A tender is an estimate (usually for a supply of goods, or the carrying out of a service) submitted in response to a prior request. The situation is similar to an auction. The person tendering makes the offer and the person who invited the tender may accept whichever tender they wish. There is no obligation to award the contract to the person submitting the lowest tender.

v) *Sales of shares.* When a company issues a prospectus inviting the public to subscribe for shares, the document will be described as an 'offer for sale'. In fact it is only an invitation to the public to make offers, which the company can accept or reject at its discretion. An acceptance must normally precisely match the offer, but where a company issues shares it will reserve the right to make a partial acceptance of subscribers' offers, because the number of shares applied for is likely to exceed the number of shares available.

c) An offer can be terminated in several ways.

i) *Withdrawal.* To be effective the withdrawal must be communicated to and received by the person to whom it was made (the offeree).

ii) *Refusal or counter-offer.* If goods are offered for sale at £1000 and the offeree refuses this offer or makes a counter-offer of, for example, £900, this will have the effect of terminating the original offer to sell at £1000. If the offeree later changes his mind and tries to 'accept' at £1000 this will be ineffective, since the offer to sell at £1000 no longer exists.

iii) *Lapse of time.* If no period is fixed an offer will lapse after a reasonable time. What is reasonable will vary depending on the goods. For example an offer to sell tomatoes may lapse after a few hours, whereas an offer to sell bricks may not lapse for several weeks.

2 Acceptance

a) An acceptance must be unconditional and must correspond to the terms of the offer. If X offers to sell 100 tons of grain for £1000, Y cannot 'accept' 50 tons at £500. (Y can of course offer to buy 50 tons for £500 which X may choose to accept). Similarly an acceptance 'subject to contract' is ineffective. It is possible to accept by conduct, for example by despatching goods in response to an offer to buy, or by returning a lost dog in response to an offer of a reward.

b) The offeror cannot impose a condition that silence shall amount to acceptance. For example it is not possible to make an agreement by saying 'if you do not telephone me by Friday I will assume that you have accepted my offer to buy your car for £5,000'.

c) In general acceptance is not effective until communicated to and received by the offeror. Thus if an acceptance is not received because of, for example, interference on a telephone line, there is no contract. However if it is the offeror's fault that acceptance is not received, then acceptance would be regarded as communicated. This would occur if, for example, the offeree accepts by Fax, but no-one in the offeror's office bothers to read it.

d) An exception to the rule that acceptance must be communicated occurs when acceptance is by post. In this case acceptance is complete when a letter is posted. A contract would therefore exist even if the letter is lost in the post.

e) In complex commercial contracts which are the result of lengthy negotiations, it can be very difficult to say exactly when an offer has been made and accepted, since the draft agreement will go through several changes as new demands are made or concessions granted. In the event of a dispute the court will need to look at all the correspondence and take evidence of any oral statements in order to decide whether the parties agreed to the same terms.

f) Problems also occur when both parties claim to have contracted on their own 'standard conditions' and these conditions conflict.

For example in BRITISH ROAD SERVICES v ARTHUR CRUTCHLEY LIMITED (1967) BRS delivered whisky for storage with a delivery note incorporating their standard terms. When taking delivery AC Ltd stamped the delivery note 'received under Arthur Crutchley Ltd's conditions'. It was held that this stamp amounted to a counter-offer which BRS had accepted by handing over the goods. The contract had therefore been made on AC Ltd's standard terms.

3 Consideration

a) This is the element of value essential for a valid contract. It may be mutual promises to do something in the future. For example X orders a garden shed from Y to be delivered and paid for next week. There are two promises for the law to enforce: X's promise to pay and Y's promise to deliver. In this situation, where the acts have not been performed, the consideration is said to be *executory*.

b) If in the above case X paid for the shed at the time it was ordered, his consideration would be *executed* and there would only be one promise for the law to enforce, namely Y's promise to deliver the shed.

c) There is no consideration if a person promises to pay for a completed act. For example if A mows B's lawn as a favour while B is on holiday and later B promises to pay, A cannot enforce B's promise to pay if B changes his mind. The act that A would be putting forward as consideration i.e. mowing the lawn, was finished before any promise to pay was made. This is know as *past consideration* and it will not support a contract.

d) Sometimes a person who has provided no consideration will get the benefit of the contract, whereas the person who paid the price will get no benefit. For example John orders flowers to be sent to Mary, who is in hospital. If the flowers are not sent, John is entitled to a remedy against the shop, because the contract is between John and the shop. The only persons who can sue on a contract are the parties to that contract, not someone outside the contract, even if the contract was made for their benefit.

e) As long as something of value supports the contract the court will not ask whether it is proportionate in value to the thing

given in return. The court is not concerned with providing remedies for people who make bad bargains. It is therefore possible to
make a valid contract to sell a valuable car for 1p.

f) Sometimes a person (P) who is in financial difficulties may have
a debtor (Q) who tries to take advantage of the situation by
offering part payment if such payment is accepted in full settlement of their debt. Such a part payment is no consideration for a
promise to release the balance. The general rule is that P may sue
for the balance, despite their previous indication that they would
not do so.

For example in D & C BUILDERS v REES (1965) Rees owed
the builders £482. She knew that they were in financial trouble
and offered them £300 in full settlement of the debt. The builders
accepted this, but later changed their mind and sued for the
remaining £182. They succeeded because the defendant's
payment of £300 was no consideration for the builders' promise
to let them off the balance.

4 Intention to create legal relations

a) Some contracts will expressly state that there is no intention to
create legal relations. This is usually the case with, for example,
football pools. Such contracts are *'binding in honour only'*.

b) If the parties do not expressly deny intention to create legal relations, what matters is not their actual intention, but the inference
reasonable people would draw from their words or conduct i.e. it
is an *objective test*.

c) In a *commercial contract* it is presumed that the parties intend to
create legal relations. If one party claimed that there was no such
intention they would have to produce evidence to have the
assumption set aside. In a *domestic situation* the opposite applies
i.e. it is presumed that legal relations are not intended unless
evidence to the contrary can be produced.

 Task 1

Last week a friend of yours, Mark, was the 'victim' of a remarkable
coincidence. He had arranged to meet his friend Ann at 'Le Corgi'
for lunch. Because it was Ann's birthday, Mark telephoned the

restaurant the day before and placed a special order for lobster. On the way to 'Le Corgi' Mark saw a handbag in a shop window priced at £35 and went in to buy it as a gift for Ann. The shopkeeper said that it had been wrongly placed there and was already sold. Mark felt that the shopkeeper could not insist on this but had to leave without making a purchase. Ann never arrived at 'Le Corgi' and Mark was presented with a bill for £47 for the lobster which had been ordered for him. He was upset because Ann had not arrived, so he stormed out without paying.

On the way home, whilst walking through the park, he came across a stray dog, a corgi. There was a tag on its collar indicating that it was owned by 'Le Corgi' restaurant. By now Mark had calmed down, so he decided to take the dog back to its owner.

The restaurant owner was delighted to be reunited with his dog and told Mark that he would tear up the bill for the lobster. Later that evening, when Mark had arrived home, he was reading yesterday's local paper when he noticed a display box which read as follows 'Lost, prize-winning pedigree corgi. £500 reward if returned to 'Le Corgi' restaurant'.

Advise Mark.

5 Carlill v Carbolic Smokeball Company (1893)

The leading case illustrating a number of important points concerned with the formation of contract, dates back to 1893. In CARLILL v CARBOLIC SMOKEBALL CO the defendant company manufactured a patent medicine, called a 'smokeball'. In various advertisements they offered to pay £100 to any person who caught influenza after having sniffed the smokeball three times a day for two weeks. They also stated that they had deposited £1000 at the Alliance Bank in Regent Street to show their 'sincerity'. Mrs Calill used the smokeball as advertised and contracted influenza after more than two weeks treatment, and whilst still using the smokeball. She claimed her £100. The company raised several defences:

a) The advertisement was too vague since it did not state a time limit in which the user had to contract influenza.

   The court said that it must at least protect the user during the period of use.

b) It was not possible to make an offer to the whole world, or to the public at large.

> *The court made a comparison with reward cases and stated that such an offer was possible.*

c) Acceptance was not communicated.

> *It was not necessary to do so in such cases. A comparison was again made with reward cases where no communication is necessary.*

d) The advertisement was a mere gimmick and there was no intention to create legal relations.

> *The deposit of £1000 would indicate to a reasonable person that there was an intention to create legal relations.*

e) Mrs. Calill provided no consideration.

> *This was the most promising defence, but it was held that the actual act of sniffing the smokeball amounted to consideration. (The purchase price could not be consideration, since it supported a contract with the seller of the smokeball, not the manufacturer).*

Discussion topic

Aleem, Asif, Munir and Pratap (see Assignment 1 page 63) have now formed their company, Indian Traders Limited, and want to know whether the company is contractually bound in each of the following situations.

a) It promised to sell an Indian carpet to Javed and gave him seven days to make up his mind. Four days later it sold the carpet to Wasim for a better price. On the sixth day it received a letter from Javed accepting the offer of Indian Traders Ltd.

b) It promised to sell a very valuable antique Indian tapestry to Priti for £3.

c) It promised to sell 20 pairs of Levis to Harry at a price to be fixed later.

d) After Eric had painted Indian Traders Ltd's office the company promised to pay Eric £800.

e) It received unsolicited goods through the post with a notice saying that it will be assumed that Indian Traders Ltd has bought them unless they are returned within seven days.

 Review questions *(answers page 293)*

1. X wrote to Y offering to sell his car for £1,000. At the same time Y wrote to X offering to buy X's car for £1,000. Is there a valid contract?

2. Name three methods by which a contractual offer may be terminated.

3. Define consideration and distinguish between executed, executory and past consideration.

4. What is an invitation to treat?

5. How much time must pass before an offer ceases to exist because of lapse of time?

6. Nigel agreed with his son-in-law Martin, that Martin would enter a car race. Martin was to drive the car and Nigel would pay the entry fee. Martin won the race and Nigel is claiming half of the prize money. Advise Martin.

20

Factors affecting the validity of a contract

This Chapter considers a number of situations which may prevent the formation of a valid contract, namely misrepresentation, mistake, illegality, duress and undue influence.

1 Misrepresentation

a) A misrepresentation is an untrue statement of fact which is one of the causes which induces a contract. For example if A is selling a second-hand car to B he may tell B that the car has done 40,000 miles (the reading on the milometer). If the car has done more than 40,000 miles, but someone has altered the milometer, this would amount to misrepresentation if B allowed it to affect his decision. If B would have bought the car whatever the mileage, no action can be brought. If A knew the mileage had been altered, the misrepresentation would be fraudulent, and if he did not know then the misrepresentation would be innocent. Misrepresentation makes a contract *voidable*. This means that the contract is valid until the victim of the misrepresentation exercises his option to avoid the contract.

b) A statement of opinion, for example that a product represents good value, will not amount to a misrepresentation unless the maker of the statement is an expert or has special knowledge. Similarly silence cannot amount to a misrepresentation unless a statement made in negotiations subsequently becomes false and is not corrected, or where silence distorts a statement which is literally true.

c) The above example shows that there are two basic types of misrepresentation, namely *fraudulent* misrepresentation and *innocent* misrepresentation. A third category, *negligent* misrepresentation, was introduced by the Misrepresentation Act 1967.

   i) *A fraudulent misrepresentation* is a statement which is known to be false, or made without belief in its truth, or made recklessly, not caring whether it is true or false. The innocent party may chose to ignore the misrepresentation and to continue with the contract. Alternatively he may rescind the contract (i.e obtain restoration to the pre-contract situation) and claim damages.

ii) *An innocent misrepresentation* is a statement which the maker honestly and reasonably believes to be true. As with fraudulent misrepresentation the victim may chose to continue with the contract. Alternatively the victim has the right to rescind the contract, but there is no right to damages. However damages may be awarded instead of rescission, if the court considers it equitable (fair) to do so. This would probably be the case if the misrepresentation was very trivial.

iii) *A negligent misrepresentation* is a false statement made by someone who had no reasonable grounds for believing it to be true. The victim has a right to damages if he has suffered loss. The remedy of rescission is also available.

d) The remedy of rescission will be lost in certain situations.

i) If the innocent party, with knowledge of the right to rescind, affirms the contract, i.e. by his conduct leads the other party to believe that he intends to continue with the contract.

ii) Lapse of time. For example in LEAF v INTERNATIONAL GALLERIES (1950) Leaf was persuaded to buy a painting by an innocent misrepresentation that it was by John Constable. Five years later he discovered the truth and immediately claimed rescission. Since he acted immediately he could not be said to have affirmed the contract, nevertheless his claim was held to be barred by lapse of time.

iii) If restoration to the pre-contract state of affairs is impossible, for example because the goods have been sold to someone else, or because they are perishable and have deteriorated.

 Task 1

In negotiations leading to the sale of his business, the seller, Samuel, made a true statement giving total figures for turnover and profits for the last five years. This gave the buyer (Barbara) the impression that the business was in a healthy state. Barbara did not ask for any further breakdown of the figures. If she had they would have shown a steady decline in profitability. Barbara, having completed the purchase, has now discovered the true state of affairs.

Advise Barbara as to her remedies, if any.

2 Mistake

People frequently make mistakes when they purchase goods. A person may realise too late that a new pair of shoes are too small, or that a briefcase which had been assumed to be leather is in fact imitation leather. The general rule for such mistakes is that the contract is binding, i.e that mistakes about the quality or characteristics of goods do not invalidate the contract or give any remedy to the person who made the mistake. However there are some types of mistake which will render a contract *void*.

a) Mistake as to the existence of the subject matter, i.e the parties make a contract relating to something which (unknown to both of them) does not exist.

b) Mistake as to the possibility of performing the contract i.e the parties make a contract which (unknown to both of them) cannot possibly be performed.

c) Mistake as to the identity of the subject matter. For example A intended to buy product X, but B intended to sell product Y.

d) Mistake as to the identity of other party. This is a much more complex situation. It will normally occur when a fraudulent person Mr Crook induces a vendor Mr Baker to sell goods by representing himself as some other person. If the courts are to hold that a mistake as to identity makes the contract void, it is essential that

   i) The parties do not deal face to face, and

   ii) Mr Crook represents himself as someone else who actually exists, not a fictitious person, and

   iii) The identity of the purchaser is important to Mr Baker.

   If these conditions are satisfied Mr Baker will be able to recover the goods, since title cannot pass under a void contract.

   In LEWIS v AVERAY (1971) Lewis advertised his car for sale and was induced to accept a cheque from a crook who said he was the famous actor Richard Greene (who played Robin

Hood in a BBC television series). The cheque was worthless. Lewis was able to trace the car to Averay who had purchased it from the crook in good faith. Lewis was unable to recover the car because the contract with the crook was not void for mistake since the parties had dealt face to face. Lewis' mistake was as to the credit worthiness of the other party and not to his identity. The contract between Lewis and the crook was therefore only voidable for fraud. The importance of this distinction is explained in more detail in e. below.

e) It is very important to distinguish a contract which is *void for mistake* from one which is merely *voidable for misrepresentation*. The distinction is of little importance to the original parties, since the goods or money can be recovered from the other party to the contract if they are still in his possession. The distinction is however very significant if the goods have been sold to a third party. For example if Ann 'sells' her car to Brenda and then Brenda re-sells the car to Carol, if the contract between Ann and Brenda is void for mistake, then Ann can recover the car from Carol, because no title passes under a void contract.

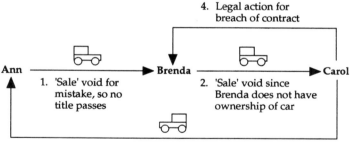

If Brenda is a crook and cannot be found in order to commence the legal action, Carol will bear the loss.

In the next example the sale from David to Eric is only voidable for misrepresentation (by Eric). Eric then sells the car to Fred. Fred will become the owner of the car provided the second sale took place before David could avoid the contract with Eric. This is because 'voidable' means 'valid until avoided'.

Example: Avoidance before second sale

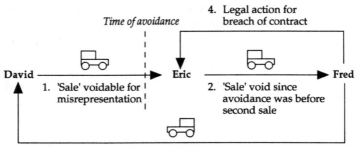

If Eric is a crook and cannot be found in order to commence the legal action, Fred will bear the loss.

Example: Avoidance after second sale

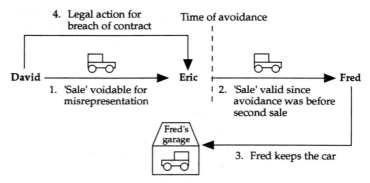

If Eric is a crook and cannot be found in order to commence the legal action, David will bear the loss.

In each of the above situations the crook (Brenda or Eric)will obtain the car without paying for it, for example by giving a forged cheque. The crook will then sell on for cash and disappear.

3 Duress

Duress occurs when physical violence or the threat of violence causes someone to make a contract. The effect is that the contract is *voidable*.

4 Undue influence

a) Sometimes, where there is a relationship based on trust, for example a solicitor and client or parent and child, the person in whom trust is placed brings pressure to bear on the other to such an extent that they make a contract that it to their disadvantage and which they would not otherwise have made. This is known as undue influence and its effect is to make the contract *voidable*.

b) Another type of undue influence occurs when a party to a contract abuses a position of economic power. This is known as *economic duress*. For example in ATLAS EXPRESS v KAFCO (1989) Kafco had a contract with Woolworths for the delivery of its goods to about 800 Woolworths stores. Kafco then made a contract with Atlas Express for carriage of the goods. Atlas later decided that the carriage charge was too low and presented Kafco with a new invoice showing higher carriage charges. They also refused to accept any goods for delivery unless the invoice showing the higher charges was signed. Kafco protested and tried to resist the increase, but since they were committed to Woolworths (who would withdraw their business if the goods were not delivered) they signed the invoice. Subsequently Kafco refused to pay the increased charge and was sued by Atlas Express. Kafco's defence of economic duress was accepted by the court. It was also held that Atlas Express had provided no consideration for Kafco's signature of the invoice since they had not promised to do anything over and above what was already in the contract.

5 Illegality

The courts will not enforce contracts prohibited by statute or contracts to commit crimes or civil wrongs, for example an agreement to divide the proceeds of theft or a contract drawn up to deceive the Inland Revenue. However there are many more contracts, which are neither prohibited by statute, nor involved with anything criminal, but which will not be enforced by the courts because they are *contrary to public policy*. The most important of these are contracts in *restraint of trade* i.e. a contract which restricts anyone from freely exercising their trade or profession. When looking at such contracts the court tries to balance two conflicting interests. On the one hand it is in the interest of the parties to be able to contract on whatever terms they wish. On the other hand any restraint of trade is likely to be against the public interest, since it will give them less choice or less bargaining power. The basic rule is therefore that a contract in restraint of trade is illegal and void. In four exceptional situations a restraint of trade may be upheld if it is reasonable.

a) *Restraints imposed on ex-employees.* An employer is entitled to protect his trade secrets and business connections provided the area of the restraint and its duration are not unreasonable. In MASON v PROVIDENT CLOTHING (1913) the company's ex-employee was restrained from working in a similar post within 25 miles of London. This restraint was held to be void since the area was too wide, being about one thousand times as large as the area in which he was employed. The reasonableness of the duration of the restraint depends on the type of business to be protected. If it is one to which clients are likely to resort for a long time, a lifetime restraint may be valid. Thus in FITCH v DEWES (1921) a lifetime restraint preventing a legal executive from practicing within seven miles of his former employer's office was upheld.

b) *Restraints imposed on the vendor of a business.* Provided there is a genuine sale of the goodwill, then a restraint that is of reasonable duration and covering a reasonable area will be upheld. What is reasonable will depend on the nature of the business.

c) *Restraints arising from agreements between traders.* Such restraints often involve a fixing of a minimum price below which goods could not be sold. For example the 'Net Book Agreement' operated by the Publishers' Association enables publishers to enforce minimum retail prices for individual books, known as 'net books'. Clearly such contracts are contrary to the public interest and protection has been given by, for example, the Restrictive Trade Practices Act 1976 and the Resale Prices Act 1976. The RTPA requires certain types of restrictive trading agreement to be brought before the Restrictive Practices Court to determine whether the restriction is contrary to the public interest. If it is then the offending provisions are void. The RPA 1976 provides that if an agreement between a supplier and dealer establishes a minimum price to be charged by the dealer, that provision will be void, although there is a power for the Restrictive Practices Court to grant exemption in certain cases. The Net Book Agreement has been approved by the Restrictive Trade Practices

Court to protect small bookshops from price cutting by larger more powerful competitors.

d) *Solus agreements* i.e. where a trader agrees to restrict his orders to one supplier. Such agreements are often made in the petrol industry, with garages agreeing to buy, for example, Shell or Esso petrol. Duration is the most important factor in assessing the legality of these agreements. In ESSO PETROL v HARPERS GARAGE (1967) a four and a half year restraint was upheld, whereas in PETROFINA v MARTIN (1966) a twelve year restraint was declared void.

 Task 2

Garage Limited entered into an agreement with Petrol plc under the terms of which Garage Ltd would receive a 3% discount on petrol bought from Petrol plc. The agreement included a promise by Garage Ltd not to buy and sell the petrol of any other company for eight years from the date of the agreement. After the agreement had been in force for two years, Garage Ltd decided to buy its petrol from another supplier.

Your tasks are:

a) Draft a memo to the managing director of Petrol plc setting out the legal position.

b) Enclose with your memo a draft letter from the managing director to Garage Ltd.

6 Conclusion

We have seen that the parties to a contract can usually agree whatever terms they wish (either verbally or in writing) and the court will enforce their agreement. The majority of rules concerned with the question of how contracts are made are contained in hundreds of cases on offer, acceptance, consideration, intention to create legal relations and so on. These are supported by statutory rules in specific areas, dealing with for example misrepresentation, capacity of children to make contracts and traders who seek to take advantage of consumers.

Review questions (answers page 295)

1. Define a fraudulent misrepresentation.

2. What would cause the victim of an innocent misrepresentation to lose the right to rescind the contract?

3. Andrew advertised his car for sale for £5,000 in a local newspaper. Brian saw the advertisement and telephoned Andrew and offered him £4,500 for the car. Andrew eventually offered to sell Brian the car for £4,800 and Brian said he would need to drive the car before he could agree such a price. They agreed to time to meet at Andrew's house at the weekend for a test drive. On Friday Andrew sold the car to Charles for £4,500. Advise Brian.

4. Carol was short of money and wished to sell some of her jewellery. She took it to a local shop where Denise offered her £300 which Carol accepted. Denise offered Carol a cheque, but Carol asked for cash. Denise then produced a card which suggested that she was a famous actress and Carol agreed to take the cheque. The cheque proved worthless and Denise has disappeared having re-sold the jewellery to Eileen for £200. Advise Carol.

5. What is economic duress?

6. What are the main factors that will determine the reasonableness of a restraint of trade clause imposed on an ex-employee?

21

What do contracts contain?

The contents of a contract are mainly determined by the words used by the parties. These will be the express terms of the contract. Where a contract is in writing, the general rule is that the court will not look beyond these written terms to determine what the contract contains. Contracts will also contain other terms which have not been expressly agreed or stated, but which are implied either because the parties intended them to be implied, or because the law, for example the Sale of Goods Act 1979, has included them in the contract.

This Chapter first considers the question of whether the statements made by the parties are mere representations which remain outside the contract, or contract terms. It explains the difference between the two types of contract term, namely conditions and warranties and goes on to consider implied terms and exemption clauses. Finally the main provisions of the Unfair Contract Terms Act 1977 are outlined.

1 Contract terms and representations

a) Sue wants to sell her car privately and places the following advertisement in her local paper.

'1991 Ford Escort 1.6 GL, blue, 30,000 miles, two owners, extras, excellent condition, £5,000, telephone 071 123 4567'.

A possible buyer, John telephones Sue and in response to a number of questions Sue tells John that:

i)   The car had a new clutch three months ago

ii) It has just been serviced

iii) It has never been in a crash

iv) It does 34 miles per gallon

v)   It has never broken down

vi) She is selling it because she has been offered a company car.

John then visits Sue's house to drive and inspect the car. He is not very thorough and does not notice that there is no spare wheel. During their discussion Sue assures John that the mileage is genuine, and that mechanically the car is perfect. John then buys the car for £4,800.

b) In the negotiations leading to the sale of the car many statements have been made relating to the sale. Some are very specific and likely to be regarded by John as important, for example the statement that the car has done 30,000 miles. Others are just as important but much less specific, for example Sue's assurance that 'mechanically the car is perfect'. Other statements may be very specific, but much less important, such as the reason given for the sale. Finally there are matters which would concern some buyers but not others, for example the statement that the car had never been in a crash. Some buyers would automatically reject a car that had been involved in a serious crash, others would assume that it had been properly repaired and would not be put off purchasing it.

c) All these statements will be either representations, or express terms. The express terms will be either warranties or conditions.

Representations

i) These are statements which induce the formation of a contract, but which do not form part of the contract. If a representation is untrue the innocent party (in this case John) will have a remedy for misrepresentation. In Chapter 20.1 it was shown that a misrepresentation may be innocent, negligent or fraudulent.

Express terms

ii) *Warranties* are statements which, unlike representations, do become part of the contract, but are not regarded as the most important contract terms. If a warranty is broken the innocent party is entitled to damages, but does not have the right to treat the contract as being at an end.

In this book the term 'warranty' will always mean this type of contract term. There is another meaning which applies when a seller gives a warranty with goods sold to a customer. In this situation it means the same as 'guarantee'. It is important not to confuse a warranty given with goods sold with 'warranty' meaning a particular type of contract term.

A *condition* is a vital contract term. They are so important to the contract that if a condition is broken the innocent party may treat the contract as at an end and claim damages.

d) Even in the simple example of the sale of a second-hand car it is very difficult to classify all the statements, since classification as a representation, condition or warranty depends on the intention of the parties. This will vary because different buyers will attach varying degrees of importance to similar statements. John may regard the mileage of 30,000 as very important whereas another buyer may be much more heavily influenced by the statement that the car has never broken down. The intention of the parties is assessed objectively by reference to their words or conduct. If a dispute arises a person cannot say that their intention was one thing if it would appear to a reasonable observer that their intention was something else. When judging intention the courts will consider a number of factors, for example

i) The stage of negotiations at which the statement was made. The later it was made the more likely it is to be a contract term.

ii) Whether the statement was reduced to writing after it was made. If it was it is clearly regarded as more important, and is therefore probably a contract term.

iii) Whether the person making the statement suggests that the other party should check it. If so it is more likely to be a representation.

iv) Whether the maker of the statement possessed special skill or knowledge as compared with the other party. For example in DICK BENTLEY PRODUCTIONS v HAROLD SMITH MOTORS (1965) the dealer sold a Bentley car stating that it had done only 20,000 miles since a replacement engine, whereas it in fact had done 100,000 miles. This statement was held to be a contract term since the dealer was in a much better position to know the mileage than the purchaser.

2 Standard form contracts

a) Many contracts are in standard printed form. The basic terms are set out and applied to all contracts of the same kind. There will be a number of blanks to be filled in, for example with the buyer's name, the price of the goods or services, the delivery date and so on.

b) A major advantage of such contracts is that they save time. It would clearly be impractical, particularly for businesses dealing with the public, to negotiate and settle new contracts for each transaction.

c) One disadvantage is that consumers rarely read the 'small print' and even if they do, it would be most unusual for a consumer to insist on changing the terms. This has sometimes led to businesses taking advantage of the situation by including terms in the standard form contract which exclude or limit their liability in the event of their own breach of contract.

d) The law has now redressed the balance of power to some extent by passing the Unfair Contract Terms Act 1977 (see 5. below). This Act makes some exemption clauses void, while others are only valid if they satisfy a test of reasonableness.

e) A typical standard form contract for the purchase of a second-hand car from a large main dealer (Perry Group plc) is included in Appendix E.

 Group activity 1

Working in groups of two or three, go into several high street stores or any other businesses that deal with consumers. Ask them for a copy of their standard form contract. Explain that you will only use it for educational purposes. Try to obtain several different standard form contracts. Back at college study the small print.

a) Can you identify any exemption clauses? If so do you consider them to be reasonable?

b) Do you think the contract should be re-drafted so that it is fairer to the consumer? If so what would you change?

3 Implied terms

a) It has been shown that the contract between Sue and John contains a number of conditions and warranties that had been expressly agreed between them, either verbally or in writing. It will also contain contract terms that will not have been expressly agreed and which Sue and John may not even have thought of. These are known as implied terms.

b) Some terms are implied by custom. This means that the parties are presumed to have contracted by reference to the customs prevailing in the trade or locality in question. Terms may also be implied by the courts either because:

i) The term is so obvious that the parties must have intended it to be included, or

ii) The term has been implied because the law seeks to maintain certain standards of behaviour. Thus for example in contracts of employment the employee impliedly promises to serve the employer faithfully and that he is reasonably skilled. The employer impliedly promises that he will not require the employee to do an unlawful act and that he will provide safe premises.

c) The most important implied terms are contained in the Sale of Goods Act 1979, which repeated provisions first enacted in 1893. The main implied conditions are:

   i) That the seller has a *right to sell* (S.12 SGA 1979). Thus John does not have to agree with Sue that it is her car or that she is selling as the owner's agent. If it is later discovered that the car was not Sue's because it was stolen, then John can sue Sue for breach of this implied condition (even if Sue was unaware that she was selling a stolen car). The car itself will of course have to be returned to the true owner.

   ii) That goods sold in the course of the business are of *merchantable quality* (S.14[2] SGA 1979). 'Merchantable quality' means that *the goods must be as fit for their usual purpose as is reasonable to expect having regard to any description applied to them, the price and all other relevant circumstances.* Thus defects which would render new goods unmerchantable will not necessarily be unacceptable if they occur in second-hand goods. Second-hand goods will however be unmerchantable if the defect is sufficiently serious. In SHINE v GENERAL GUARANTEE FINANCE (1988) it was held that a 20-month old second-hand car was not of merchantable quality at the time of the sale when the buyer later discovered that 8 months earlier it had been written off by insurers, since it had been totally submerged in water for over 24 hours.

   iii) That goods sold in the course of a business are *fit for their purpose* (S.14[3] SGA 1979). It is possible that goods which are of merchantable quality are not fit for a particular purpose which the buyer makes known to the seller. Thus if the buyer makes his purpose known to the seller and he relies on the seller's skill and judgment, he will have a remedy for breach of condition if the goods are found not to be fit for that purpose.

d) The Sale of Goods Act 1979, as the name implies, only covers sales of goods, it does not cover contracts where goods are supplied as an incidental part of, for example, a contract for work and materials. In such cases the Supply of Goods and

Services Act 1982 implies conditions for goods supplied similar to the conditions implied by the Sale of Goods Act for goods sold.

e) Another important type of contract concerns *consumer services*. For example contracts for storage, repairs, cleaning, transport, holidays, banking, law, accounting, advertising, dentistry, teaching and so on. These contracts lead to thousands of disputes each year about, for example, the quality of workmanship, delays in carrying out work and the price charged. The Supply of Goods and Services Act 1982 therefore implies conditions that:

   i) Where the supplier is acting in the course of a business he will carry out the service with *reasonable care and skill* (S.13 SGSA 1982).

   ii) Where the supplier is acting in the course of a business and the time for the service to be carried out is not fixed by the contract or determined by the course of dealings between the parties, the supplier will carry out the service within a *reasonable time* (S.14 SGSA 1982).

   iii) That where the price is not determined by the contract or in a manner agreed in the contract or by the course of dealings between the parties, the person dealing with the supplier will pay a *reasonable price* (S.15 SGSA 1982).

4 Exemption and limitation clauses

a) An *exemption clause is* a term in a contract which seeks to exempt one of the parties from all liability. A *limitation clause* seeks to limit a party's liability to a specific sum if certain events occur, such as breach of condition, negligence, or theft of the goods.

b) An exemption clause may become a term of the contract by *signature* or *notice*. If the contract is not signed the exemption or limitation clause will only apply if:

   i) The party knows of the clause, or if

   ii) Reasonable steps are taken to bring it to his attention before the contract is made.

In OLLEY v MARLBOROUGH COURT (1949) Olley booked in at the Marlborough Court Hotel. When she went to her room she saw a notice on the wall stating that the hotel would not be liable for articles lost or stolen unless they were handed in for safe-keeping. Olley left some furs in the bedroom and closed the self-locking door. She then hung the key on a board in reception. Her furs were stolen. It was held that the exemption clause was not effective because the contract was completed at the reception desk before she went up to the bedroom. Thus the notice in the bedroom was seen too late to be part of the contract.

c) The more outlandish the clause (whether it is an exemption clause, a limitation clause or an agreed damages clause) the greater the effort that must be made to bring it to the other party's attention. In INTERFOTO PICTURE LIBRARY v STILETTO VISUAL PROGRAMMES (1988) an advertising agency (Stiletto) hired 47 transparencies from Interfoto. They arrived with a delivery note requiring them to be returned by a specified date. The delivery note included nine 'small print' conditions which Stiletto never read. One of the conditions stated that it if the transparencies were returned late there would be a charge of £5 per transparency per day. Stiletto returned the transparencies 14 days late and was billed for over £3,500. Interfoto's claim failed since the clause imposed an unusual and exorbitant charge and they had not taken sufficient steps to bring it to the attention of a person with whom they had never previously dealt.

d) Even if a person signs a contract containing an exemption clause, the person signing may not be bound by it if the other party misrepresented the terms of the contract. In CURTIS v CHEMICAL CLEANING (1951) Curtis took a white satin wedding dress, trimmed with beads and sequins to the cleaners. The assistant gave her a form to sign and when asked about its contents she said that it excluded the company's liability for damage to the beads and sequins. Curtis then signed the form, which in fact contained a clause excluding the company from all liability. When the dress was returned it was badly stained. The company attempted to rely on their exemption clause, but it was held that they could not do so since the assistant had misrepresented the effect of the form.

e) The use of exemption clauses may be defended on the grounds that people should have freedom to contract on whatever terms they wish. They also make it possible for contracting parties to agree different rates according to the risks to be borne by each of them. On the other hand there is a need to protect the public from exemption clauses in standard form contracts used by large companies. For example some years ago it was impossible to buy a new car from a dealer without 'signing away' all the rights given by the Sale of Goods Act. Limitations on the use of exemption clauses are now contained in the Unfair Contract Terms Act 1977.

5 The Unfair Contract Terms Act 1977

a) The Act uses two methods for controlling exemption clauses. Some clauses are completely ineffective, whereas others are subject to a test of reasonableness. It is also relevant that the Act only applies to liability which arises in the course of a business. The main provisions are set out below.

b) *S.2. Exclusion of negligence liability.*

   i) A person cannot, by reference to any contract term, restrict his liability for death or personal injury caused by his negligence.

   ii) In the case of other loss or damage (for example damage to the other person's property) a person cannot restrict his liability for negligence unless the term is reasonable.

c) *S.3. Standard term contracts and consumer contracts.* The party who imposes the standard term contract or who deals with the consumer cannot, unless the term is reasonable:

   i) Restrict his liability for his own breach, or

   ii) Claim to be entitled to render substantially different performance, or no performance at all.

d) *S.5. 'Guarantee' of consumer goods.* Where goods are of a type ordinarily supplied for private use or consumption and loss or damage arises because the goods are defective and the manufacturer or distributor was negligent, liability cannot be excluded or restricted by reference to a term contained in a 'guarantee' of the goods.

e) *S.6. Sale of goods.*

   i) S.12 SGA 1979 (implied condition as to title) cannot be excluded.

ii) S.13-15 SGA 1979 cannot be excluded in a consumer sale, but can be excluded in a non-consumer sale if the exemption clause is reasonable.

S.14 was discussed above. S.13 implies a condition that in a *sale by description* the goods shall correspond with the description and S.15 implies a condition that where goods are *sold by sample* the bulk will correspond with the sample.

f) *S.11. The requirement of reasonableness.* The Act states that reasonableness must be assessed by reference to all of the circumstances, but it also lays down some guidelines, for example:

i) The strength of the bargaining positions of the parties relative to each other.

ii) Whether the customer received an inducement (such as a lower price) to agree to the term. If he did the term is more likely to be reasonable.

iii) Whether the customer knew or ought reasonably to have known of the existence and extent of the clause.

iv) Where the term excludes or restricts liability if some condition is not complied with, whether it was reasonable at the time of the contract to expect compliance with the condition.

v) Whether the goods were manufactured to the special order of the customer. If they were the term is more likely to be reasonable.

An example of an unreasonable exemption clause was recently considered by the House of Lords. In SMITH v ERIC BUSH (1989) Smith wished to purchase a house. She approached the Abbey National Building Society for a mortgage and paid for a survey including a valuation report by the surveyor (Eric Bush) hired by the building society. Smith did not hire her own surveyor, but relied on the building society's survey and valuation. Bush however negligently failed to notice that removal of the chimney breasts had left the chimneys in a dangerous state. A few months after Smith moved in they collapsed, causing considerable damage. Although Smith was allowed to see the valuation report, her mortgage application form stated that neither the Abbey National, nor the surveyor gave any warranty that the report was accurate, and that it was supplied without responsibility on their part. The House of Lords held that this disclaimer of responsibility was unreasonable in circumstances where the surveyor knows that the borrower will be supplied with a copy of the report and is likely to rely on it despite the disclaimer. Smith was therefore successful in her action.

 Task 1

To: Chief Administrative Officer, Central College

From: Principal, Central College

Date: 1st September 1994

I have had several telephone conversations with the Training Director of the Egyptian National Power Company (ENP). We have a 'gentleman's agreement' that the College will provide a six month training course in computer aided design for 10 young employees of ENP. The course will include one day per week English tuition provided by our English as a Foreign Language Section. We have also agreed to provide whatever help we can with regard to student accommodation. Please prepare a formal draft contract to send to the Training Director of ENP. Please send this to me together with some explanatory notes. Thank you.

 Group activity 2

The class should work in groups of four for this activity. In each group two students play the part of landlord and two play the part of tenants. The landlords have recently purchased a house which they intend to let. The tenants will each have a bedroom and shared use of the dining room, lounge, kitchen and bathroom. In total there will be four tenants in the house. The group should hold a meeting at which they will agree the terms of a tenancy agreement. Prior to the meeting each side should have prepared their position.

 Review questions *(answers page 296)*

1. Explain the terms condition and warranty.

2. What provisions in the Unfair Contract Terms Act 1977 apply to an attempt to exclude negligence liability by means of a contract term?

3. What is meant by 'merchantable quality' in a contract for the sale of goods?

4. What is the difference between an exemption clause, a limitation clause, and an agreed damages clause?

5. By what methods may an exemption clause become part of a contract?

6. What conditions are implied by the Supply of Goods and Services Act 1982 in a contract for the provision of consumer services?

22

Ending a contract

There are four ways by which the rights and obligations of the parties may come to an end. These are performance, agreement, frustration and breach.

1 Performance

a) A person who performs a contract in accordance with its terms is discharged from any further obligations.

b) If a person's obligation is to pay money, then he will not be discharged unless he tenders exactly the right amount of cash. For example a contract will not be discharged by offering a £20 note in settlement of a £10 debt, because it is not reasonable to compel the other party to provide change. Of course if the creditor provides change without any objection the contract will be discharged. If a debtor pays by cheque, he will not be discharged until the cheque is honoured by his bank.

c) If a person's obligation is to deliver goods, the goods must be tendered at a reasonable hour. For example a contract will not be discharged if a vendor leaves goods on the buyer's doorstep in the middle of the night. The goods must also comply exactly with the contract terms. If the seller tenders too few goods, too many goods, or the right amount of goods mixed with other goods, the buyer may reject all of them, because performance is not exact. The same applies if the goods are not packed in accordance with the contract. For example in Re MOORE AND LANDAUER (1921) a supplier of tinned fruit agreed to supply the goods in cases containing 30 tins each. When he delivered the goods about half were packed in cases of 24 tins each. The correct total amount of tins were delivered, and the market value of the goods was unaffected. However there was a breach of contract, because the performance was not exact. This entitled the buyer to reject the whole consignment.

d) Many contracts state the order in which the parties must perform their obligations. For example if Fred agrees to work for Abdul for £200 per week, payable in arrears, clearly Abdul need not pay Fred until Fred has done the weeks work.

2 Agreement

a) The parties may agree to end a contract before it has been performed. This may occur when both parties have obligations outstanding. In the example in the previous chapter (page 145) John agreed to purchase a second-hand car from Sue for £4,800. Assume they agreed that John would bring the cash on Saturday and take the car away. On Friday John is told that he is being made redundant from his job. He therefore decides that he can no longer afford the car. He tells Sue this on Friday evening. Sue is quite entitled to insist that the contract stands. It does not matter that nothing has changed hands yet (since executory consideration will support a contract – see page 131) nor is it relevant that John has a very good reason to want to get out of the contract. Sue may however agree to end the contract. Consideration (value) for this agreement to end the contract is automatically present, since both John and Sue give up something of value, namely the right to insist on the other party's performance.

b) A contract may also be discharged by agreement when a party who has performed his obligations decides to release the other party from the obligation to perform. For example Bill may agree to mow Henry's lawn for £20. After mowing the lawn Bill may decide to make a generous gesture and release Henry from his obligation to pay. In the vast majority of cases this would be the end of the matter. However an interesting situation arises if Bill later changes his mind and insists on payment. The basic rule is that Bill would succeed because Henry has not given anything in return for being released from his obligation to pay. An exception would however occur if, in reliance on the promise to release the debt, Henry has changed his position, such that it would be unfair to allow Bill to go back on his promise.

3 Frustration

a) A contract may be discharged by frustration if, after its formation, events occur making its performance illegal or impossible. In general such an event will only discharge a contract if:

i) it was not thought of by the parties when the contract was made,

ii) it completely changes the nature of the contract,

iii) neither party was responsible for it,

iv) it results in a situation to which the parties did not intend to be bound.

For example in TAYLOR V CALDWELL (1863) Caldwell contracted to let a music hall to Taylor for 4 days. Before the first day the music hall was accidentally burnt down. Taylor claimed damages alleging that Caldwell had broken the contract by not providing a music hall. However it was held that Caldwell was discharged from his obligation when the music hall burnt down. The contract was discharged by frustration.

b) A contract is not frustrated just because is becomes more expensive for one of the parties. For example in DAVIS CONTRACTORS V FAREHAM UDC (1956) the contractors agreed to build 78 houses at a price of £94,000 in 8 months. Labour shortages caused the work to take 22 months at a cost to Davis of £115,000. Davis wanted to claim that the contract was frustrated so that they could bring a new claim for the value of work done and at least recover their £115,000. The court said that hardship, loss or inconvenience did not amount to frustration, the obligation must change such that it becomes completely different from the thing originally contracted for.

c) If, when a contract is discharged by frustration, one party has paid money, the court may order the money to be repaid.

Similarly if somebody has received a benefit the court may order that person to pay the other party something for it.

4 Breach

a) Breach occurs:

i) if a person fails to perform one of his contractual obligations, for example he does not perform on the agreed date, or he delivers goods of inferior quality, or he refuses to pay the agreed price, or

ii) if a person, before the date fixed for performance, indicates that he will not perform on the agreed date. This is known as *anticipatory breach*.

b) Breach does not automatically end the contact.

i) Breach of *warranty* only entitles the innocent party to damages, it does not give him a right to treat the contract as ended.

ii) Breach of *condition* entitles the innocent party to damages and gives him the choice of whether to treat the contract as still in existence or terminated. In such a case if the innocent party chooses to end the contract he is not bound to accept further performance and he may sue for damages at once. Similarly if there is an anticipatory breach, the innocent party does not have to wait for the time fixed for performance, but may sue for damages as soon as the other party has indicated that they are not going to perform the contract.

c) *Instalment contracts.* If in an instalment contract there is a breach with regard to one or some instalments, the main tests as to whether the breach entitles the innocent party to treat the contract as at an end are:

i) The ratio that the breach bears to the contract as a whole, and

ii) The degree of probability that the breach will be repeated.

 Task 1

In the last week of the college holidays you decided to hire a 'luxury two berth cruiser' from Driftwood Boats Limited for a one week holiday cruise on the Thames. When you arrived to collect the cruiser Driftwood Boats Ltd provided you with a four berth cruiser, because it was the only one they had available. You were pleased to have a larger boat, but you were very dissatisfied that both the interior and exterior paintwork was cracked and peeling, which gave the boat a very scruffy appearance. You also missed one full day of the holiday, since the engine failed and Driftwood Boats Ltd needed 24 hours to carry out repairs.

When you returned the boat you were presented with a bill for £75, being the difference in price between a two berth cruiser and a four berth cruiser. You refused to pay this, and in fact regret having paid the full price for the holiday in advance, since it was spoilt by the events set out above.

Driftwood Boats Ltd seem very determined to pursue their claim for £75. Your task is to write a letter to the managing director of Driftwood Boats setting out your position.

Group activity 1

The class should work in groups of four for this activity. In each group two students act as publishers and two students act as authors. The publishers are college lecturers, who have published three booklets written by colleagues. To date they have never had any formal written contracts, relying only on verbal agreements to pay authors 10% of the selling price of each booklet sold. The booklets have all sold well and the publishers are now considering publishing a textbook written by two lecturers at another college. All parties feel that a formal contract should be entered into. The activity is to role play a meeting between the authors and publishers at which the main contract terms are agreed. Each side should come to the meeting having previously prepared their position.

Discussion topic

1. Jenny accepted an engagement to play the piano at the Blue Moon Club in Manchester for two weeks commencing 1st December 1994. On 30th November Jenny was arrested by the police for being in possession of drugs and was held in custody

until 4th December. The Blue Moon Club now refuse to engage Jenny. Advise Jenny.

2. Roy placed an advertisement in 'Antiques Monthly' that an auction of paintings would take place in Birmingham on 30th March. James travelled 200 miles to the auction, but when he arrived at the advertised venue there was a notice on the door saying 'Auction postponed for one week'. James attended the auction one week later and bid £3,000 for a painting. He then changed his mind and called out 'bid withdrawn'. The auctioneer apparently did not hear him and banged his hammer. Advise James.

 Review questions *(answers page 298)*

1. What is meant by frustration of contract?
2. Is a person justified if he or she terminates a contract which has become unprofitable?
3. What is an anticipatory breach of contract?
4. Jack agreed to deliver to Arnold 12,000 golf balls packed in boxes of three. He delivered the specified number of golf balls, but packed in boxes of twelve. Advise Arnold.
5. What is a effect of a breach of warranty?
6. Eric has booked a room in a London hotel to visit a jazz festival which is to be held in Hyde Park. Two days before the festival is due to take place, the organisers cancel it. Eric therefore wishes to cancel his reservation. Advise Eric.

23

Remedies for breach of contract

A breach of contract is a civil wrong that will entitle the innocent party to refuse further performance of the contract and seek a remedy. The possible remedies are:

a) Damages i.e. monetary compensation.

b) To make a 'quantum meruit' claim for work done.

c) Specific performance i.e. a claim for the actual performance of the other person's promise.

d) Injunction i.e. an order to prevent a person from doing something.

1 Damages

a) The usual remedy for breach of contract is *damages*. This is a payment of money by the party in breach to the innocent party. A claim for damages raises two questions:

i) Is the loss suffered by the innocent party (the plaintiff) sufficiently closely linked to the breach? If there is not a sufficient link, the loss is said to be too *remote* and the plaintiff will not get compensation for that loss even if it would not have occurred but for the defendant's breach of contract.

For example, Sally purchases a prawn and avocado sandwich for her lunch. The prawns are bad and she is ill. As a result she misses work the next day, so her car is parked outside her house instead of in the office car park. Unfortunately the car is badly damaged by a careless lorry driver who does not stop. Sally will be able to recover the purchase price of the sandwich, and claim compensation for her illness. However the damage to her car is not sufficiently closely linked to the sale of a bad sandwich to entitle her to compensation.

This example is very obvious, but often cases are much more borderline. The law therefore requires a 'rule' for remoteness. This is set out in b. below.

ii) What payment should the plaintiff receive in respect of loss which is not too remote i.e how should damages be *measured* (see c below)?

b) *Remoteness.*

i) The loss is not too remote if it arises *naturally from the breach itself,* or if it is *foreseeable as the probable result of the breach.* An example of loss arising naturally from the breach itself is PINNOCK V LEWIS (1923) where the seller of poisonous cattle food was held liable for the loss of the cattle to which it was fed. An example of the second part of the rule (loss foreseeable as probable) occurred in INTERNATIONAL MINERALS AND CHEMICALS CORPORATION V HELM (1986) where a debt was due to be paid to an American plaintiff in Belgium francs. As a result of late payment the value of Belgium francs as against US dollars fell by 40%. It was held that the loss was recoverable since the defendant could foresee that such a loss was a probable consequence of their breach of contract.

ii) An example illustrating both parts of the rule occurred in PILKINGTON V WOOD (1953). When Pilkington bought a house in Hampshire his solicitor, Wood, failed to notice that the title was defective. (This did not mean that there was anything wrong with the building itself, but that the title documents, the deeds, were incomplete). Wood was held liable for the difference between the value of the house with good title and with defective title, since this was loss naturally arising from the breach itself. However Pilkington's job shortly moved to Lancashire and he wanted to sell the house. The defective title delayed the sale and meant that Pilkington could not pay off a bank overdraft using the sale proceeds. It was held that Wood was not liable for this additional loss since it could not be foreseen that Pilkington would shortly wish to move or that he would have an overdraft that he expected to pay off out of the sale proceeds.

c) *Measure of damages.*

i) The rule is that the plaintiff recovers his actual loss i.e. he is placed in the same position as if the contract had been performed (not the position he would have been in if the contract had never been made). Therefore when assessing damages for breach of a contract of employment the court will take into account the plaintiff's liability to taxation.

ii) In assessing the amount of damages the court may take into account inconvenience, annoyance and disappointment. For example in JARVIS V SWAN TOURS (1973) Jarvis paid £63 for a two week winter sports holiday. It was very different from the advertisement, as there was little of the holiday atmosphere promised because the staff did not speak English and in the second week Jarvis was the only guest at the hotel.

He recovered £125 damages for the disappointment and annoyance resulting from his ruined holiday.

d) *Mitigation.* There is a rule that the plaintiff must do what is reasonable to minimise the total loss i.e. the plaintiff cannot recover for a loss that he ought to have avoided. For example if someone is wrongfully dismissed from their job, they must seek to minimise the loss by trying to find another suitable job as quickly as possible. They cannot do nothing and then try to claim damages for months or years out of work.

e) *Liquidated damages.* Sometimes a term of the contract will state the amount of damages to be paid in the event of a breach. These are known as liquidated damages. Provided this is a genuine estimate of the loss, the court will uphold the sum stated, even if the actual loss is a greater or lesser sum. If however the amount in the contract is far more than the greatest loss which could have resulted from a breach of contract, the court will regard it as a penalty clause and declare it to be void.

 Task 1

On May 10th 1994 Mrs. Windsor placed an order with Castle Stationers Limited for 500 copies of a wedding announcement in respect of her daughter's forthcoming marriage. The price agreed was £320. On May 12th, before Castle Stationers Ltd had started the printing, Mrs. Windsor telephoned them to cancel the order because the engaged couple had had a row and the wedding had been called off.

You are the managing director of Castle Stationers Ltd and your company is in desperate financial trouble. Your task is to write to Mrs.Windsor explaining, with reasons, what you require from her.

2 Quantum Meruit

a) Where there is a breach of contract and the innocent party has done work under that contract, they may claim payment for what has been done rather than sue for damages.

b) A quantum meruit claim may also be made when work has been done and accepted under a void contract. For example in CRAVEN-ELLIS v CANONS LTD (1936) Craven-Ellis was employed as managing director of the company. The directors who made the contract were not authorised to do so and the contract was held to be void. However Craven-Ellis had rendered services and sued for remuneration. He was successful in this quantum meruit claim.

3 Specific performance

This is an order by the court ordering a person to carry out his contractual obligations. It will not normally be awarded if damages would be an adequate remedy. It is most likely to be awarded in contracts for the sale of land. An award of specific performance is at the discretion of the court, in contrast the remedy of damages exists as a right.

4 Injunction

There are two main types of injunction:

a) A *mandatory injunction* orders a person to take action to undo a breach of contract. For example he may be ordered to take down an advertising sign erected in breach of contract.

b) A *prohibitory injunction* is an order of the court which prohibits a person from doing something. For example an injunction may be granted to prevent somebody who has just sold a business from starting up a competing business nearby, in breach of a reasonable restraint of trade clause in the contract of sale.

5 Limitation periods

A plaintiff must commence an action within *six years* of the breach of contract. Failure to discover the breach does not alter this rule. However if the breach is concealed by the fraud of the defendant or the action is for relief from the consequences of a mistake, the plaintiff has six years from when the fraud or mistake was, or ought to have been discovered, whichever is the earlier.

Discussion topic

1. Susan agreed to sell a painting to Fred for £400. The painting needed a new frame and Susan told Fred that the painting would be ready for him to collect in three weeks time. However, when Fred came to collect and pay for the painting Susan refused to give it to him. Advise Fred.

2. Dennis owns a road haulage company. He agreed with Winston that he would deliver grain to Winston's warehouse in Northampton. Winston then asked Dennis to deliver the grain to a different warehouse, 30 miles away in Birmingham, offering him extra remuneration. Winston did not pay this additional amount. Advise Dennis.

3. Dennis (the owner of a road haulage company) also had a contract with Richard to deliver Richard's steel to Geoff. Geoff agreed to help Dennis unload the steel. When the steel was delivered Geoff refused this assistance. Advise Dennis.

4. Dennis also had a contract to deliver a consignment of apples by 5 o'clock on 2nd September. The contract also provided for the payment of liquidated damages of £500 in the event of a breach of contract. Dennis delivered the apples at 2.00pm on 3rd September. The buyer accepted the goods, but three weeks later Dennis received a demand for £500 damages for breach of contract. Advise Dennis.

 Task 2

You are a farmer. Potatoes are one of your main crops. You sell large quantities each year to three different crisp producers X, Y and Z. To assist planning you try to sell the entire crop at a fixed price about two months before it is harvested. This year in April you signed three contracts.

i) 300 tons to X at £35 per ton, delivery 15th June.

ii) 400 tons to Y at £34 per ton, delivery 30th June.

iii) 300 tons to Z at £33 per ton, delivery 15th July.

The weather during May was disastrous for potatoes. You were able to make delivery to X and Y, but could only supply 100 tons to Z. It is now mid-August and you have just received the following letter.

Dear Mr. Giles,

Re: Breach of Contract

I am sure you admit the breach of contract last month when you only delivered 100 tons of the agreed 300. Fortunately I was able to use them, but as you know I could have rejected the whole consignment. Since I was good enough to accept part performance I am sure you will be prepared to accept payment of £17.50 per ton, rather than £33 per ton. Of course I then had to buy 200 tons elsewhere. On 15th July the market price was £34 a ton. I thought it would fall, so in an attempt to save you money I decided to wait a few days. Unfortunately by 20th July the price had shot up to £42 per ton and I was forced to buy 200 tons at that price, otherwise I would have let down my own customers. The result of all this is that you owe me £50. Please send me your cheque as soon as possible.

Yours sincerely

Z

1. Why does Z claim that Giles owes him £50?

2. Write a reply from Giles to Z.

 **Review questions** (answers page 299)

1. What is the rule for remoteness of damage in contract?

2. What are liquidated damages?

3. When are the courts likely to grant an injunction as a remedy for breach of contract?

4. An award of damages places the innocent party in the position he would have been in prior to the contract. True or false?

5. What is meant by mitigation of damage?

6. Give two examples of contracts where specific performance would be an appropriate remedy for breach?

24

Special types of contract: agency, cheques and insurance

The rules that have been covered in previous Chapters apply to ordinary contracts, in particular contracts for goods and services. However there are many special types of contract which have their own particular rules. These are often set out in Acts of Parliament. We have already looked at the contract of partnership and contracts of employment. Contracts for the sale of goods and consumer credit agreements are considered in the next two Chapters.

This Chapter gives a brief introduction to three important types of contract namely agency, cheques and insurance. There are several other categories which are beyond the scope of this book for example sales of land, mortgages, carriage of goods, contracts of guarantee and money lending contracts.

AGENCY

1 Definition

a) An *agent* is a person who is able to make a contract on behalf of another person known as the *principal*. The agent may be an employee of the principal, for example a salesman in a shop, or he may be an independent contractor, for example an estate agent. Directors are agents of their companies, and partners are agents of the other partners in the firm. Whatever the type of agent the distinctive characteristic of the relationship is that the agent has the power to make a binding contract between the principal and a third party without personally becoming a party to that contract.

b) In everyday language the word 'agent' is often used to describe anybody who buys and sells goods. For example a car dealer may be described as the 'sole agent' for a particular make of car. This does not mean that the dealer acts as the legal agent of the manufacturer when selling a car to a customer. In practice the dealer acts on his own account when he buys from the manufacturer and sells to the customer. This wider use of the word 'agent' must be distinguished from the narrower legal use with which we are concerned.

2 Appointment of agents

Agency may be created in four ways:

a) *Express agreement.* This is the usual method of appointing an agent. The appointment may be made verbally or in writing.

b) *Implication.* Agency may arise when, although there is no specific agreement, an agency relationship can be implied from the conduct of the parties. Since the test is objective an agency relationship will be held to exist if the principal and agent would appear to a reasonable person to be acting as if there was an agency relationship, even if they did not intend or recognise the fact themselves.

c) *Ratification.* Sometimes an appointed agent will exceed his authority, or a person with no authority will purport to act as an agent. In general the principal will not be bound by such a contract. However the principal may choose to ratify (i.e. adopt) the contract at a later date.

d) *Necessity.* Occasionally a person may find themselves in a situation with regard to contract goods where an emergency has arisen and they cannot get instructions from the owner of the goods. If in this situation they act in good faith, and in the interests of all the parties, by for example disposing of the goods or incurring some expense in relation to them, the principal will be held to the contract. For example in GREAT NORTHERN RAILWAY V SWAFFIELD (1874) a horse was sent by rail and on arrival at its destination there was no-one to collect it. GNR incurred the expense of stabling the horse for the night. It was held that GNR was an agent of necessity, with authority to incur the expense in question.

3 Duties of the principal and agent

a) The principal must pay the agent the agreed commission or other remuneration and must indemnify the agent for any losses incurred in the course of the agency.

b) The agent must:

i) Carry out the principal's lawful instructions.

ii) Exercise reasonable care and skill in the performance of the duties.

iii) Act in good faith and for the benefit of the principal. This means that he must not misuse confidential information regarding the principal's affairs, that he must not let his own interest conflict with his duty to the principal and that he must not make any profit over and above the agreed commission or remuneration. For example in LUCIFERO V CASTEL (1887) an agent appointed to purchase a yacht for his principal bought the yacht himself and then sold it to his principal at a profit, the principal being unaware that he was buying the agent's own property. It was held that the agent had to pay this profit to the principal.

4 The authority of the agent

a) Where an agent is given express authority, an act performed within the scope of this authority will bind the principal and the third party.

b) Where an agent is employed to conduct a particular trade or business he has implied authority to do whatever is incidental to such trade or business, even if the principal told the agent that he did not have such authority, unless the third party knew of the lack of authority. For example in WATTEAU V FENWICK (1893) the manager of a public house was instructed by the owner (Fenwick) not to purchase tobacco on credit. Watteau, who has not aware of this restriction, sold tobacco to the manager. Fenwick was held liable to pay for this, because it was within the usual authority of a manager of a public house to purchase tobacco.

5 Termination of agency

a) The parties may agree at any time to terminate their agency arrangement, or the principal may withdraw the agent's authority at any time. In this case, if the agent is also an employee, then proper notice must be given to terminate the contract of employment. The principal should also give notice of the termination to third parties with whom the agent has dealt, otherwise he will not be able to deny the authority of the agent, if the agent should make subsequent contracts with these third parties.

b) An agency relationship will also be terminated:

    i) On the death or insanity of either the principal or the agent.

    ii) On the bankruptcy of the principal.

    iii) If a fixed term agency agreement comes to an end.

    iv) If the purpose for which the agreement was created has been accomplished, or

    v) If the subject matter or the operation of the agency agreement is frustrated or becomes illegal.

 Task 1

A friend of yours, Peter, wants to buy his father's car, but he is having difficulty selling his existing car. Last week, when he was buying petrol at his local garage (A.1 Autos Ltd) the garage owner remarked that Peter had had a 'for sale' sign in the back window of the car for the last three weeks and that if Peter left the car on A.1 Autos Ltd's forecourt they would sell the car for him and keep 10% of whatever they could get for it. The garage owner said there was no need to write anything down because they were a big company and they would probably sell the car within a couple of days. Peter is unsure about this arrangement.

Your task is to write a letter to Peter explaining the possible problems and giving him some advice as to how he might protect his position.

CHEQUES

1 Introduction

a) A person who opens a bank account makes a contract with their bank. The contractual duties of the customer and the bank are set out below. The basic relationship between bank and customer is one of debtor and creditor. While the customer has money in the bank the bank is the debtor. If the customer is overdrawn the bank is the creditor and the customer is the debtor.

b) One advantage of having a bank account is that the customer can pay for goods and services by cheque. When a customer writes a cheque he is not in fact making a new contract with the bank, he is giving the bank an order to pay the person named on the cheque. The person who writes the cheque is known as the 'drawer' and his bank is the 'paying bank'. The person who is receiving payment is the 'payee' and his bank is the 'collecting bank'.

2 Crossings

a) Most cheques are crossed. This means that two parallel lines are drawn on the cheque. When a cheque is crossed the payee cannot go into a bank and obtain cash over the counter. The crossing means that the cheque must be paid into the payee's bank account. Therefore someone who does not have a bank account should not accept a crossed cheque in payment for goods or services.

b) A crossing provides some protection against theft of the cheque. For example Ann writes a cheque for £100 payable to Gary. It is then stolen from Gary by Ken. If the cheque is uncrossed Ken can go into a bank, pretend to be Gary (he would need identification which would not be a problem if he also stole Gary's driving licence) forge Gary's signature (he would be asked to sign the back of the cheque) and obtain payment. All this could be done within five minutes of stealing the cheque. If the cheque was crossed Ken would have to open a bank account in Gary's name and wait for the cheque to be sent to Ann's bank (the paying bank). This would take several days, during which time Gary might discover the theft and tell Ann, who would then stop the cheque.

3 The duties of the customer and the bank

a) *Customers duties.*

    i) To indemnify the paying bank when it makes authorised payments on his behalf.

    ii) To take reasonable care when writing cheques to prevent alteration of the amount.

iii) To inform the bank if his cheque book is stolen or if he is aware of any forgeries.

b) *Duties of the banker.* When a person opens an account his bank will be the paying bank in respect of cheques written by the customer and it will be the collecting bank in respect of cheques made payable to the customer. The main duties are:

i) To take reasonable care in the conduct of the customer's business.

ii) To honour cheques i.e. make payments if there are funds in the account or up to any agreed overdraft limit.

iii) To keep the customer's affairs secret, unless there is an acceptable reason for disclosure, for example if the customer has given the banker's name as a reference, and

iv) To collect for the customer's account cheques paid in by the customer.

INSURANCE

1 Definition

a) Insurance is a contract whereby the insurance company, in return for a sum of money called the *premium*, contracts with the insured to pay a specified sum of money on the happening of a particular event, for example the death of the insured, or to indemnify the insured against any loss caused by the risk insured against, for example fire. '*Indemnity*' means that the insured will be compensated for the actual loss, so far as it does not exceed the sum stated in the policy.

b) Insurance companies accept substantial risks on the basis of answers given by the insured on an insurance proposal form. They do not rely on anything else (such as a meeting with the insured) to assess their risk or decide on the premium. Insurance contracts are therefore known as contracts *uberrimae fidei*. This means of utmost good faith. The consequence of this is that the insured is under an obligation to disclose any facts that might influence the insurance company's decision about the risk or the premium to be charged, even if an appropriate question does not appear of the proposal form. If a material fact is not disclosed (albeit innocently) the insurance company can avoid the contract.

c) A contract of insurance will only be valid if the insured has an *'insurable interest'* in the subject matter i.e. if he stands to lose by its destruction. A person therefore has an insurable interest in his own car, but not in a car belonging to anyone else.

 Task 2

You work in the Claims Department of a large insurance company. You have just received a claim from Woodland Timber Ltd. It appears that the company's main asset, an estate of 20,000 Christmas trees, has just been destroyed by fire. It seems clear from the company's notepaper that the sole shareholder and director is Mr.Charles Woodman and that the company was incorporated on 1st March 1994. On checking your records you find that Mr.Woodman took out insurance on the timber estate in 1990, when it was in his sole personal ownership. Write a letter to Mr.Woodman explaining why your insurance company will not be paying him any compensation.

2 Main types of insurance contract

a) There are only two classes of insurance required by law. They are motor insurance and employers' liability insurance. These are covered in Chapter 9.4 page 56. Some of the other main types of insurance contract are set out below.

b) *Fire insurance.* This is generally regarded as essential for both businesses and private individuals. The contract will indemnify the insured for loss caused by fire during a specified period. The contract will cover not only items burned or damaged by smoke, but will include damage caused by water used to fight the fire. It will not however cover damage caused by mere overheating, there must actually be ignition. A business will also be advised to have a consequential loss policy, since the business will suffer additional loss while waiting for machinery, stock and so on to be replaced. A consequential loss policy will enable the business to keep going and should put it in the same position as it would have been in if the fire had not occurred.

c) *Public liability insurance.* A business should protect itself against legal liability for injury or damage caused to any member of the public as a result of a negligent act by an employee acting in the course of employment. *Product liability insurance* should also be considered if there is any possibility of any products sold or supplied by the business causing injury or damage to members of the public as a result of a defect in the product.

d) *Theft insurance.* This is also advisable for both business and private individuals. Like fire insurance it is a contract to indemnify the insured for any loss suffered. If at the time of the contract the insured deliberately over-values an item, the insurance company will be able to avoid the contract.

e). *Accident insurance.* This is not a contract of indemnity since it will provide for the payment of a specified sum if a certain event occurs, for example the death by accident of the insured person, or a smaller sum in the event of his disablement.

f) *Life insurance.* Like accident insurance this is not a contract of indemnity. The policy will specify a sum to be paid to the insured's executor on the insured's death. (An executor is a person appointed in a Will to distribute the deceased's assets to the persons named in the Will). A person has an insurable interest in their own life or in the life of their husband or wife. A creditor also has an insurable interest in the life of the debtor up to the amount of the debt. Generally a person does not have an insurable interest in anyone else's life, even the lives of close relatives such as parents, children, brothers and sisters.

 Discussion topic

1. Pamela asked her agent Annabel to sell 12 computers for her. She instructed her that they should not be sold for less than £500 each. What is the legal position if:

   a) Annabel sells the computers for £475 each.

   b) Annabel buys the computers herself for £500 each without informing Pamela and later sells them to Cheapside Training Limited for £550 each.

   c) Annabel sells the computers to the Surefire Recruitment Agency for £550 each and is paid a 'finder's fee' by the recruitment agency of £250.

2. Pauline appointed Albert to sell a car. She then withdrew Albert's authority, but Albert nevertheless went ahead and sold the car to Sidney. Is this a valid sale? What would be the position if the authority had not been withdrawn, but the sale had taken place after Pauline's death?

 **Review questions** *(answers page 300)*

1. Explain the different forms of an agent's authority. How can this authority be terminated?

2. How is agency created?

3. What is the extent of an agent's right to be paid for his services?

4. What is the effect of crossing a cheque?

5. Explain the term 'insurable interest'.

6. What duties are owed by a customer to the bank in relation to cheques?

7. What is meant by 'indemnity'.

 **Part 3 assignments**

Assignment 5

Refer to the standard consumer contract in Appendix E (page 266). A friend of yours, Damien Mansell, is considering purchasing a second-hand car from Perrys. Write a letter to him explaining the most important terms in Perrys' standard contract and advising him of any practical matters that he should bear in mind.

You are also asked to advise Damien of other methods of purchasing a second-hand car, for example car auctions and private sellers. Point out to him the legal and practical differences between the various methods and the advantages and disadvantages of each.

Assignment 6

Study the negotiated business contract in Appendix F (page 270). This has been drawn up by the Registrar of Central College. The use of agents to recruit overseas students is a new venture for Central

175

College and the Principal is taking a special interest in the venture. In particular the Principal would like your advice on the following:

a) The Principal has heard that there are certain formal requirements which must be complied with if a contract is to be valid. The Principal would like you to state how the proposed contract meets each of these requirements.

b) The Principal would also like you to report on the strengths and weaknesses of this contract, both from the point of view of Central College and the other party.

c) Finally the Principal wishes to know whether you would recommend any changes.

Part 4

Business consumers

Element 9.4 Investigate the rights of business customers and consumers

Consumers are people who buy goods or services from businesses. In general the law will not interfere with any person's freedom to make any contract, but there are several reasons why it is reasonable for the law to modify this freedom to contract in order to give special protection to consumers. For example:

a) Consumers will usually have much less technical knowledge of the product or service than the seller. They will therefore rely on the seller to give them accurate and truthful information.

b) Some consumers are susceptible to skilled sales techniques, sometimes in their own homes. As a result, they may make a purchase that they soon regret or enter into a credit agreement that they cannot afford.

c) A coordinated group of traders may make agreements between themselves (for example to all charge the same high price), which will restrict free competition and therefore have an adverse effect on consumers.

This part of the book describes the main methods by which the law seeks to rectify the imbalance between traders and consumers. It explains the main consumer protection legislation, for example the Sale of Goods Act 1979, the Consumer Credit Act 1974, the Fair Trading Act 1973 and the Data Protection Act 1984. It also describes the role of 'consumer watchdogs', ie organisations which look after the interests of consumers, for example the Consumers' Association, the British Standards Institute and the Ombudsman. There is an outline of UK and EC competition rules (ie rules to prevent the distortion of free trade) and the final chapter gives a brief outline of the County Court small claims procedure.

On successful completion of Part 4 activities and review questions, students will have knowledge of the main rights of consumers (performance criteria 1) and the key legislation and organisations which exist to protect their interests (performance criteria 2). Students will also understand how consumer disputes may be resolved either out of court or as a result of legal action (performance criteria 3). The end of part assignments will generate the evidence required for your portfolio of coursework.

BTEC guide to coverage of performance criteria

The performance criteria and evidence indicators are listed in the left-hand column. The Assignment column contains the number of the assignment which covers the criteria indicated.

The Task and Group Activity columns indicate the chapter numbers as well as task or group activity numbers. For example '2.1' in the Task column indicates Chapter 2 Task 1 covers that particular performance criteria. '2.1' in the Group Activity column would indicate Chapter 2 Group Activity 1 covers the criteria in question.

9.4   Investigate the rights of business customers and consumers

Performance Criteria and Evidence Indicators	Assignment	Task	Group activity
9.4.1 The nature and scope of consumer protection is investigated	8	25.1, 28.1 30.1, 31.1	
9.4.2 Key rights of consumers are identified	7, 8	26.1, 28.1 31.1	26.1, 27.1 28.1, 28.2
9.4.3 Procedures for dispute settlement between customer and business are described	7, 8	28.1, 31.1	
Evidence indicator. A case study containing consumer problems which the student will identify, suggest solutions to and explain the procedure to be followed to attain a successful outcome	7, 8		

25

Legislation protecting buyers of goods and services

There are numerous Acts of Parliament that protect buyers of goods and services. Some of these are covered in other Chapters, for example the Unfair Contract Terms Act 1977, the Consumer Credit Act 1974, the Fair Trading Act 1973, the Restrictive Trade Practices Act 1976, the Resale Prices Act 1976 and the Competition Act 1980 (see Index for page references). There are also a number of specialist statutes that are not appropriate for this book, for example the Estate Agents Act 1979 and the Lotteries and Amusements Act 1976.

This Chapter concentrates on the main consumer protection statutes, namely:

a) the Sale of Goods Act 1979,

b) the Supply of Goods and Services Act 1982,

c) the Consumer Protection Act 1987,

d) the Trade Descriptions Act 1968.

SALE OF GOODS ACT 1979

1 Introduction and definitions

a) A sale of goods is the most common type of commercial contract. The general law of contract, for example the rules on offer and acceptance and all the other rules in Chapters 18 to 24, apply to contracts for the sale of goods, together with specific rules contained in the Sale of Goods Act 1979.

b) A contract for the sale of goods is *'a contract whereby the seller transfers or agrees to transfer the property in goods to the buyer for a money consideration called the price'* (S.2 SGA 1979). The definition covers both a sale i.e. where the property in the goods passes at the time of the contract, and an agreement to sell i.e. where the transfer of property is to take place at a future time.

c) In this context *'property'* means the legal right of ownership of the goods, it does not mean possession of the goods. It is of course possible to pass ownership without passing possession, or to pass possession without ownership, for example hire purchase contracts.

d) In some contracts the goods will be identified and agreed on at the time of sale, for example 'my Ford Escort K123 ABC'. These are known as *specific goods*. Sometimes the contract will be for what are known as *future goods* i.e. goods to be manufactured or acquired by the seller after the contract is made, for example 'a wedding cake'. Alternatively the contract may be for goods that form part of a larger class or consignment e.g a contract for half of a particular lorry-load of sand. These are known as *unascertained goods*.

e) A contract for *work or labour* is sometimes difficult to distinguish from a sale of goods. For example if my car is serviced at a garage I will receive some goods, for example new oil and spark plugs, but a large element of the contract will be the skill and labour of the mechanics. The test is whether the real substance of the contract is skill and labour or the supply of goods. Contracts for work and labour are governed by the Supply of Goods and Services Act 1982. The implied terms contained in this Act were discussed in Chapter 21.3 page 150.

2 The terms of the contract

a) In Chapter 21 we looked at several questions which are also relevant to sales of goods:

  i) Is a statement made in negotiations a mere representation inducing the contract, or a term which is part of the contract?

  ii) If it is a term, is it a condition or warranty?

  iii) If a term has not been expressly agreed, can it be included in the contract by implication?

  iv) Are any exemption or limitation clauses valid?

b) We also considered the main terms implied in a contract for the sale of goods:

  i) By S.12 SGA there is an implied condition that the seller has the right to pass good *title* to the goods.

ii) By S.13 SGA where goods are sold by description there is an implied condition that they will correspond with the *description*.

iii) By S.14 SGA where goods are sold in the course of a business there are implied conditions that the goods will be of *merchantable quality* and *fit for their purpose*.

iv) By S.15 SGA there is an implied condition that where goods are sold by *sample* the bulk will correspond with the sample and that there are no defects which would not be apparent on a reasonable examination of the sample.

c) The Unfair Contract Terms Act 1977 (Chapter 21.5 page 152) also contains provisions relevant to the sale of goods. In particular:

i) S.12 SGA can never be excluded.

ii) S.13-15 SGA cannot be excluded in a consumer sale, but can be excluded in a non-consumer sale if the exemption clause is reasonable.

3 The transfer of the property in goods

a) It is very important to know when the property (title to the goods) passes. If we refer back to the example at the start of Chapter 21, Sue sold her car to John for £4,800. Assume that John gives Sue a cheque for £3,000 on Tuesday and arranges to collect the car and give her the other £1,800 in cash on Saturday. They agree that from Tuesday to Saturday the car will remain parked in Sue's drive while John's cheque is cleared by his bank. What would be the situation if the car is stolen on Friday? Must Sue find another similar car for John, must she give him back his money, or must John still pay the remaining £1,800? It is important to know when property (not possession) passes because risk passes with property. Therefore the owner will have to bear any loss arising from, for example, theft or vandalism. In this case, where there is a *contract for the sale of specific goods, the property passes when the contract is made,* even if the time of payment and/or delivery is postponed. John's contract was made, and the property therefore passed on Tuesday. All of the loss therefore falls on John, who still has to pay Sue the remaining £1,800 even though the car no longer exists.

There are two ways in which John could have avoided this situation:

i) He could have agreed with Sue that the property did not pass until he collected the car on Saturday. If he had done so Sue would have to bear all the loss and return the £3,000 already paid by John.

ii) He could have insured the car against theft, such insurance to run from Tuesday. It is relevant to note that even if Sue had not terminated her insurance on the car neither John nor Sue could claim on her policy. Sue could not claim because it is not her car and John could not claim because it is not his insurance policy.

b) The rule that in a contract for the sale of *specific goods* property passes when the contract is made, is subject to any contrary agreement by the parties. It is therefore quite common in commercial contracts for the seller to hand over possession of goods, but specify that the property will not pass until the buyer has paid for them. This is known as a *'reservation of title'* clause. For example in ALUMINIUM INDUSTRIE BV v ROMALPA (1976) the plaintiffs, who were sellers of aluminium, provided in their conditions of sale that 'the ownership of the material to be delivered by AIV will only be transferred to the purchaser when he has met all that is owing to AIV no matter on what grounds'

After having taken delivery of a consignment of aluminium the purchaser went into liquidation. AIV, who had not received the purchase price, sought to enforce the above provision by physically recovering the goods. Clearly this would be much better for them than to claim as an unsecured creditor in the liquidation of an insolvent company. The court held that AIV could rely on the clause and recover the consignment.

A reservation of title clause will not normally apply where the goods have been subjected to a manufacturing process. For example in RE PEACHDART (1983) leather was sold on reservation of title terms. It was held that the supplier's title ceased to exist when the leather had been made into handbags, despite the fact that the goods had not yet been paid for.

To increase the protection afforded by a reservation of title clause it is advisable for the seller:

i)   to require the goods to be kept separate from the buyer's other stock; and

ii) to reserve a right of access to the buyer's premises.

4 Sale by a person who is not the owner

a)   The general rule is that if there is a 'sale' by a person who is not the owner, the buyer will acquire no title and will have to return the goods to the true owner. The buyer may of course sue the seller for breach of S.12 SGA, but will not be entitled to any compensation from the true owner. This general rule has several exceptions which are listed below.

b)   If the seller has the authority or consent of the owner, or if the owner is prevented by his own conduct from denying the seller's authority to sell, then the buyer will acquire good title.

c)   Where goods are sold in an open, public and legally constituted market, or in a shop in the City of London between sunrise and sunset and the goods are of a kind usually sold in the market, the buyer will acquire a good title provided he buys in good faith. He would not therefore acquire title if he knew that the goods were stolen.

d)   If the seller has a voidable title, but this title has not been avoided at the time of sale, the buyer will acquire good title provided he buys in good faith and without notice of the seller's defect in title. This provision only applies to contracts that are voidable for fraud or misrepresentation, not to those that are void for mistake. (See Chapter 20.2.e page 139).

e)   If an agent, who is in possession of goods or documents of title with the consent of the owner, sells the goods in the agent's ordinary course of business to a genuine purchaser who is not aware of any defect in the agent's authority, the buyer will obtain good title.

f)   Sometimes a seller will remain in possession after the sale, as for example in the sale from Sue to John described in the previous paragraph. If in this situation Sue were to 'sell' the car for a second time to Fred on Thursday for £4,600, allowing Fred to take the car away, Fred would obtain good title to the car provided he purchased in good faith without notice of the previous sale to John.

g) A similar situation exists where a buyer obtains possession after an agreement to sell. Remember that when there is an agreement to sell, although there is a contract, the title to the goods has not yet passed. If however the buyer has possession with the seller's consent, any sale by him to a person acting in good faith and without notice of the lack of good title will have the same effect as if the sale was made with the owner's consent. Title will therefore pass to the buyer.

5 The rights of an unpaid seller

a) The remedies of the seller depend on whether or not possession of the goods has passed to the buyer. If the seller still has the goods he may retain them until the contract price has been paid. This is known as the right of *lien*. The seller may not re-sell the goods unless:

   i)   they are perishable,

   ii) the seller gives notice to the buyer that he intends to re-sell and the buyer does not pay within a reasonable time, or

   iii) the seller has expressly reserved the right to re-sell if the buyer defaults in payment.

b) If the seller has parted with possession of the goods to a carrier he can *stop the goods in transit* and re-take possession if the buyer becomes insolvent i.e. if the buyer is unable to pay his debts as they fall due.

c) If the contract contains a reservation of title clause the seller may be able to *re-possess* the goods even if they are in the possession of the buyer.

d) If possession and property have passed to the buyer the seller may bring an *action for the contract price*.

e) If the buyer refuses to accept delivery of the goods the seller may bring an *action for non-acceptance*. In such cases if there is a market for the goods the measure of damages would normally be the difference between the contract price and the market price on the date fixed for acceptance, or if no date was fixed at the time of refusal to accept.

6 The remedies of the buyer

If the seller is in breach of contract the buyer may:

a) If it is a breach of condition, *terminate the contract and sue for damages.*

b) If it is a breach of warranty, either *sue for damages* or seek an appropriate reduction in the contract price.

c) Sue to *recover any money paid* to the seller.

d) Sue for *specific performance.* As previously mentioned this remedy is not a right, but is at the discretion of the court and will not be granted if damages are adequate. It would be appropriate if the goods have a special value or if they are unique, for example a classic car or a painting.

e) If the seller's breach is non-delivery the buyer can bring an action for *damages for non-delivery.* If there is a market for the goods the measure of damages would normally be the difference between the contract price and the market price on the date fixed for delivery, or if no date was fixed, at the time of refusal to deliver.

 Task 1

You are a car dealer. On 1st July you signed a contract to supply a new Ford Mondeo to a Mr. Austin for £14,000, delivery date August 1st. Your profit will be exactly £1,400. At 10.00am on 1st August Mr. Austin came to the showroom. You were expecting him to pay the money and take the car. Instead he informed your junior sales assistant, Cleo, that he did not want the Mondeo because he had just made an impulse purchase of a second-hand Jaguar. As he left the showroom you overheard the end of the conversation between Mr. Austin and Cleo.

Mr.Austin	'I know we had a deal, but you've lost nothing, Mondeos are very popular, you'll still make your profit when you sell it to somebody else'
Cleo	'You're right, I've got someone coming in this afternoon who wants a blue Mondeo. I am sure everything will be OK'.

You rushed out of your office to try to speak to Mr. Austin, but by the time you reached the showroom door he had driven off.

a) Write a letter to Mr. Austin seeking to recover as much compensation as possible, and

b) Write a memo to the group managing director, enclosing a copy of your letter to Mr. Austin, explaining why your attempt to recover compensation may be unsuccessful.

7 Auction sales

S.57 SGA 1979 applies to auction sales.

a) Each lot is the subject of a separate contract of sale.

b) Each sale is complete when the auctioneer announces its completion by the fall of the hammer or in some other customary manner. Until this happens the bidder may retract the bid or the seller may withdraw the goods.

c) A sale may be subject to a reserve price i.e. a minimum price below which the goods cannot be sold.

 Discussion topic

1. Is it reasonable that in general, when a person purchases goods in good faith from someone who is not their owner and who does not sell with the authority or consent of the owner, that person acquires no title to the goods and must return them to the true owner?

2. Dave recently qualified from London University with a degree in Electronics. When he graduated he was 41 years old and found it difficult to get a job. He decided to take a stall in the local marketplace and sell reconditioned electrical goods that he had purchased from junk shops and reconditioned himself. He attached a note to each item saying that it was second-hand and purchased at the purchaser's risk, with no liability on Dave's part. Some of the items are sold to other market traders and some direct to the public. When reconditioning some of the items, Dave used faulty wiring, with the following results.

   a) Ann, who bought one of Dave's microwaves from another trader in the market, received a severe electric shock.

b) Brian, who bought a television from Dave suffered damage to curtains when the television caught fire.

c) Carol, Brian's wife, was burned when she attempted to put out the fire.

Advise Dave.

3. Dave has five young children. When he was in the market he purchased 30 boxes of washing powder from another trader (Pete) at 50p a box. The brand appeared to be new on the market, since Dave had never heard of it. Four of Dave's children developed a severe rash after wearing clothes washed in the powder. Subsequent tests indicated that the powder would probably cause similar rashes in 25% of children and 10% of adults. Dave wants his money back and additional compensation from Pete for the childrens' injuries. Advise Dave.

THE SUPPLY OF GOODS AND SERVICES ACT 1982

The Act has two main parts. Part I amends the law with respect to terms implied in certain contacts for the supply of goods. Part II codifies the common law rules applicable when a person agrees to carry out a service.

1 Part I

a) Many commercial transactions where property is transferred do not fall within the definition of a sale of goods. For example:

i) Contracts for *work and materials,* for example building, car repair, and contracts to install central heating or double glazing.

ii) Contracts of *exchange or barter.* Provided there is no money consideration these are not sales of goods. A contract of part exchange is a sale of goods.

ii) *'Free gifts'.* If a buyer is given a gift of 'product X' if he buys 10 units of 'product Y' he will own product X although it was not sold to him.

iv) Contracts for the *hire of goods.*

b) The problem was that Sale of Goods Act protection did not apply to goods supplied under such contracts. This could be unfair, for example when someone supplied work and materials the obligations in respect of the materials were implied at common law, but if he only supplied the materials he would be subject to the provisions of the Sale of Goods Act.

c) This unfairness was remedied by the 1982 Act. The Act applies to 'contracts for the transfer of property in goods' and 'contracts for the hire of goods'. Sections 2 – 5 provide statutory implied terms on the part of the seller similar to those in S.12 – 15 Sale of Goods Act 1979 thus:

   i)   By S.2 there is an implied condition that the transferor has the right to transfer the property in the goods.

   ii) By S.3 there is an implied condition that the goods will correspond with their description.

   iii) By S.4 there are implied conditions relating to quality and fitness for purpose.

   iv) By S.5 there is an implied condition that where the transfer is by reference to sample the bulk will correspond with the sample.

d) Sections 7 – 10 apply to contracts for the hire of goods and also provide statutory implied conditions similar to S.12 – 15 Sale of Goods Act 1979.

2 Part II

a) In October 1981 the National Consumer Council published a report entitled 'Service Please '. This reported widespread dissatisfaction with regard to consumer services. The main areas of complaint concerned poor quality workmanship, delays in carrying out work and complaints about the price charged. These problems are very important because of the large number of service contracts made each day, involving for example storage, repairs, cleaning, transport, holidays, banking, law, accounting, advertising, dentistry and so on. The purpose of the Act is to codify the common law relating to the three main areas of dissatisfaction referred to above, namely skill, time of performance and price.

b) The Act applies to contracts under which a person agrees to carry out a service. However it does not apply to contracts of employment, apprenticeships, services rendered to a company by a director and to the services of an advocate before a court or tribunal.

c) By S.13 there is an implied term that where the supplier is acting in the course of a business he will carry out the service with *reasonable care and skill*.

d) By S.14 there is an implied term that where the supplier is acting in the course of a business and the time for the service to be carried out is not fixed by the contract or determined by the course of dealings between the parties, the supplier will carry out the service within a *reasonable time*.

e) By S.15 there is an implied term that where the consideration is not determined by the contract, or in a manner agreed in the contract, or by the course of dealings between the parties, the party contracting with the supplier will pay a *reasonable price*.

3 Exclusion of liability

S.7 Unfair Contract Terms Act 1977 deals with contracts for the supply of goods other than contracts of sale or hire purchase. It provides that:

a) If the exclusion clause relates to title it will be void.

b) If the exclusion clause relates to description, quality, fitness or sample:

   i) If the buyer deals as a consumer the clause is void.

   ii) If the buyer does not deal as a consumer the exclusion clause must satisfy the requirement of reasonableness.

c) If the exclusion clause relates to poor quality work, i.e. a breach of *S.13*, the clause must satisfy the requirement of reasonableness (unless the negligent work causes personal injury or death, in which case it is void).

d) If there is a complaint in a consumer contract for work and materials, it will be necessary to discover the exact nature of the complaint. If it concerns defective materials the exclusion clause will be void. On the other hand if the materials are acceptable but the workmanship is negligent, the exclusion clause will have to satisfy the reasonableness test. In general it is becoming more difficult for traders to exclude liability for negligence when dealing with consumers. For example in WOODMAN v PHOTO TRADE PROCESSING (1981) Woodman took some film of a friend's wedding to a shop for developing. The shop displayed a notice limiting their liability to the cost of the film. Due to the processor's negligence the film was ruined. It was held that the exclusion clause was unreasonable and Woodman was awarded £75 to compensate for his disappointment.

 Group activity 1

Work in groups of four for this activity. Obtain several holiday brochures from local travel agents. Each group should chose one brochure and analyse its standard conditions. One or two members of each group should then make a short presentation to the whole class, explaining the most important conditions and commenting on whether they represent a fair balance between the interests of the tour operator and the holiday maker.

THE CONSUMER PROTECTION ACT 1987

1 Introduction

a) Consumer groups have argued for some time that the law governing civil liability for damage caused by defective goods is unsatisfactory. To proceed against a manufacturer, a consumer generally had to rely on the law of negligence, since his contract would usually be with someone other than the manufacturer, for example a retailer. In 1985 the European Community issued a directive on product liability. This was implemented by the Consumer Protection Act 1987. The Act has three main parts dealing with product liability, consumer safety and misleading price indications.

2 Product liability

a) Where product liability applies the consumer will not have to prove negligence when claiming compensation for injuries caused by products which are defective or unsafe.

b) To succeed in a product liability claim against a manufacturer the plaintiff must show four things:

    i)   that the product contained a defect,

    ii)   that the plaintiff suffered damage,

    iii) that the damage was caused by the product, and

    iv) that the defendant was a producer, 'own brander' or importer of the product.

c) A supplier will also be liable if he fails to identify the producer or importer when requested to do so.

d) The effect of the Act is that liability is no longer decided by reference to the fault of the manufacturer or some other person, but by reference to the state of the product in question. Even so the plaintiff may experience some difficulty proving that the defect in the product caused the injury.

e) There are three types of defect:

    i)   A *manufacturing defect* occurs when a product fails to comply with the manufacturer's product specifications and consequently deviates from the norm.

    ii)   A *design defect* occurs when the product specifications are themselves at fault and present a hazard. This type of defect is very serious and has led to major claims for compensation, particularly in defective drug cases, for example thalidomide.

    iii) A *duty to warn defect* refers to the producer's responsibility to provide appropriate warnings and instructions to enable the consumer to use the product safely.

f) A product will be judged to be defective if its safety is not such as persons are generally entitled to expect, taking all circumstances into account, for example any instructions and warnings and the use to which it could reasonably be expected to be put.

g) There are a number of defences, for example:

    i)   That the defendant did not supply the product.

    ii)   That the supply was otherwise than in the course of a business.

    iii) That the defect did not exist in the product at the time of supply.

iv) That the state of scientific and technical knowledge at the relevant time was not such that the producer might be expected to have discovered the defect.

v) More than 10 years have elapsed since the product was first supplied.

h) Defence iv. above is known as the 'state of the art' defence. It is particularly significant in the area of drugs where new products are constantly being developed on the boundaries of medical and scientific knowledge. A defect in a new drug could affect thousands of users but they would not be compensated if the defect was unknowable at the time of the product's circulation.

3 Consumer safety

This part of the Act is intended to provide the public with better protection from unsafe consumer goods. It primarily imposes criminal sanctions, but it will also assist the plaintiff in a civil action for negligence since, if a manufacturer has been found guilty of an offence under the Act, the plaintiff will be able to rely on this, instead of having to prove negligence. The main provisions are:

a) A person is guilty of an offence if he supplied consumer goods which are not reasonably safe.

b) The Secretary of State for Trade may make safety regulations (for example with regard to flammability or toxicity) governing the making and supplying of goods. These regulations cover, for example, childrens' nightdresses and electric blankets.

c) The Secretary of State may also serve a 'prohibition notice' on the supplier, prohibiting him from supplying goods which are unsafe. A 'notice to warn' may also be served, requiring the supplier to publish, at his own expense, a warning to customers about unsafe goods.

4 Misleading price indications

a) A person commits an offence if, in the course of a business, he gives consumers an indication which is misleading as to the price at which any goods, services, accommodation or facilities are available.

b) Examples of misleading price indications include:

   i) An understatement of the price.

   ii) Failing to make it clear that some other additional charge will be made.

   iii) Falsely indicating that the price is expected to be increased, reduced or maintained.

   iv) Making a false price comparison, for example by falsely stating that the price has been reduced.

c) The Act provides various defences, for example:

   i) That the defendant took all reasonable precautions and exercised all due care to avoid the commission of an offence.

   ii) That the defendant was an innocent publisher or advertising agency who was unaware, and who had no grounds for suspecting, that the advertisement contained a misleading price indication.

 Discussion topic

What is the legal effect of instructions or warnings as to the use of goods supplied to consumers?

THE TRADE DESCRIPTIONS ACT 1968

1 Introduction

The Trade Descriptions Act 1968 is a criminal statute which prohibits false trade descriptions about goods and false or misleading statements about services. It is not possible for individuals to bring a civil action for breach of the Trade Descriptions Act. They may however be able to bring an action for misrepresentation or breach of contract.

2 False trade descriptions about goods

a) A person shall be guilty of an offence if, in the course of a trade or business, they

   i) Apply a false trade description to any goods, or

   ii) Supply or offer to supply any goods to which a false trade description is applied.

b) Usually the seller will commit the offence, but a buyer can also be guilty under the Act. For example in FLETCHER v BUDGEN (1974) a car dealer told a private seller that his car could not be repaired and it was only fit for scrap. The dealer then bought the car for £2, repaired it and advertised it for sale at £315. It was held that a buyer who gave a false trade description of goods when purchasing them in the course of a business could be guilty of an offence under the Act.

c) 'Trade description' is widely defined to include any indication, direct or indirect, in relation to a number of matters referred to in the Act, for example:

    i)   Quantity or size.

    ii) Method of manufacture, production or processing.

    iii) Fitness for purpose, strength, performance or accuracy.

    iv) The results of any testing.

    v)   Place of date of manufacture, production of processing.

    vi) The person who manufactured, produced or processed the goods.

    vii) The history of the goods, for example previous ownership or use.

d) A trade description will be false if it is false or misleading to a material degree. The use of a word which is not strictly a trade description will be an offence if it is false to a material degree. For example in ROBERTSON V DICICCO (1972) a car dealer placed an advertisement in a newspaper describing the car as a 'beautiful car'. The car was arguably beautiful, but it was unfit for use. It was held that an offence had been committed since words such as 'beautiful' when applied to a car were an indication of fitness for use and quality as well as a description of appearance.

3 False trade descriptions about services

a) It is an offence if, in the course of a trade or business, a person makes a statement which is known to be false or recklessly makes a statement which is false about:

    i)   the nature or provision of any services, accommodation or facilities, or the time or manner of their provision or their evaluation, or

    ii) the location or amenities of any accommodation provided in the course of any trade or business.

b) Although the offence refers to 'knowledge' and 'recklessness' a corporation may be guilty of the offence provided the knowledge or recklessness is in the mind of the directors or other persons controlling the company.

c) A statement will be reckless if the person making it has no regard to whether it is true or false.

4 Defences

a) A person charged under the Act will have a defence if he can prove:

    i)   That the commission of the offence was due to a mistake, or to reliance on information supplied by another person, or due to some other cause beyond his control and that he took all reasonable precautions and exercised all due care to avoid committing the offence.

    ii) That in proceedings relating to the supply of goods, that he did not know and could not with reasonable care have found out, that the goods did not conform to the description.

b) A person may be able to avoid liability by the appropriate use of a disclaimer which cancels out the effect of a trade description. If a disclaimer is to be effective it must be as bold, precise and compelling as the description itself. For example if a car dealer wishes to disclaim responsibility for a possible false milometer reading a 'small print' contract term would not be effective. An appropriate disclaimer would need to be written on a label stuck on the milometer itself.

 Review questions *(answers page 302)*

1. What is the difference between a sale and an agreement to sell?

2. What are the main implied terms in the Sale of Goods Act 1979?

3. What is a 'reservation of title' clause in a contract for the sale of goods?

4. How does a product liability claim differ from a negligence claim?

5. Why is it important to know the time at which the property in goods passes?

6. What is a lien?

26

Consumer credit

Purchasing on credit is generally an expensive way to shop. In addition to the cash price the consumer will have to pay interest and other charges. A cash purchase saves money and removes worries about repayment of the debt.

Anyone who borrows money should shop around for the best deal, using the APR (annual percentage rate of charge) as a general guide. Even with 1994 interest rates at less than half the 1991/2 levels, debt is a major problem for many consumers.

Anyone considering credit should ask themselves:

a) Do I really want the item or the loan?

b) Should I try to save up the money, or use savings in order to pay the cash price?

c) Will I have enough cash left at the end of each month for essential expenditure and have something left for emergencies?

d) Will I be able to keep up payments if the interest rate rises or if my income falls?

1 The Consumer Credit Act 1974

a) The consumer credit industry is regulated by the Consumer Credit Act 1974.

b) The main purposes of the Act are:

   i) To set out a uniform system of statutory control over the provision of credit.

   ii) To protect the interests of consumers by imposing a system of licencing on those who offer credit and by increasing the protection of consumers by redressing bargaining inequalities, controlling trading malpractices and regulating the remedies for non-payment.

c) The Act regulates all forms of credit, including cash loans, sales of goods on credit, credit card transactions, and hire purchase agreements.

d) The Act only applies to credit agreements by which the creditor (who may be an individual or a corporation) provides the debtor (who must be an individual) with credit not exceeding £15,000. The term *'individual'* is defined to include partnerships and other unincorporated bodies even though they are not usually thought of as consumers. This definition includes a number of different types of credit, for example:

   i) Credit up to an agreed limit, for example a bank overdraft or a credit card.

   ii) Credit of a fixed amount, for example a bank loan or a hire purchase agreement.

   iii) Credit that must be used for a specified purpose, or

   iv) Credit that the debtor may use for any purpose, for example a bank overdraft.

2 Types of credit

a) *Hire purchase.* See 3 below.

b) *Credit sale.* This is similar to hire purchase but title passes to the buyer at the time of sale and the purchase price is paid by a number of instalments.

c) *Credit cards,* for example Access and Visa. The card company will send a monthly account for items purchased. The consumer can pay off the full amount or make a minimum repayment and pay interest on the balance.

d) *Store cards.* These are similar to credit cards, but use is restricted to a particular store or group of stores. Like credit cards they are an expensive form of credit.

e) *Charge cards.* These are used like credit cards, but the bill must be paid in full each month.

f) *Mail order catalogues.* The buyer may save time and money by purchasing from home and will usually get an interest free period within which to pay for the goods. Interest will usually be payable if goods are paid for over a period of time.

g) *Bank loans.* If a person has a bank account it may be possible to arrange a bank overdraft. The advantage is that it can be quickly arranged and the debt will be reduced as soon as the customer pays funds into the account. An overdraft is not however necessarily a cheap form of credit. Banks also offer personal loans which are repaid by fixed installments over an agreed period.

h) *Building society loans.* If a person is buying their home and their mortgage is less than the value of the house, it may be possible to raise cash by increasing the mortgage. This may involve survey fees and it would of course involve long term liability.

i) *Finance company loans.* Retailers such as car dealers, furniture dealers and electrical retailers may offer to arrange a finance company loan if a person is purchasing a large item.

j) *Secured loans.* A bank, building society or finance company may insist that a loan should be secured on a person's home. This will give extra security to the lender which may be reflected in a lower rate of interest. However if the loan is not repaid, the lender can apply for the home to be sold.

k) *Pawnbroking.* An individual leaves an article such as a piece of jewellery with a pawnbroker in return for a loan. The item will be returned when the loan plus interest has been repaid over an agreed period. If the money is not repaid the pawnbroker may sell the article. This is usually an expensive form of credit.

l) *Small moneylenders.* Such lenders often collect repayments from individuals' homes each week. This increases the cost of borrowing. The loan should be cheaper if the individual pays at the lender's premises.

Group activity 1

Working in groups of two or three, members of the class should chose one type of credit to investigate. The investigation should cover rates of interest and the main conditions typically attached to the chosen form of credit. One member of each group should then make a short presentation to the rest of the class, describing the form of credit, the rate of interest, the main terms and the advantages and disadvantages of the particular form of lending.

3 Hire purchase

a) Hire purchase is a common method of obtaining possession and use of goods before making full payment. Under a hire purchase contract the consumer obtains possession of the goods and is granted an option to purchase them. The consumer does not 'agree to buy' the goods at the time of the contract. Therefore if he sells the goods before he has exercised the option to purchase he does not pass title to them.

b) Usually when a consumer purchases goods on hire purchase the dealer does not provide the credit. The dealer will sell the goods to a finance company for cash. The finance company will then hire the goods to the consumer. The hire purchase contract will therefore be between the finance company and the consumer, not between the dealer and the consumer. The following example will help to clarify this.

David has purchased a compact disc system on hire purchase from Luton Audio (a small independent dealer) and is obtaining finance from Audio Finance plc, a finance company. The following two diagrams illustrate the situation. The first summarises the effect of signing a hire purchase agreement. The second illustrates what happens at the end of the period of the agreement.

i. When the hire purchase agreement is signed, the following takes place:

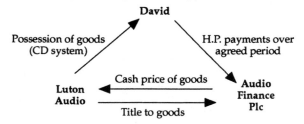

ii. At the end of the agreed period, title passes to David:

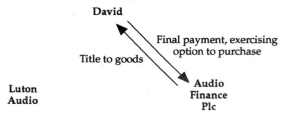

4 Formation of the agreement

a) *Licencing.* Any person who wishes to carry on a consumer credit business must first obtain a licence from the Director General of Fair Trading, who must be satisfied that the applicant is a fit person to engage in such business.

b) *Seeking business.*

i) Any advertisement must give a fair and comprehensive picture of the credit offered and must include the true rate of interest. In METSOJA v NORMAN PITT (1989) a car dealer advertised a new car with a 0% credit facility. The dealer also operated on a part-exchange basis, however the part-exchange allowance was lower if a new car was bought on credit than it would be if the new car were purchased for cash. It was held that the lower allowance on part-exchange for persons purchasing on credit was a hidden charge for credit contrary to the Act.

ii) The Act also creates several criminal offences related to canvassing for business, for example it is an offence to solicit entry by an individual into certain consumer credit agreements off trade premises, unless in response to a written request.

iii) It is also an offence to send someone an unsolicited credit card (i.e. a credit card that had not been requested by the consumer), for example of the type commonly issued by large retail chains.

c) *Formal requirements.* Prior to making the agreement certain information must be disclosed to ensure that the debtor is aware of his rights and duties, the amount and rate of the total charge for credit and the remedies available under the Act. The agreement itself must:

i) be in writing,

ii) contain all express terms in a clearly legible form,

iii) be signed by the debtor personally and by or on behalf of the creditor or owner,

iv) comply with detailed regulations as to form and content, and

v) if it is a cancellable agreement (see e. below), it must contain a notice in statutory form indicating the right of the consumer to cancel the agreement and how and when this right can be exercised.

Immediately after signing the agreement the consumer must receive a copy of the signed agreement. Within seven days the consumer must receive a second copy of the completed agreement. This second copy is only necessary if the agreement was not completed by the consumer's signature i.e. if the creditor has not previously signed it. If it is a cancellable agreement this copy must be sent by post and must contain details of the debtor's right to cancel. If the agreement was completed by the consumer's signature no second copy is required. However if the agreement is cancellable a notice must be sent by post within seven days giving the consumer details of cancellation rights.

d) *The annual percentage rate of charge.* All lenders must work this out in the same way so that consumers can make a fair comparison. To calculate the APR a lender will add all interest and other charges together and take into account how and when payments are made.

e) *The right to cancel.*

    i)   A consumer credit agreement is normally cancellable if the consumer signed it at a place other than the place of business of the owner, creditor or any person acting on their behalf. This provision gives individuals a 'cooling off' period during which time they may reconsider their purchase, having been persuaded, usually in their own homes, to enter into a consumer credit contract. As stated above the consumer must receive their second statutory copy, or the notice of their right to cancel, within seven days of signing the agreement. They then have a further five days within which to cancel the agreement.

    ii) The effect of cancellation is that the agreement is treated as if it had never been entered into. Therefore any deposit paid, or goods handed over in part-exchange by the consumer must be returned. The consumer need not send the goods back, but must retain them and permit their collection in response to a written request.

5 Matters arising during the agreement

a) The consumer is entitled to receive, in return for a request in writing and a small payment, another copy of the agreement and a statement of the current financial position.

b) The consumer is also entitled, at any time, to pay the amount outstanding on his account and discharge his indebtedness.

c) The agreement may contain a variation clause, for example allowing the finance company to increase the rate of interest. Such a variation will not take effect until proper notice is given to the consumer.

d) In a three-cornered consumer credit agreement of the type described in 3. above the Act provides that if the consumer has a claim against the dealer for misrepresentation or breach of contract, the consumer will have a similar claim against the creditor. This is an important additional remedy which guards against the possibility of the dealer being unable to meet the consumer's claim. For example if a debtor uses a Barclaycard to pay for goods then a claim may be made against the creditor (the credit card company) rather than the supplier, provided the cash price for the goods is more than £100.

6 Default

a) When a consumer defaults the creditor cannot take any action to enforce the agreement unless a default notice has been served on the consumer. This must specify:

   i) the alleged breach,

   ii) the action to put it right if it is capable of remedy,

   iii) what sum, if any, is required to be paid as compensation, and

   iv) the date by which such action must be taken, which must be no less than seven days after the service of the default notice.

b) In addition where goods are bought on hire purchase the Act provides that once one third or more of the total price of the goods has been paid, the creditor cannot recover possession except by order of the court. Such goods are known as *'protected goods'*.

c) Entry on to any premises by the creditor to take possession of goods is prohibited except by court order.

d) The charging of default interest at a higher rate than the basic rate of interest is prohibited.

7 Termination

a) The consumer may, at any time before the final payment falls due, terminate a consumer credit agreement by giving written notice to the person authorised to receive payments.

b) The consumer's liability is to pay amounts already due, plus the amount, if any, by which one half of the total price exceeds the total money already paid, or such lesser amount as may be specified in the agreement. The consumer may also have to compensate the creditor for any damage to goods if he has failed to take reasonable care of them.

c) If any term in the agreement is inconsistent with these provisions, by for example imposing additional liability on the consumer, the term will be void.

8 Control by the court

a) *Enforcement orders.* In several situations, for example if the agreement has been improperly executed, the Act requires the creditor to obtain an enforcement order from the court before he can enforce the agreement. Such an order will not be granted if the agreement was a cancellable one, but the consumer was not given proper notice of the right to cancel.

b) *Time orders.* On the application for an enforcement order, or on an application to recover possession of goods after service of a default notice, the court may grant a time order giving the consumer more time to pay.

c) *Return orders.* Where the consumer is in breach and the creditor seeks to recover the goods, the court may issue a return order, ordering the consumer to return the goods.

d) *Transfer orders.* If the consumer is in breach and the goods can be divided up, the court may make a transfer order giving ownership of part of the goods to the consumer and returning the rest to the creditor.

e) *Extortionate credit bargains.* If the court finds that a credit bargain is extortionate it may re-open the agreement in order to do justice between the parties. Thus it can relieve the consumer of liability to go on paying money, or it can order the return of money already paid by him. The court will consider whether the total charge for credit is exorbitant and whether the agreement as a whole contravenes principles of fair dealing. It will therefore look at, for example, the interest rates prevailing when the agreement was made, the degree of financial pressure placed on the consumer and the financial risk taken by the creditor.

 Task 1

Write a reply to the following letter:

Dear Sir,

Seven months ago I purchased a television set on hire purchase at the price of £320. I made a down-payment of £2 and I have paid 6 monthly installments of £12. Can I avoid further payment by returning the set to the dealer?

A few days ago my husband signed a hire purchase agreement for a set of Encyclopedia Britannica. We now realise that this was a terrible mistake. Can we get out of the contract?

Yours faithfully

June Smith

 Review questions *(answers page 304)*

1. What is a hire purchase contract?

2. What is the liability of a person who wishes to terminate a consumer credit agreement before the end of its term?

3. Explain what is meant by a cancellable consumer credit agreement.

4. What are protected goods?

5. What is a time order?

6. John borrows £1,000 to pay for a new car. The loan is to be repaid over one year by monthly installments of £100. Therefore by the end of the year John will have repaid £1,200. If no other charges are involved, what is the APR?

27

The Data Protection Act 1984

Computers are increasingly used throughout society to collect, store, process and distribute information about individuals. This information is referred to in the Act as *'personal data'*. The increase in personal data held on computers has led to concern over individual privacy, the use to which such information is put and the damage that a person might suffer if the information is wrong. In an attempt to deal with these issues the Data Protection Act 1984 was passed.

1 Purpose of the Act

The basic purpose of the Act is to improve practice among computer users, thus raising public confidence in computer record keeping. In particular the Act:

a) Gives rights to individuals about whom information is recorded on computer. They may find out information about themselves, challenge it if appropriate and claim compensation in certain circumstances.

b) Places obligations on those who record and use personal data (data users). They must be open about that use and follow sound and proper practices.

2 What the Act covers

a) The Act only applies to automatically processed information – broadly speaking information which is processed by a computer. It does not cover information which is held and processed manually in for example ordinary paper files. The Act does not cover all computerised information but only that which relates to living individuals. It does not for example cover information which relates only to a company.

b) The Act also exempts certain personal data from the requirement to register, for example:

i) Personal data held by an individual (for example a home computer user) in connection with personal, family or household affairs.

ii) Personal data used only for calculating and paying wages and pensions, keeping accounts or keeping records of purchases and sales in order to ensure that the appropriate payments are made.

iii) Personal data held by an unincorporated members' club, for example a sports club, which is not a registered company.

iv) Personal data which the law requires the user to make public, for example personal data in the electoral register.

3 The requirement of registration

a) Every user who holds personal data must be registered, unless all the data is exempt. The register entry contains the data user's name and address together with broad descriptions of:

   i) The personal data which the data user holds.

   ii) The purposes for which the data is used.

   iii) The sources from which the data user intends to obtain the information, and

   iv) The people to whom the data user may wish to disclose the information.

b) Data users who should have registered, but have not, commit a criminal offence. It is also a criminal offence to operate outside the descriptions contained in the register entry.

c) The register is open to public inspection at the Registrar's office in Wilmslow, Cheshire. Inspection of the register is free. Official copies of individual register entries are available from the Registrar's office for £2 per entry.

4 The data protection principles

a) Registered data users must comply with the Data Protection Principles in relation to the personal data they hold. The Principles broadly state that personal data shall:

   i) Be obtained and processed fairly and lawfully.

   ii) Be held only for the lawful purposes described in the register entry.

   iii) Be used only for those purposes and only be disclosed to those people described in the register entry.

   iv) Be adequate, relevant and not excessive in relation to the purposes for which they are held.

   v) Be accurate and, where necessary, kept up to date.

   vi) Be held no longer than is necessary for the registered purpose.

   vii) Be surrounded by proper security.

The Principles also provide for individuals to have access to data held about themselves and, where appropriate, to have the data corrected or deleted.

b) To enforce compliance with the Principles, the Registrar can serve three types of notice:

   i) An *enforcement notice,* requiring the data user to take specified action to comply with the particular Principle. Failure to comply with an enforcement notice is a criminal offence.

   ii) A *de-registration notice,* cancelling the whole or part of a data user's register entry. The data user would commit a criminal offence if it carried on as if the registration was valid.

   iii) A *transfer prohibition notice,* preventing the data user from transferring personal data overseas if this is likely to lead to a Principle being broken.

5 Individuals' rights

The Act gives legal rights to individuals concerning personal data held about them.

a) *Compensation.* A person is entitled to seek compensation if damage has been caused by the loss, unauthorised destruction or unauthorised disclosure of personal data. If damage is proved, the court may also order compensation for any associated distress. Compensation may also be sought if damage is caused as a result of inaccurate data.

b) *Correction or deletion.* If personal data is inaccurate the individual may complain to the Registrar or apply to the court for correction or deletion of the data.

c) *Subject access.* An individual is entitled, on making a written request, to be supplied with a copy of any personal data held about him or her. The data user may charge a fee of up to £10 for supplying this information. Sometimes this right will not exist, for example where giving the information would be likely to prejudice the prevention or detection of a crime.

d) *Complaint to the Registrar.* An individual who considers there has been a breach of one of the provisions of the Act is entitled to complain to the Registrar. If the complaint is justified and cannot be resolved informally, the Registrar may use his powers to prosecute or to serve one of a number of notices within his power, for example an enforcement notice requiring the data user to take specified action to comply with the Act or a de-registration notice, cancelling the whole or part of a data user's register entry.

6 Disclosure of personal data

a) The Act does does not prevent a data user from disclosing information about an individual if the person to whom the disclosure is made is described in the disclosures section of the data user's register entry.

b) There is no general right for an individual to object to the disclosure of personal data. Although data users are required to be careful not to deceive or mislead anyone about the purpose for which the information is held, used or disclosed.

7 The Data Protection Tribunal

The Act established the Data Protection Tribunal, consisting of a legally qualified chairman and lay members, to consider appeals by data users against the Registrar's decisions. Appeals may relate to the refusal of a registration application or to the service of an enforcement or de-registration notice. The Tribunal can overturn the Registrar's decision and substitute whatever decision it thinks fit. On questions of law there is an appeal from the Tribunal to the High Court.

 Group activity 1

Work in groups of four for this activity. In each groups two students should act as college administrators and two students as legal advisers. The Chief Administrative Officer of Central College has just found out about the Data Protection Act. He has not seen the Act and he does not know what action, if any, the College ought to take. He has therefore asked the College legal advisers to give the College appropriate advice. Role play a meeting at which the advice is given. The College administrators should prepare for the meeting by finding out what records the College keeps and how this information is stored. The legal advisers should prepare by choosing suitable questions to ask the administrators.

Helpful booklets may be obtained free of charge from the office of the Data Protection Registrar, Wycliffe House, Water Lane, Wilmslow, Cheshire SK9 5AF. Telephone 0625 535777.

 **Review questions** *(answers page 305)*

1) What information does the Data Protection Act 1984 apply to?
2. What information is contained in a data user's register entry?
3. What rights does the Act give to data subjects?
4. What is the role of the Data Protection Tribunal?
5. What is the consequence for a data user who fails to register as required by the Act?
6. What is an enforcement notice?

28

Consumer watchdogs

As long ago as 1962 the Malony Report on Consumer Protection said that:

'The business of making and selling is highly organised, often in large units, and calls to its aid at every step complex highly expert skills. The business of buying is conducted by the smallest unit, the individual consumer, relying on the guidance afforded by experience if he possesses it, and if not, on instinctive but not always rational thought processes'.

This chapter introduces the main statutory and independent organisations which seek to redress this imbalance between sellers and buyers and generally protect the interests of consumers. They do this in a wide variety of ways, for example:

a) Trying to ensure that the interests of consumers are taken into account by decision makers in industry and government.
b) Establishing performance and safety standards.

c) Taking steps to correct unfair and anti-competitive business practices.

d) Enforcing consumer protection legislation concerning for example, trade descriptions and weights and measures.

e) Investigating consumer complaints about public services.

1 The Office of Fair Trading

a) *Introduction.* The post of Director General of Fair Trading was set up by the Fair Trading Act 1973. The 'Office of Fair Trading' (OFT) is the Director's staff. There are no local branches, although the OFT works closely with trading standards departments run by local authorities. The aim of the OFT is to protect consumers by encouraging competition among businesses and looking after consumers by making sure that trading practices are as fair as possible.

b) *Looking after consumers.* The OFT carries out a range of activities that look after consumer interests.

   i) Examining consumer problems by monitoring consumer complaints made to trading standards departments, environmental health departments, citizens advice bureaux and other bodies. The OFT cannot give help or advice on individual disputes, but will analyse trends and identify problem sectors and practices that adversely affect consumers. As a result the OFT may recommend changes in business practice or in the law.

   ii) The OFT encourages traders to raise standards and set out ways of dealing with complaints. Codes of practice have been negotiated with and adopted by a number of trade associations with these objectives in mind. Areas covered include for example buying by post, buying double glazing, funerals, dry cleaners, package holidays and so on.

   iii) The OFT will take action against traders who persistently commit offences or break their obligations to customers, for example car dealers who sell defective cars. Such traders can be asked to give a written assurance that they will mend their ways. If they refuse to give the assurance, or break one that has been given, they can be taken to court.

iv) The OFT issues licences (under the Consumer Credit Act 1974) to traders who wish to carry on any credit business and keeps a public register of licenced traders. Licences can be refused or revoked if the Office considers that the trader is not fit to have one. Estate agents do not need licences, but under the Estate Agents Act 1979, the Director General can ban someone from engaging in estate agency work if he considers that the person is unfit to do so. The Office keeps a register of estate agents who have been banned.

v) If a complaint about a misleading advertisement is referred to the Director General by the Advertising Standards Authority or a trading standards department, the Director General can ask the High Court to ban the advertisement. Such action is a last resort which will only be used when other methods have failed and where it is in the public interest that the advertisement should be stopped.

vi) The Office publishes a range of leaflets and booklets giving information on consumer rights and obligations. These are available from trading standards departments, citizens advice bureaux or by writing to the Office of Fair Trading, Room 306, Field House, 15-25, Breams Buildings, London EC4A 1PR.

c) *Encouraging competition.* Lack of competition in business is likely to be against the public interest, since it may restrict public choice and/or lead to the fixing of higher prices. The Director General has duties in relation to monopolies, mergers and trade practices which may be restrictive or anti-competitive. These will be discussed in the next Chapter.

d) *Investment business.* Under the Financial Services Act 1986, detailed arrangements have been made to control investment businesses, including life insurance. The OFT examines the rules and other arrangements for the management of these businesses. If they are anti-competitive, the Director General reports to the Secretary of State who can then impose changes.

Group activity 1

One member of the group should write to the Office of Fair Trading at the address given in 1.b.vi above and ask for sufficient copies of a consumer information pack for all members of the group. You will find that each pack contains a number of separate leaflets on for example, buying by post, problems with shoes, buying used cars, problems of debt and so on. The class should split into groups of two or three. Each group will then study one of the leaflets and give a ten minute presentation to the whole class explaining the issues dealt with by the leaflet and passing on the advice contained in it.

In some cases it may be possible to have a class discussion based on actual problems faced by class members.

2 Trading standards departments

a) These are part of local county or borough councils. Their main function is to enforce consumer protection legislation concerning safety, trade descriptions, prices, weights and measures, food quality and the fairness of consumer credit contracts.

b) They can bring prosecutions under the Trade Descriptions Act 1968 where traders give false descriptions of goods or services. They can prosecute under the Weights and Measures Act 1985 where traders give short measures. They also test weighing machines and equipment used in shops. Under the Consumer Protection Act 1987 they can issue suspension notices preventing traders selling goods which are believed to be unsafe. Under this Act they can also prosecute traders for giving misleading price indications or for selling goods which are in breach of safety regulations. They also have powers of enforcement under several other Acts, including the Consumer Credit Act 1974.

3 Environmental health departments

a) Environmental health officers normally work for local borough councils. Selling food which is unfit for human consumption is a criminal offence. Environmental health officers have an important role in ensuring that food is prepared in hygienic surroundings and is safe to eat. They inspect, markets, food shops and restaurants. If a consumer purchases contaminated food, or finds a 'foreign body' such as a piece of glass in food he or she should contact the local environmental health department.

b) Environmental health officers also deal with poor quality housing, health and safety at work (under the Health and Safety at Work Act 1974), pest control and air pollution.

4 The Consumers' Association

a) The Consumers' Association was formed in 1957. It now has about 800,000 members who subscribe to its main publication 'Which?'.

b) The main work of The Consumers' Association is to provide independent and technically-based advice on a full range of goods and services available to consumers and to publish the results in its magazines. Its method is to test products (in its own laboratory) and investigate services in order to provide comparative reports on performance, quality and value. These reports will always identify the supplier and/or the brand.

c) In addition to Which? The Consumers' Association publishes several other magazines (for example 'Gardening Which?' and 'Money Which?') and numerous annual guides and action packs. Action packs include for example 'Buying a Secondhand Car', 'Choose your Pension', 'Work for Yourself' and 'Baby on the Way'.

d) The Consumers' Association also seeks to help consumers by persuading suppliers to improve safety, performance or quality and by encouraging the Government to pass legislation to protect consumers. For example it was influential in the passing of the Unfair Contract Terms Act 1977.

e) The Consumers' Association is an independent organisation funded by members' subscriptions. To ensure that it maintains independence its magazines carry no advertising and it receives no money from manufacturers, suppliers or the Government.

f) It operates as a registered charity. Overall policy is controlled by a Council of approximately 20 members elected by subscribers to Which? They are unpaid and must not have a top post in a business which makes, sells or promotes consumer goods or services. They are elected for a three year term. The Council appoints a Chief Executive who is in charge of day to day operations.

Overall The Consumers' Association employs approximately 480 staff.

 Task 1

In each of the following situations is the statement made by the shop true or false?

1. You purchase a tennis racket in a half-price sale. The racket is marked 'seconds'. The first time you use the racket you hit an overhead smash off centre and the frame cracks. The shop says you cannot have you money back, because you knew it was imperfect at the time of purchase.

2. You purchase a pair of shoes in a sale. A few days later the heel comes off. You can't find the receipt, but you still take the shoes back to the shop. The shop says it does not have to give you a refund because you do not have a receipt.

3. You book a table for two at an expensive restaurant. Unfortunately you catch a cold and decide not to go to the restaurant. You also forget to telephone to cancel your reservation. The restaurant says it is entitled to sue you for the profit it would have made on your meal.

4. You buy a new electric razor which works from the mains power supply. Later the same day, before you have taken it out of its box, you change your mind and take it back to the shop, because you have decided you would prefer a battery powered razor. The shop says it is entitled to refuse to change the goods.

5. You book your car into the local garage for a change of oil and spark plugs. Without telling you the garage replace the head-gasket and present you with a bill for £200. They say you have to pay because it was essential work.

6. You purchase a hair dryer for your mother's birthday. It is faulty, so she takes it back to the shop where you bought it. The shop says she is not entitled to a refund.

The answers to these questions are at the end of the Chapter (page 223).

5 The National Consumer Council (NCC)

a) The NCC is a Government funded body working directly on consumers' behalf. It was set up in 1975. Its main role is as a pressure group. It tries to ensure that the interests of all consumers are taken into account by decision makers in business, industry, the professions and Government. It is a campaigning organisation, so it does not test consumer products nor deal directly with consumer complaints.

b) At present it is very concerned with consumer problems of credit and debt. Also public utilities (Gas, Electricity and Water), housing and health policies and high street legal services. The NCC's research and policy recommendations are published in books and reports which are on sale at its offices.

6 The British Standards Institution (BSI)

a) The job of the BSI is to establish performance and safety standards. It tests products for performance and safety and/or specifies product dimensions. It may also recommend the way in which goods should be used or maintained by consumers. Where a product is marked 'BS' followed by a number this indicates that the manufacturer has complied with the particular standard for that product. If the product has a kite mark or safety mark this means that the BSI has independently tested the product against the standard and that the standard has been complied with in every respect.

The **BSI Safety Mark** indicates that the product meets safety standards.

The **BSI Kitemark** indicates that the product meets standards to do with safety, quality or performance.

b) BSI standards also apply to some services as well as products. For example some colleges have achieved BS5750, the standard for quality procedures.

7 Advertising Standards Authority (ASA)

a) The ASA scrutinises advertisements and sales promotions in non-broadcast media to check that the advertising is *'legal, decent, honest and truthful'*. It examines over 850 advertisements each month to see if they comply with its own guidelines – The British Code of Advertising Practice. The Code includes, for example, detailed rules on advertising health and slimming products, cigarettes and alcohol, advertisements offering employment and advertisements aimed at children.

b) The ASA also checks sale promotions by monitoring press advertisements and postal special offers. Sales promotions must comply with the British Code of Sales Promotion Practice. Both these Codes are voluntary, but the ASA will publish monthly case reports of complaints received and of its ruling in each case.

8 Regulation of public services

a) *Electricity*. The Office of Electricity Regulations (OFFER) is an independent body established under the Electricity Act 1989 to regulate the activities of the electricity supply industry and

217

protect the interests of customers. It has 14 regional offices throughout the UK and in each region there is a Regional Electricity Consumers Committee to represent the interests of customers in that area. OFFER is headed by the Director General of Electricity Supply.

b) *Gas.*

i) The Office of Gas Supply (OFGAS) was set up by the Gas Act 1986. It is an independent body whose main duty is to ensure that British Gas plc complies with its statutory duties. It also seeks to ensure that gas is supplied to consumers wherever possible and it monitors the prices charged to customers. These prices are controlled by a formula set out following privatisation. Control is also exercised over prices charged by landlords who resell gas to tenants.

ii) There is also a Gas Consumers Council. This is an independent agency, set up in 1986 by an Act of Parliament. It represents the interests of all 17 million domestic and commercial gas users. It has 12 regional offices which deal with complaints about gas supply, gas appliances and fittings.

c) *Water.* The Office of Water Supply (OFWAT) is an independent body set up in 1989. It deals with customer protection policy, including prices and complaints. There are 10 Customer Service Committees, one for each water region. These investigate consumer complaints about water and sewerage and will try to resolve the problem on the customer's behalf. Complaints will only be referred to the Director General of Water Services (the head of OFWAT) if they cannot be resolved by the appropriate Customer Service Committee.

d) *Telecommunications.* The Office of Telecommunications (OFTEL) regulates the activities of UK telecommunications companies, in particular British Telecom. It looks after the consumers' interests with regard to prices and the quality of service. It also has a duty to investigate complaints.

e) *The Post Office.* The Post Office Users' National Council (POUNC) is an independent body, funded by the DTI to represent customer interests concerning for example the quality of service, proposed prices and overall policy. It will also investigate complaints.

f) *Rail travel.* The Central Transport Consultative Committee was originally established by the Transport Act 1947. It is a statutory consumer body representing the interests of users of British Rail's services and facilities. Although funded by Government its views are independent from both British Rail and the Government. The CTCC monitors British Rail performance and policies and has a legal right to recommend changes to the British Railways Board.

g) *Air travel.* The Air Transport Users Committee is a non-statutory body set up by the Civil Aviation Authority to represent passengers' interests. It can investigate complaints and make recommendations, although it cannot give rulings. Each airport also has a Consumer Consultative Committee which will liaise with the Air Transport Users Committee.

9 Other bodies

There are many other organisations which advise and help consumers. Some of the more important are set out below.

a) *Citizens Advice Bureaux.* CABs provide free and confidential advice. There are over 1,300 outlets in the UK dealing with roughly 7 million enquiries per year. Consumer and debt enquiries are the second largest area dealt with by the CAB. The CAB will also act as a pressure group, bringing particular problems to the attention of policy makers on both the national and local level. Approximately 23,000 people work in the CAB service, 90% of whom are part-time volunteers.

b) *The National Federation of Consumer Groups.* Local consumer groups were first established during the 1960s, to investigate local problems and publish results locally. These groups are members of the NFCG which produces various publications, for example a consumer newsletter and a handbook of consumer law. The NFCG campaigns nationally on issues of concern to members and provides consumer representatives for many industry consumer committees.

c) *Law Centres Federation.* This is the co-ordinating body for law centres. It also provides information about their work to the general public and to local and national government. There are approximately 60 local law centres which provide free advice and representation to individuals and groups on matters such as education, housing, employment, immigration, sex discrimination and social security.

d) *The Securities and Investments Board.* Under the Financial Services Act 1986, detailed arrangements were made to control investment businesses, including life assurance. The SIB was set up in 1988, its basic aim is to achieve a high level of investor protection by ensuring that anyone providing any form of investment service meets standards of honesty, competency and solvency. Investment businesses must therefore be authorised by the SIB or one of the other bodies set up under the Financial Services Act.

10 Ombudsman

a) An ombudsman is a person whose job is to investigate complaints relating to the exercise of administrative functions. The intention is to give the public further safeguards against maladministration in addition to those provided by courts and tribunals.

b) When people refer to 'the Ombudsman' they generally mean the Parliamentary Commissioner for Administration. This post was established in 1967. The ombudsman is appointed by the Crown and his role is to investigate complaints relating to the administrative acts of government departments. Jurisdiction is however rather limited in that the ombudsman can only investigate where the allegation is that the correct procedure has not been followed. There is no power where the procedure was correct, even if the resulting decision was wrong. A further limitation is that the ombudsman has no power to initiate investigations. Access to the ombudsman is also restricted because he will only act at the request of a Member of Parliament. A person with a complaint must therefore bring it to the notice of an MP. Most complaints are made against the Department of Social Security, followed by the Inland Revenue.

c) In addition to the Parliamentary Commissioner there are a number of other ombudsmen set up under various Acts of Parliament, including:

   i) Health Service Ombudsman, to investigate certain specified complaints relating to the National Health Service.

ii) Local Government Ombudsman, to investigate alleged injustice resulting from maladministration by local government, police authorities or water authorities.

iii) Legal Ombudsman, to investigate complaints against members of the legal profession where such complaints have not been resolved by either the Law Society or the Bar Council. These are the governing bodies for solicitors and barristers.

iv) Banking Ombudsman, Insurance Ombudsman, Building Society Ombudsman, Pensions Ombudsman and Stock Exchange Ombudsman. In each case the Ombudsman deals with particular complaints relating to their industry or profession.

11 Citizens Charter

In many areas of public life the Government has published Citizens Charters. Of particular interest to students are the Charters for Further Education and Higher Education.

The Charter for Further Education was published in 1993. The 30 page document aims to promote high standards of service for everyone who uses colleges. It:

a) Recognises that colleges provide a service to a range of people including full-time and part-time students of all ages, employers and other members of the community.

b) Sets out principles and targets (where appropriate) that colleges and others involved in further education are expected to meet, with regard to, for example:

   i) Reliable, impartial and timely advice about the choices available.

   ii) Clear and accurate information about courses, qualifications, facilities and entry requirements.

   iii) Prompt payments of grants.

   iv) High quality teaching and effective management of learning.

   v) Regular information on progress and achievements.

   vi) Access to reliable and unbiased careers advice.

c) Sets out what an employer or member of the local community has the right to expect. For example:

   i) Enquiries to be handled efficiently.

   ii) Information about available facilities and any charges made.

d) Explains what everyone has a right to expect if things go wrong, in particular that the college will have open, fair and effective complaints procedures.

e) Explains how to contact the various organisations involved in further education.

f) Makes it clear that by Summer 1994 every college should have developed its own charter, following consultation with customers and containing precise targets wherever possible.

 Group activity 2

Obtain a copy of the Charter for Further Education from your college or from:

> Charters
> Freepost EDO 3138
> London E15 2BR

If your college has its own charter, or a 'learner contract' based on the Charter for Further Education, you should also obtain a copy of these documents.

If your college does not have a learner contract, work in groups of three or four to produce a draft contract, setting out as precisely as possible, the obligations of each party to the contract i.e. the college and the individual student.

If your college has a learner contract, write a report on its strengths and weaknesses, suggesting any improvements that you feel should be made.

 Review questions (answers page 306)

1. What are the main aims of the Office of Fair Trading?

2. Briefly describe the work of environmental health officers.

3. How is the Consumers' Association funded ?

4. What is a kite mark?

5. How are the main public services regulated?

6. Describe the role of the Parliamentary Commissioner for Administration.

Answers to Consumer Quiz

1. *False.* If goods are marked as seconds the consumer cannot expect them to be perfect, but they must still be of merchantable quality and fit for their purpose. Provided the defect was not obvious, the buyer is entitled to a refund.

2. *False.* It does not matter that the goods were purchased in a sale, nor are consumer rights affected by the absence of a receipt, although a dispute is less likely if the receipt has been retained. In the absence of a receipt, a credit card slip, or cheque book stub will provide evidence of the purchase.

3. *True.* When you book a table at a restaurant you make a contract with the restaurant. Failure to purchase a meal is a breach of contract and the restaurant may sue for its loss of profit. Precise quantification of the compensation may be difficult, since different meals will vary in price.

4. *True.* Someone who makes a mistake or who changes their mind is not entitled to a refund or a credit note. Some shops will of course replace goods to retain customer goodwill.

5. *False.* You only have to pay for work which you have previously agreed will be carried out.

6. *False.* You have a contract with the shop, your mother does not. Only the person who purchased the goods is entitled to a refund. Since you could take the goods in on behalf of your mother, the shop would probably change the item out of goodwill.

29

Competition policy and how it helps consumers

Competition policy controls anti-competitive practices such as agreements between suppliers to fix minimum prices, the creation of monopolies that reduce the number of suppliers, limiting the production or import of particular goods, agreements to share the market for particular goods and many more. Any such conduct is likely to affect consumers. It may restrict choice, lead to higher prices, cause them to travel further to obtain specific goods or services and so on.

At common law (i.e case law developed in the courts) all these restrictions would be valid since the common law places almost no restrictions on a person's freedom to contract. Legislation was therefore needed to protect the consumer. All of this legislation is comparatively recent. The most important Acts are:

a) the Fair Trading Act 1973

b) the Restrictive Trade Practices Act 1976

c) the Resale Prices Act 1976

d) the Competition Act 1980.

In addition there are several European Union articles and regulations dealing with competition across EU states. These are dealt with in the next Chapter.

1 Monopolies and mergers

a) *Monopolies.* If a company or group of companies controls at least one quarter of the national or local market for the supply of particular goods or services, the *Director General of Fair Trading* must be notified and he will consider whether the case should be referred to the *Monopolies and Mergers Commission*. If it is and the Commission finds that an aspect of the monopoly operates against the public interest, the Secretary of State for Trade and Industry can take steps to remedy the matter. This may involve asking the Office of Fair Trading to negotiate appropriate remedial actions and subsequently monitor and review them from time to time.

b) *Mergers.* The Director General must be notified of all mergers that either lead to or strengthen a monopoly situation, or where the gross value of the assets taken over exceeds £30,000,000. The OFT will conduct an initial examination of the merger and advise the Secretary of State for Trade and Industry as to whether it should be referred to the *Monopolies and Mergers Commission.* The Commission will then investigate whether it would be against the public interest for the merger to proceed. If they conclude that it is, the Secretary of State has powers to prohibit or disband it. The OFT may advise whether conditions should be imposed before allowing a merger to proceed.

2 Restrictive trade practices

a) The Restrictive Trade Practices Act 1976 requires certain types of restrictive trading agreement, for example agreements designed to fix prices and/or regulate the supply of goods or services, to be registered with the Director General of Fair Trading. The agreement is placed on a register open to public inspection. Unless the restrictions are insignificant the Director General must refer the agreement to the Restrictive Practices Court to determine whether the restriction is contrary to the public interest. If it is, then the offending provisions are void. Failure to register a registerable agreement also renders the restrictions in it void.

b) Any restriction is presumed to be contrary to the public interest unless it falls within one or more of eight *'gateways'* referred to in the Act, for example

   i) The agreement benefits the public because it reduces the risk of injury.

   ii) The agreement maintains export trade.

   iii) Removal of the restriction would have a serious adverse affect on the level of unemployment.

Task 1

One agreement approved by the Restrictive Practices Court is the Net Book Agreement. The Agreement, operated by the Publishers' Association, enables any publishers who are signatories, to enforce minimum retail prices (i.e the net price) for individual books, known as 'net books'. Most books sold in the UK are net books, although school books are normally sold non-net (i.e. not subject to the Agreement). This means that a net book cannot be discounted below the price set by the publisher.

Write a report setting out the advantages and disadvantages of the Net Book Agreement for publishers, authors, small bookshops, large bookshops and the public?

Although the Agreement is approved by the Restrictive Practices Court, in July 1992 the European Court of Justice outlawed the operation of the Net Book Agreement in trade across EC frontiers.

3 Resale price maintenance

a) Suppliers are allowed to recommend minimum resale prices for their goods. They cannot however impose prices on retailers, for example by threatening to withhold further supplies. If a supplier breaks this law (The Resale Prices Act 1976) the Director General can take proceedings in the Restrictive Practices Court or alternatively accept a written promise from the suppliers that they will not impose minimum prices on shopkeepers.

b) There is a power for the Restrictive Practices Court to grant exemption if the restriction is in the public interest, for example if any after sales service would be reduced unless the resale price agreement was enforced. Only two exemption orders have ever been made. These relate to books and certain drugs.

4 Anti-competitive practices

Under the Competition Act 1980 the OFT can look into the conduct of any single business which may restrict, distort or prevent competition concerning goods and services. Businesses with a turnover of less than £5m a year are not covered unless they have more than a quarter of a particular market. If, after investigation, a practice is found to be anti-competitive, the Director General can refer it to the *Monopolies and Mergers Commission* to see if it is against the public interest. Alternatively the Director General may accept a written promise to end the practice.

 Discussion topic

Why may the existence of a monopoly be disadvantageous to consumers?

 Review questions *(answers page 307)*

1. When is a monopoly deemed to exist?

2. What is the role of the Monopolies and Mergers Commission?

3. What is a restrictive trading agreement?

4. Is it possible for a manufacturer to require their goods to be sold at a certain price?

5. In what circumstances may a restrictive trading agreement be upheld by the Restrictive Trades Practices Court?

6. What is the difference between a merger and a take-over?

30

The role of the European Union in consumer protection

The European Community (EC) (which was later known as the European Union, EU) was first established by the Treaty of Rome 1957. The original six members were France, West Germany, Belgium, Italy, The Netherlands and Luxembourg. The United Kingdom, Denmark and Eire joined in 1973. Greece joined in 1981 and Spain and Portugal in 1986. In October 1990 Germany was unified and the former East Germany became subject to EU law.

1 The aim of the European Union

a) The basic aim of the EU is to establish a common market where there can be free movement of goods, services, persons and capital between the member states. This is expected to lead to the development and expansion of economic activity, closer relationships between member states and a general rise in standards of living.

b) In the early 1980s it became apparent that, despite many improvements, the basic aim was not being achieved sufficiently quickly. Trade barriers between member states meant that the EU did not make full use of its strength as a market and was losing ground to the USA and Japan. It was therefore decided to pass the Single European Act 1986. This was ratified by all member states and had the main objective of the creation of a single market by December 31st 1992. The Act gave further powers to the European Commission and the European Parliament to push through appropriate legislation. Many barriers still exist, however the Act did lead to some acceleration of legislative activity designed to remove trade barriers.

2 Competition in the European Union

a) EU policy is based firmly on the belief that healthy and workable competition stimulates economic activity since it gives freedom of action to manufacturers and suppliers and freedom of choice to consumers. The Treaty of Rome therefore contains several rules (known as Articles) which seek to ensure that competition in the EU is not distorted by trade barriers.

b) There are a number of ways by which national governments and manufacturers or suppliers can distort competition, for example:

   i) Agreements between suppliers to share markets i.e. two companies operating in the same sector agreeing not to export to the other's country.

   ii) Import duties imposed by governments to discourage imported goods and protect home manufacturers.

   iii) State aid to home industries, to reduce their costs and make them more competitive.

iv) The establishment of monopoly power by particular companies or groups.

c) Controlling trade barriers and ensuring compliance with EU
competition law is a difficult task. Trading conditions within
member states vary considerably. There are different tax systems
and levels, different labour costs, different technical requirements and so on. An obvious example of technical differences
concerns lefthand and righthand drive cars. Such diverse trading
conditions inevitably lead to prices of the same products varying
between member states. This tempts manufacturers or suppliers
of goods with higher costs and prices to make it more difficult
for purchasers in their own countries to buy the same goods
cheaper elsewhere. For example the price of cars on the continent
is much cheaper than in the UK. However if you try to order a
right-hand drive car in Belgium to bring into the UK, many
manufacturers will quote an excessive delivery time, for example
one year, in order to discourage the purchase.

3 Article 85 Treaty of Rome

a) This is one of two key anti-competitive provisions in the Treaty
of Rome. It defines in broad terms a general prohibition on
agreements which have as their object or effect the prevention,
restriction or distortion of competition within the Common
Market. The Article then gives some examples such as:

i) Directly or indirectly fixing purchase or selling prices or any
other trading conditions.

ii) Limiting or controlling production, markets, technical devel-
opments or investment.

iii) Sharing markets or sources of supply.

iv) Applying dissimilar conditions to equivalent transactions
with other trading parties, thus placing them at a competitive
disadvantage.

b) Agreements which contravene Article 85 are void and the
persons concerned can be fined.

c) Article 85 exempts certain agreements, for example agreements
improving the production or distribution of goods and services
or agreements promoting technical or economic progress,

provided consumers are allowed a fair share of the resulting benefit.

4 Article 86 Treaty of Rome

a) This Article prohibits any abuse, by one or more undertakings, of a dominant position within the Common Market, or in a substantial part of it insofar as it may affect trade between member states. It goes on to give examples similar to those given in Article 85 concerning, for example, imposing unfair purchase or selling prices and/or limiting production and markets to the detriment of consumers.

b) There have been very few cases on Article 86, partly because of difficulties in deciding the meaning of 'dominant position'. Basically it means a position of economic strength which is sufficient to enable the undertaking to prevent effective competition.

c) Abuses of a dominant position which have been held to exist include for example:

   i) Selling at too high a price.

   ii) Selling at such a low price that competition is eliminated.

   iii) Giving discriminatory benefits according to nationality.

   iv) Granting varying price concessions to customers buying the same products in the same quantities, such concessions depending on whether or not the buyer has also purchased supplies from a competitor of the dominant company.

5 The relationship of European Union law and United Kingdom law

a) If a merger or restrictive trade practice agreement affects only the UK market, it will fall within the exclusive jurisdiction of the UK courts.

b) If such an agreement affects trade between two or more member states EU law will also apply. If in such a case there is an overlap or conflict between EU law and UK law, EU law will apply. For example if an agreement has granted exemption from the effect of Article 85, it cannot be challenged in the UK courts under provisions in the Restrictive Trade Practices Act or the Resale Prices Act.

 ## Task 1

Make contact with the Department of Trade and Industry, Ashdown House, 123 Victoria Street, London SW1E 6RB. Try to find out, through their published literature, how current EU legislation (EU Directives) on consumer protection, is likely to affect British consumers over the next few years.

 Review questions *(answers page 308)*

1. What is the main aim of the European Union?

2. What was the purpose of the Single European Act 1986?

3. Briefly summarise Article 85 Treaty of Rome.

4. Briefly summarise Article 86 Treaty of Rome.

5. Does the European Union have any jurisdiction over mergers or trade practices which only affect the UK market?

6. Give two examples of practices which would distort free competition.

31

Enforcing consumer rights

Consumer rights may ultimately be enforced through proceedings in the County Court or in the High Court. Court action is however a last resort and every effort should be made to resolve the dispute before such drastic steps are taken.

For example if a person has a complaint about goods purchased in a shop, they should stop using the goods and take them back, together with the receipt (if possible). If the situation is complicated it may be better to write, sending in photocopies of receipts, guarantees or other relevant documents. The buyer should of course keep a photocopy of the letter of complaint. If a complaint is made by telephone the buyer should take notes of what has been said and obtain the name of the person who took the call. The call should be followed by a letter confirming what was agreed, or what is still in dispute.

This Chapter deals with the situations when such personal approaches to the seller have been unsuccessful and legal action has become necessary.

1 Seeking advice

Most of the consumer watchdogs described in Chapter 27 will provide some free advice to domestic consumers.

a) *Environmental health departments* will give advice on health matters such as unfit food and drink or unclean restaurants.

b) *Trading standards departments* will investigate, for example, misleading descriptions or inaccurate weights and measures.

c) *Citizens advice bureaux* have staff able to advise on consumer law and may be prepared to negotiate with traders on behalf of individual consumers. Complex problems can be transferred to local solicitors, with funding through the Legal Aid Scheme in some cases.

d) *Consumer advice centres* are run by local authorities. Like the citizens advice bureaux they will help consumers to resolve disputes with traders or help them to commence county court proceedings.

e) *Local law centres* are generally located in deprived areas. They provide a comprehensive legal service for the local community. Consumer problems are a relatively small part of their work since local matters such as housing, social security and employment are often very pressing.

f) *Solicitors.* If suitable free advice is not available it may be necessary to consult a solicitor. Solicitors are the general practitioners of the legal profession. They give advice and represent clients in court. If legal aid is not available advice can be extremely costly (£100 to £150 per hour) so it is important to make sure that other sources of advice have been tried first. As with any other contract it is wise to 'shop around' to find the best available service at the lowest price.

Even if all the advice indicates that an individual has a very strong case, many people are extremely reluctant to commence legal proceedings. Modern county court forms and procedures are however reasonably straightforward. In addition clear and helpful leaflets (approved by the Plain English Campaign) may be obtained from county court offices. These should enable most people to bring their own small claim without the need for a solicitor.

 Discussion topic

What is the difference between solicitors and barristers?

2 County courts

a) In the English legal system civil cases (for example contract, trespass or negligence) are heard in different courts from criminal cases (such as murder, theft or dangerous driving). The lowest level civil court is the *County Court*. It will hear all cases where the amount claimed is less than £25,000. It will also hear most cases between £25,000 and £50,000. If the sum involved exceeds £50,000 the case will be heard in the *High Court*.

b) If the claim is for £1,000 or less a special, less formal, small claims procedure can be followed. Since most consumer contracts fall below this limit the Chapter focuses on this procedure.

c) There are about 400 county court districts which are grouped into 'circuits'. *Circuit Judges* preside over each circuit and will hear cases at a number of different courts. Cases are also heard by assistant judges known as *District Judges*. The term 'county court' is rather misleading since neither the circuit, nor the courts' jurisdiction are based on county boundaries.

d) County courts play a very important role in the legal system. Over one and a half million actions are started each year, although only about 5% result in trial, since most are discontinued or settled out of court before the trial stage is reached.

3 Small claims procedure

a) A small claim is a claim for £1,000 or less. Most claims are for money owed for goods or services. However there are many other possible reasons for a claim, for example bad workmanship, faulty goods or goods not supplied. The person making the claim is called the *'plaintiff'* and the person being claimed from is the *'defendant'*.

b) Making the claim.

    i) The plaintiff must fill in the *county court summons* (form N1, see Appendix C). Three copies are needed, for the plaintiff, the defendant and the court. The forms are sent to the court with the court fee (£10 to £60 depending on the amount claimed). The fee is added by the plaintiff to the amount claimed.

    ii) It is important to describe the claim clearly. In a claim for money owed the plaintiff should state how much is owed, why it is owed, the date on which it should have been paid and how much (if any) has already been paid.

    iii) Once the fee has been paid the court will post the summons and a reply form to the defendant. The defendant has 14 days to reply.

c) A defendant who received a summons can do one of four things:

    i) Pay the whole amount.

    ii) Ignore the summons. If this happens the plaintiff fills in form N205A (Appendix C) and obtains *'judgment by default'*. The court will then order payment to be made.

    iii) Agree that he owes the money and send back form N9A (Appendix C). If this happens the plaintiff fills in the bottom of form N205A, which asks the court to send the defendant an order to pay.

    iv) Disagree with the claim (or part of it) saying that he owes only some of the money or none at all. The defendant must complete form N9B (Appendix C) saying why the claim is not acceptable.

d) If the claim is disputed a District Judge will look at the claim and the defence and decide whether:

i) a *'preliminary appointment'* to see both the plaintiff and defendant is necessary, or

ii) an *'arbitration hearing'* should take place, or

iii) the case is too complex to be dealt with under the informal small claims procedure and order *trial in 'open court'*.

e) If a preliminary appointment is made the District Judge will read the claim and the defence, ask questions and seek to settle the dispute. If this cannot be achieved he will refer it to arbitration or to a hearing in open court.

f) If an arbitration hearing is ordered the court will send a form to the plaintiff giving details of the date and place of the hearing and giving 'directions', for example that any expert's report to be offered in evidence by the plaintiff be sent to the defendant at least 14 days before the hearing.

g) Both arbitration and preliminary appointments take place in private in the District Judge's room (called 'chambers'). Each party can take someone with them, for example a friend or relative to speak on their behalf as a 'lay representative'. They may also take witnesses.

h) At the hearing the District Judge will try to find out the facts by reading or listening to the evidence of the parties and any witnesses. Usually the plaintiff goes first and then the defendant replies. The District Judge will decide whose evidence is most likely to be right. If the Judge thinks that each party's evidence is equally likely (or unlikely) to be right, the case will be dismissed, because the onus is on the person who starts a claim to prove it.

 Task 1

There are many different methods of purchasing goods, for example

a) In a shop

b) At a car boot sale

c) From a mail order catalogue

d) Over the telephone

e) From a Book Club or Music Club

f) From a private individual.

Select two different methods (either from the above list, or your own examples). For each method write a short, five point, plan advising potential customers how best to protect themselves at the time of purchase and how to safeguard their position (as far as possible) should the goods turn out to be faulty.

 Review questions (answers page 309)

1. What is the financial limit for the informal small claims procedure?

2. Which court hears claims for sums in excess of £50,000?

3. Who will hear cases in the county court?

4. What is a preliminary appointment?

5. What happens to a defendant who ignores a summons?

6. If a judge is undecided about the evidence and the claims of the parties, who will win the case, the plaintiff or the defendant?

 Part 4 assignments

Assignment 7

Barry Brown's Claim

Last Thursday Garage Ltd fitted a new clutch to your car at a cost of £260. Earlier this week (Tuesday) the new clutch failed when you were driving on the M25. Since the car was stuck in first gear you were unwilling to drive it and it was towed to the nearest garage at a cost of £65. This garage told you that the work done last week was incompetent and caused the failure of the new clutch. They fitted another new clutch at a cost of £290.

Later the same day (Tuesday) when you approached Garage Ltd, they assured you that all their mechanics were City and Guilds qualified (with certificates to prove it) and that all their work was checked by the Chief Mechanic. They said that it was just bad luck that the clutch failed again so soon. You do not accept this explanation and have decided to take legal action.

1. Write a letter to the managing director of Garage Ltd, setting out your position and giving them a chance to settle the matter out of court.

2. On the assumption that your letter has not been answered, complete a county court summons (Form N1 in Appendix C).

Garage Ltd's Claim

Last Thursday you fitted a new clutch to Barry Brown's car. When Barry telephoned you late Thursday morning, you offered to do the work the following Monday, and you told him that you would need the car for four hours. He said it was urgent and the work must be done immediately. You agreed that for an extra £25, you would do the work the same afternoon (Thursday) between 3.00pm and 6.00pm. When Barry collected the car he said he was unsure of his bank balance, so he gave you a cheque for £140 and £120 cash.

When Barry came back earlier this week (late on Tuesday) demanding compensation because the new clutch had failed, you explained that the mechanics were well qualified and that their work was checked by the Chief Mechanic. You explained that you thought it was either very bad luck that the clutch had failed, or that there was some concealed defect that was the fault of the manufacturer. You therefore refused to pay him anything and he stormed out.

Since this visit Barry's cheque has been returned unpaid by his bank, because there was no money in his account. In the same post you have received a summons.

1. Write an appropriate letter to Barry Brown setting out the terms on which you would settle.

2. On the assumption that your letter has not been answered, complete the county court defence and counter-claim (Form N9B in Appendix C).

Assignment 8

This assignment involves the investigation of one type of selling, or the selling of a particular product or service. Choose a sales method, product or service which is often associated with consumer problems, for example (a) doorstep selling, (b) timeshare selling, (c) telephone selling, (d) party selling, (e) second-hand car sales, (f) home extensions, (g) mail order shopping, (h) holidays and (i) restaurants.

Write a report which, for your chosen topic:

1. Identifies potential problems.
2. Describes the main relevant consumer protection legislation.
3. Identifies the key rights of consumers.
4. Describes the procedures to be followed in the event of a dispute between the customer and the business.

Part 5

Appendices

These appendices contain various forms and types of contract, which are referenced from the text to illustrate specific points. There is also a section containing answers to review questions.

A

Company forms

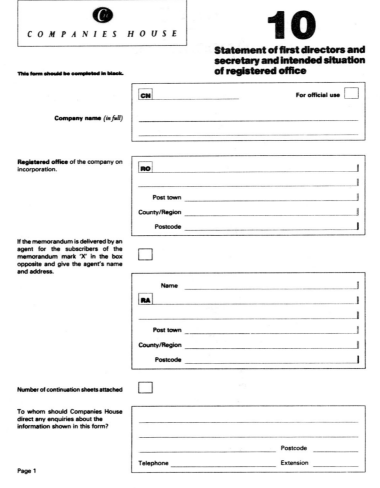

COMPANIES HOUSE

This form should be completed in black.

10

Statement of first directors and secretary and intended situation of registered office

CN _____   For official use [ ]

Company name *(in full)* _____

Registered office of the company on incorporation.

RO _____

Post town _____

County/Region _____

Postcode _____

If the memorandum is delivered by an agent for the subscribers of the memorandum mark 'X' in the box opposite and give the agent's name and address.

[ ]

Name _____

RA _____

Post town _____

County/Region _____

Postcode _____

Number of continuation sheets attached [ ]

To whom should Companies House direct any enquiries about the information shown in this form?

_____

Postcode _____

Telephone _____   Extension _____

Page 1

240

Company Secretary *(See notes 1 - 5)*

Name	*Style/Title	**CS**
	Forenames	
	Surname	
	*Honours etc	
	Previous forenames	
	Previous surname	

Address

Usual residential address must be given. In the case of a corporation, give the registered or principal office address.

AD

Post town

County/Region

Postcode _____ Country _____

I consent to act as secretary of the company named on page 1

Consent signature   Signed   Date

Directors *(See notes 1 - 5)*
Please list directors in alphabetical order.

Name	*Style/Title	**CD**
	Forenames	
	Surname	
	*Honours etc	
	Previous forenames	
	Previous surname	

Address

Usual residential address must be given. In the case of a corporation, give the registered or principal office address.

AD

Post town

County/Region

Postcode _____ Country _____

Date of birth **DO**   Nationality **NA**

Business occupation **OC**

Other directorships **OD**

* Voluntary details

I consent to act as director of the company named on page 1

Page 2   **Consent signature**   Signed   Date

A Company forms

Directors (continued)

(See notes 1 - 5)

Name

*Style/Title   **CD**

Forenames

Surname

*Honours etc

Previous forenames

Previous surname

Address   **AD**

Usual residential address must be given.
In the case of a corporation, give the
registered or principal office address.

Post town

County/Region

Postcode   Country

Date of birth   **DO**   Nationality   **NA**

Business occupation   **OC**

Other directorships   **OD**

* Voluntary details   I consent to act as director of the company named on page 1

Consent signature   Signed   Date

Delete if the form
is signed by the
subscribers.

Signature of agent on behalf of all subscribers   Date

Delete if the form
is signed by an
agent on behalf of
all the subscribers.

All the subscribers
must sign either
personally or by a
person or persons
authorised to sign
for them.

Signed	Date
Signed	Date
Signed	Date
Signed	Date
Signed	Date
Signed	Date

Page 3

242

Notes

1 Show for an individual the full forenames NOT INITIALS and surname together with any previous forenames or surname(s).

If the director or secretary is a corporation or Scottish firm - show the corporate or firm name on the surname line.

Give previous forenames or surname except that:

· for a married woman, the name by which she was known before marriage need not be given,

· names not used since the age of 18 or for at least 20 years need not be given.

In the case of a peer, or an individual usually known by a British title, you may state the title instead of or in addition to the forenames and surname and you need not give the name by which that person was known before he or she adopted the title or succeeded to it.

Address:

Give the usual residential address.

In the case of a corporation or Scottish firm give the registered or principal office.

2 Directors known by another description:

A director includes any person who occupies that position even if called by a different name, for example, governor, member of council. It also includes a shadow director.

3 Directors details:

Show for each individual director their date of birth, business occupation and nationality. **The date of birth must be given for every individual director.**

4 Other directorships:

Give the name of every company of which the individual concerned is a director or has been a director at any time in the past 5 years. You may exclude a company which either **is** or at **all times during the past 5 years** when the person was a director **was:**

· dormant,

· a parent company which wholly owned the company making the return,

· a wholly owned subsidiary of the company making the return,

· another wholly owned subsidiary of the same parent company.

If there is insufficient space on the form for other directorships you may use a separate sheet of paper.

5 Use photocopies of page 2 to provide details of joint secretaries or additional directors and include the company's name.

6 The address for companies registered in England and Wales is:-

The Registrar of Companies
Companies House
Crown Way
Cardiff
CF4 3UZ

or, for companies registered in Scotland:-

The Registrar of Companies
Companies House
100-102 George Street
Edinburgh
EH2 3DJ

243

A Company forms

COMPANIES FORM No. 12

Statutory Declaration of compliance with requirements on application for registration of a company

12

Please do not write in this margin

Pursuant to section 12(3) of the Companies Act 1985

Please complete legibly, preferably in black type, or bold block lettering

To the Registrar of Companies
(Address overleaf)

For official use

For official use

Name of company

* insert full name of Company

*

I, _____

of _____

† delete as appropriate

do solemnly and sincerely declare that I am a [Solicitor engaged in the formation of the company]†
[person named as director or secretary of the company in the statement delivered to the registrar
under section 10(2)]† and that all the requirements of the above Act in respect of the registration of the
above company and of matters precedent and incidental to it have been complied with,

And I make this solemn declaration conscientiously believing the same to be true and by virtue of the
provisions of the Statutory Declarations Act 1835

Declared at _____

Declarant to sign below

the _____ day of _____

One thousand nine hundred and _____

before me _____

A Commissioner for Oaths or Notary Public or Justice of
the Peace or Solicitor having the powers conferred on a
Commissioner for Oaths.

Presentor's name address and
reference (if any):

For official Use
New Companies Section

Post room

A Company forms

COMPANIES FORM No. 287

Notice of change in situation of registered office

287

Please do not
write in
this margin

Pursuant to section 287 of the Companies Act 1985
as substituted by section 136 of the Companies Act 1989

**Please complete
legibly, preferably
in black type, or
bold block lettering**

To the Registrar of Companies
(Address overleaf)

Company number

Name of company

* insert full name
of company

gives notice of a change in the situation of the registered office of the company to:

Postcode

‡ insert
Director,
Secretary,
Administrator,
Administrative
Receiver or
Receiver
(Scotland) as
appropriate

Signed

Designation‡

Date

Presentor's name address
telephone number and reference (if any):

For official use
D.E.B.

Post room

245

COMPANIES HOUSE

288

Change of director or secretary or change of particulars.

Please complete in black using typescript or block lettering

Company number **CN**

Company name

Appointment

(Turn over page for resignation and change of particulars).

		Day Month Year
Date of appointment	**DA**	

Appointment of director **CD** ⎫ *Please mark the appropriate box.*
Appointment of secretary **CS** ⎬ *If appointment is as a director and secretary mark both boxes.*

NOTES

Show the full forenames. NOT INITIALS
If the director or secretary is a Corporation or Scottish firm, show the name on surname line and registered or principal office on the usual residential address line.

Give previous forenames or surname except:
- for a married woman the name before marriage need not be given.
- for names not used since the age of 18 or for at least 20 years.
A peer or individual known by a title may state the title instead of or in addition to the forenames and surname.

Name *Style/title

Forenames

Surname

*Honours etc

Previous forenames

Previous surname

Usual residential address **AD**

Post town

County/region

Postcode Country

Date of birth† **DO** Nationality† **NA**

Other directorships.

Give the name of every company incorporated in Great Britain of which the person concerned is a director or has been a director at any time in the past 5 years. Exclude a company which either is, or at all times during the past 5 years when the person was a director, was
- dormant
- a parent company which wholly owned the company making the return
- a wholly owned subsidiary of the company making the return
- another wholly owned subsidiary of the same parent company

Business occupation† **OC**

Other directorships†

I consent to act as director/secretary of the above named company

Consent signature Signed Date

*Voluntary details †Directors only

A serving director etc must also sign the form overleaf.

Resignation

(This includes any form of ceasing to hold office e.g. death or removal from office).

Date of resignation etc   **DR**

Resignation etc, as director   **XD**

Resignation etc, as secretary   **XS**

Please mark the appropriate box.
If resignation etc is as a director and secretary mark both boxes.

Forenames

Surname

Date of birth *(directors only)*   **DO**

If cessation is other than resignation, please state reason *(eg death)*

Change of particulars *(this section is not for appointments or resignations).*

Complete this section in all cases where particulars of a serving director/ secretary, have changed and then the appropriate section below.

Date of change of particulars   **DC**

Change of particulars, as director   **ZD**

Change of particulars, as secretary   **ZS**

Please mark the appropriate box.
If change of particulars is as a director and secretary mark both boxes.

Forenames   *(name previously*
Surname   *notified to*
  Companies House)

Date of birth *(directors only)*   **DO**

Change of name *(enter new name)*   Forenames   **NN**

Surname

Change of usual residential address *(enter new address)*   **AD**

Post town

County/region

Postcode   Country

Other change   *(please specify)*

A serving director, secretary etc must sign the form below.

Signature

Signed _____ Date _____

(by a serving director/secretary/administrator/ administrative receiver/receiver). *(Delete as appropriate)*

After signing please return the form to the Registrar of Companies at

   or

Companies House, Crown Way, Cardiff CF4 3UZ
for companies registered in England and Wales

Companies House, 100-102 George Street, Edinburgh EH2 3DJ
for companies registered in Scotland.

To whom should Companies House direct any enquiries about the information on this form?

Tel: _____

COMPANIES HOUSE

This form should be completed in black.

363a
Annual Return

| Company number | CN _____ | ☐ |

| Company name | _____ |

Date of this return *(See note 1)*
The information in this return is made up to

	Day Month Year
DA				
	Show date

Date of next return *(See note 2)*
If you wish to make your next return to a date earlier than the anniversary of this return please show the date here. Companies House will then send a form at the appropriate time.

| DB | : | | | |

Registered Office *(See note 3)*
Show here the address **at the date of this return.**

| RO | _____ |

Any change of registered office **must** be notified on form 287.

Post town	_____
County/Region	_____
Postcode	_____

Principal business activities
(See note 4)
Show trade classification code number(s) for principal activity or activities.

| PA | | | | | | | | | | |

If the code number cannot be determined, give a brief description of principal activity.

1

Register of members

(See note 5)
If the register of members is not kept at the registered office, state here where it is kept.

RM	
Post town	
County/Region	
Postcode	

Register of Debenture holders

(See note 6)
If there is a register of debenture holders and it is not kept at the registered office, state here where it is kept.

RD	
Post town	
County/Region	
Postcode	

Company type *(See note 7)*

Public limited company.............................

Private company limited by shares............

Private company limited by guarantee without share capital...................................

Private company limited by shares exempt under section 30............................

Private company limited by guarantee exempt under section 30........................

Private unlimited company with share capital...

Private unlimited company without share capital...

T1	
T2	
T3	
T4	*Please mark the appropriate box.*
T5	
T6	
T7	

Company Secretary *(See note 8)*
(Please photocopy this area to provide details of joint secretaries).

Name	*Style/Title
	Forenames
	Surname
	*Honours etc
	Previous forenames
	Previous surname

Details of a new company secretary **must** be notified on form 288.

CS	

Address

Usual residential address must be given. In the case of a corporation, give the registered or principal office address.

* Voluntary details

AD	
Post town	
County/Region	
Postcode		Country	

2

249

A Company forms

Directors *(See note 8)*
Please list directors in alphabetical order.

Details of new directors **must** be notified on form 288.

Name	*Style/Title	**CD**
	Forenames	
	Surname	
	*Honours etc	
	Previous forenames	
	Previous surname	

Address

Usual residential address must be given.
In the case of a corporation, give the
registered or principal office address.

AD

Post town

County/Region

Postcode _____ Country

Date of birth **DO** | | | | | | Nationality **NA**

Business occupation **OC**

Other directorships **OD**

Name	*Style/Title	**CD**
	Forenames	
	Surname	
	*Honours etc	
	Previous forenames	
	Previous surname	

Address

Usual residential address must be given.
In the case of a corporation, give the
registered or principal office address.

AD

Post town

County/Region

Postcode _____ Country

Date of birth **DO** | | | | | | Nationality **NA**

Business occupation **OC**

Other directorships **OD**

* Voluntary details

3

250

Issued share capital *(See note 9)*
Enter details of all the shares in issue at the date of this return.

Class	Number	Aggregate Nominal Value
Totals		

List of past and present members
(Use attached schedule where appropriate)

A full list is required if one was not included with either of the last two returns.
(See note 10)

Please mark the appropriate box(es)

There were no changes in the period ☐

	on paper	not on paper
A list of changes is enclosed	☐	☐
A full list of members is enclosed	☐	☐

Elective resolutions *(See note 11)*
(Private companies only)

If an election is in force at the date of this return to dispense with annual general meetings, *mark this box* ☐

If an election is in force at the date of this return to dispense with laying accounts in general meetings, *mark this box* ☐

Certificate
I certify that the information given in this return is true to the best of my knowledge and belief.

Signed ....
Secretary/Director*
(delete as appropriate)*

Date ....

This return includes .... continuation sheets.
(enter number)

To whom should Companies House direct any enquiries about the information shown in this return?

....
....
....
.... Postcode ....

Telephone .... Extension ....

When you have signed the return send it with the fee to the Registrar of Companies at

Companies House, Crown Way, Cardiff CF4 3UZ
for companies registered in England and Wales
or
Companies House, 100-102 George Street, Edinburgh EH2 3DJ
for companies registered in Scotland.

4

251

A Company forms

Directors (continued)

Name

*Style/Title   `CD`

Forenames

Surname

*Honours etc

Previous forenames

Previous surname

Address   `AD`

Usual residential address must be given.
In the case of a corporation, give the
registered or principal office address.

Post town

County/Region

Postcode   Country

Date of birth   `DO`   Nationality   `NA`

Business occupation   `OC`

Other directorships   `OD`

Name

*Style/Title   `CD`

Forenames

Surname

*Honours etc

Previous forenames

Previous surname

Address   `AD`

Usual residential address must be given.
In the case of a corporation, give the
registered or principal office address.

Post town

County/Region

Postcode   Country

Date of birth   `DO`   Nationality   `NA`

Business occupation   `OC`

Other directorships   `OD`

* Voluntary details

5

252

Directors (continued)

Name	*Style/Title	**CD**	
	Forenames		
	Surname		
	*Honours etc		
	Previous forenames		
	Previous surname		

Address

Usual residential address must be given.
In the case of a corporation, give the
registered or principal office address.

Post town

County/Region

Postcode _____ Country

	Date of birth	**DO**		Nationality	**NA**	
	Business occupation	**OC**				
	Other directorships	**OD**				

Name	*Style/Title	**CD**	
	Forenames		
	Surname		
	*Honours etc		
	Previous forenames		
	Previous surname		

Address

Usual residential address must be given.
In the case of a corporation, give the
registered or principal office address.

Post town

County/Region

Postcode _____ Country

	Date of birth	**DO**		Nationality	**NA**	
	Business occupation	**OC**				
	Other directorships	**OD**				

* Voluntary details

6

253

B

Tax forms

I understand you may now be self employed (this includes subcontracting in the Construction Industry). If so please let me have the information asked for below and over the page as soon as possible.

If this is the first time you have been self employed, you may find booklet IR28 'Starting in Business' helpful. You can get this from any Tax Enquiry Centre or Tax Office. If you need any further help I shall be pleased to arrange an appointment for you to see me.

When you become self employed, you normally pay National Insurance contributions (Class 2). Please get in touch with your local office of the Contributions Agency (DSS) about this.

Enquiries about yourself and any business partners

Yourself

Your surname

Your first names

Your private address

Postcode

Tax Office to which last Income Tax Return made

Reference in that Office

National Insurance number

Date of birth ... ...

Day . Month Year

Business partners

	Partner 1	Partner 2	Partner 3
Partner's surname			
Partner's first names			
Partner's private address			
	Postcode	Postcode	Postcode

If you have more than three business partners please give the names and addresses of any other partners on a separate sheet

41G(1993)

Please turn over

254

Enquiries about the business	Replies

1. In what name is the business carried on, if not in your own name?

1. [   ]

2. What is the business address, including postcode, if different from your private address?

2. [Postcode   ]

3. What is the nature of the business?

3. [   ]

4. When did you start in this business?

4. [19   ]

5. If you took over an existing business, who did you acquire it from?

5. Name
   Address
   Postcode

6. To what date do you propose to make up your business accounts?

6. [19   ]

   If they are to be prepared by a firm of accountants, please give their name and address, including postcode.

   Name
   Address
   Postcode

7. If you are not already operating PAYE as an employer, have you any employees earning
   • more than £66.50 a week or £288 a month?
   • more than £1 a week who have other employment?

7. Yes   No
   • □   □
   • □   □   *Please tick '✓' appropriate box*

Personal enquiries	Replies

8. Were you employed or were you self employed before you started this business?

8. Employed □   Self employed □   *tick '✓' one box*

   What was the name and address of the business or employer? Please give this information even if you had a period of unemployment between leaving employment and starting your own business.

   Name
   Address
   Postcode

   If you still have the leaving certificate form P45 handed to you by your last employer, please attach it and give the leaving date.

   [19   ]

9. If this is your first occupation since leaving full time education on what date did the education finish?

9. [19   ]

10. If as well as running your business you are in paid employment, or are continuing an existing business, please give the name and address of the employer/existing business.

10. Name
    Address
    Postcode

    Is this an existing business or employment?

    Existing business □   Employment □   *tick '✓' one box*

Signature [   ]   Date [19   ]

Please say whether you are single, married, widowed, separated or divorced [   ]

255

B Tax forms

Inland Revenue

Summary of profits from _____ **to** _____

You can use this form to give the information the Tax Office will need .
Make sure you read this leaflet before you start to fill in the form and you will know exactly what to do.

To		District	Reference *from your Tax Return or Assessment*
			Your National Insurance no

Please use CAPITALS

My name is

The nature of my business is

My business address is

Postcode

Turnover	£	show your total business earnings before expenses
Expenses	£	show your total business expenses
Profit	£	take your expenses from your turnover to give your profit

To the best of my knowledge and belief the information I have given above is correct and complete.

Signature _____ Date _____

If you bought or sold any vehicles or machinery which you use in your business please give details over the page.

41K

Capital allowances

Before you give the details below you may find it useful to read leaflet IR106 ' Capital Allowances for Vehicles and Machinery '. You can get a copy from any Tax Office.

Items bought in the period of the summary shown over the page
Enter the total cost, including any part exchange allowance. Do not include finance charges if you buy the item on credit or any part of the cost covered by a grant or subsidy.

Date bought	Items bought	Cost	*Business use
		£	
		£	
		£	

* *Enter here the fraction or the percentage of business use (for example 1/2 or 50%)*

Items sold or part - exchanged in the period of the summary shown over the page

Date sold	Items sold	Sale price or part - exchange value	*Business use
		£	
		£	
		£	

* *Enter here the fraction or the percentage of business use (for example 1/2 or 50%)*

C

County court forms

 County Court Summons

Case Number
In the

County Court

The court office is open from 10am to 4pm Monday to Friday

(1)

Plaintiff's
full name
address

(2)

Address for
service (and)
payment
(if not as above)
Ref/Tel no.

Telephone:

Seal

(3)

Defendant's
name
address

This summons is only valid if sealed by the court
If it is not sealed it should be sent to the court.

What the plaintiff claims from you

Brief
description
of type of
claim

Particulars of the plaintiff's claim against you

Amount claimed

Court fee

Solicitor's costs

Total amount

Summons issued on

What to do about this summons

You can

- **dispute the claim**
- **make a claim against the plaintiff**
- **admit the claim in full and offer to pay**
- **pay the total amount shown above**
- **admit only part of the claim**

**For information on what to do or if you
need further advice, please turn over.**

Signed
Plaintiff's solicitor)
(or see enclosed particulars of claim)

N1 Default summons (fixed amount) (Order 3, rule 3(2)(b))

Keep this summons, you may need to refer to it

257

You have 21 days from the date of the postmark to reply to this summons

(A limited company served at its registered office has 16 days to reply.)

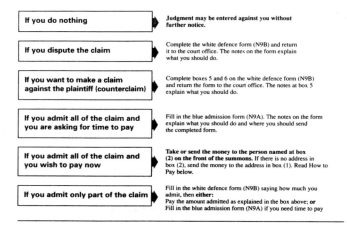

If you do nothing	Judgment may be entered against you without further notice.
If you dispute the claim	Complete the white defence form (N9B) and return it to the court office. The notes on the form explain what you should do.
If you want to make a claim against the plaintiff (counterclaim)	Complete boxes 5 and 6 on the white defence form (N9B) and return the form to the court office. The notes at box 5 explain what you should do.
If you admit all of the claim and you are asking for time to pay	Fill in the blue admission form (N9A). The notes on the form explain what you should do and where you should send the completed form.
If you admit all of the claim and you wish to pay now	Take or send the money to the person named at box (2) on the front of the summons. If there is no address in box (2), send the money to the address in box (1). Read How to Pay below.
If you admit only part of the claim	Fill in the white defence form (N9B) saying how much you admit, then **either:** Pay the amount admitted as explained in the box above; **or** Fill in the blue admission form (N9A) if you need time to pay

Interest on Judgments

If judgment is entered against you and is for more than £5000, the plaintiff may be entitled to interest on the total amount.

Registration of Judgments

If the summons results in a judgment against you, your name and address may be entered in the Register of County Court Judgments. **This may make it difficult for you to get credit.** A leaflet giving further information can be obtained from the court.

Further Advice

You can get help to complete the reply forms and information about court procedures at any county court office or citizens' advice bureau. The address and telephone number of your local court is listed under "Courts" in the phone book. When corresponding with the court, please address forms or letters to the Chief Clerk. Always quote the whole of the case number which appears at the top right corner on the front of this form; the court is unable to trace your case without it.

How to pay	To be completed on the court copy only
● PAYMENT(S) MUST BE MADE to the person named at the address for payment quoting their reference and the court case number.	Served on
● DO NOT bring or send payments to the court. THEY WILL NOT BE ACCEPTED.	
● You should allow at least 4 days for your payments to reach the plaintiff or his representative.	By posting on
● Make sure that you keep records and can account for all payments made. Proof may be required if there is any disagreement. It is not safe to send cash unless you use registered post.	Officer
● A leaflet giving further advice about payment can be obtained from the court.	Marked "gone away" on
● If you need more information you should contact the plaintiff or his representative.	

Printed in the UK for HMSO 07/92 D 8365366 C30000 36625

Notice of Issue of Default Summons - fixed amount

To the plaintiff ('s solicitor)

In the	
	County Court

The court office at

is open between 10 am & 4 pm Monday to Friday
Tel:

Case Number	Always quote this	

Plaintiff *(including ref.)*

Defendants

Issue date	
Date of postal service	
Issue fee	£

Your summons was issued today. The defendant has 14 days from the date of service to reply to the summons. If the date of postal service is not shown on this form you will be sent a separate notice of service (Form N222).
The defendant may either

- Pay you your total claim.
- **Dispute the whole claim.** The court will send you a copy of the defence and tell you what to do next.
- **Admit that all the money is owed.** The defendant will send you form of admission N9A. You may then ask the court to send the defendant an order to pay you the money owed by completing the request for judgment below and returning it to the court.
- **Admit that only part of your claim is owed.** The court will send you a copy of the reply and tell you what to do next.
- **Not reply at all.** You should wait 14 days from the date of service. You may then ask the court to send the defendant an order to pay you the money owed by completing the request for judgment below and returning it to the court.

For further information please turn over

- -

Request for Judgment

- *Tick and complete either A or B. Make sure that all the case details are given and that the judgment details at C are completed. Remember to sign and date the form. Your signature certifies that the information you have given is correct.*
- *If the defendant has given an address on the form of admission to which correspondence should be sent, which is different from the address shown on the summons, you will need to tell the court.*

A ☐ The defendant has not replied to my summons
Complete all the judgment details at C. Decide how and when you want the defendant to pay. You can ask for the judgment to be paid by instalments or in one payment.

B ☐ The defendant admits that all the money is owed
Tick only one box below and return the completed slip to the court.

☐ **I accept the defendant's proposal for payment**
Complete all the judgment details at C. Say how the defendant intends to pay. The court will send the defendant an order to pay. You will also be sent a copy.

☐ **The defendant has not made any proposal for payment**
Complete all the judgment details at C. Say how you want the defendant to pay. You can ask for the judgment to be paid by instalments or in one payment. The court will send the defendant an order to pay. You will also be sent a copy.

☐ **I do NOT accept the defendant's proposal for payment**
Complete all the judgment details at C and say how you want the defendant to pay. Give your reasons for objecting to the defendant's offer of payment in the section overleaf. Return this slip to the court together with the defendant's admission N9A (or a copy). The court will fix a rate of payment and send the defendant an order to pay. You will also be sent a copy.

I certify that the information given is correct

Signed .... Dated ....

In the	
	County Court

Case Number	Always quote this	

Plaintiff

Defendant

Plaintiff's Ref.

C Judgment details
I would like the judgment to be paid

☐ (forthwith) *only tick this box if you intend to enforce the order right away*

☐ (by instalments of £   per month)

☐ (in full by   )

Amount of claim as stated in summons
(including interest at date of issue) ....

Interest since date of summons (if any) ....
Period .... Rate .... %

Court fees shown on summons ....

Solicitor's costs (if any) on issuing summons ......

                                    Sub Total

Solicitor's costs (if any) on entering judgment

                                    Sub Total

Deduct amount (if any) paid since issue ....

            Amount payable by defendant

N205A Notice of issue (default summons) and request for judgment (Order 3. rule (2)(d)(1), Order 9 rules 3 and 6)   MCR 601222 5/93 F

C County court forms

Further information

- The summons must be served within 4 months of the date of issue (or 6 months if leave to serve out of the jurisdiction is granted under Order 8, rule 2). In exceptional circumstances you may apply for this time to be extended provided that you do so before the summons expires.

- If the defendant does not reply to the summons or if he delivers an admission without an offer of payment you may ask for judgment. If you do not ask for judgment within 12 months of the date of service the action will be struck out. It cannot be reinstated.

- You may be entitled to interest if judgment is entered against the defendant and your claim is for more than £5000.

- You should keep a record of any payments you receive from the defendant. If there is a hearing or you wish to take steps to enforce the judgment, you will need to satisfy the court about the balance outstanding. You should give the defendant a receipt and payment in cash should always be acknowledged. You should tell the defendant how much he owes if he asks.

- **You must inform the court IMMEDIATELY if you receive any payment before a hearing date or after you have sent a request for enforcement to the court.**

Objections to the defendant's proposal for payment

Case Number

N205A

260

Admission

In the

County Court

Case Number *Always quote this*

Plaintiff *(including ref.)*

Defendant

When to fill in this form

- Only fill in this form if you are admitting all or some of the claim **and** you are asking for time to pay
- If you are disputing the claim or you wish to pay the amount claimed, read the back of the summons

How to fill in this form

- Tick the correct boxes and give as much information as you can. **Then sign and date the form.**
- Make your offer of payment in box 11 on the back of this form. **If you make no offer the plaintiff will decide how you should pay.**
- You can get help to complete this form at **any** county court office or citizens' advice bureau.

Where to send this form

- **If you admit the claim in full**
  Send the completed form to the address shown at box (2) on the front of the summons. If there is no address in box (2) send the form to the address in box (1).
- **If you admit only part of the claim**
  Send the form **to the court** at the address given on the summons, together with the white defence form (N9B).

What happens next

- **If you admit the claim in full and offer to pay**
  If the plaintiff accepts your offer, judgement will be entered and you will be sent an order telling you how and when to pay. If the plaintiff does **not** accept your offer, the court will fix a rate of payment based on the details you have given in this form and the plaintiff's comments. Judgement will be entered and you will be sent an order telling you how and when to pay.
- **If you admit only part of the claim**
  The court will tell you what to do next.

How much of the claim do you admit?

- ☐ I admit the full amount claimed as shown on the summons **or**
- ☐ I admit the amount of £ _____

---

1 Personal details

Surname _____

Forename _____

☐ Mr ☐ Mrs ☐ Miss ☐ Ms

☐ Married ☐ Single ☐ Other *(specify)*

Age _____

Address _____

Postcode _____

---

2 Dependants *(people you look after financially)*

Number of children in each age group

under 11 ☐   11-15 ☐   16-17 ☐   18 & over ☐

Other dependants *(give details)* _____

3 Employment

☐ I am employed as a _____

My employer is _____

Jobs other than main job *(give details)* _____

☐ I am self employed as a _____

Annual turnover is...................... £ _____

☐ I am not in arrears with my national insurance contributions, income tax and VAT

☐ I am in arrears and I owe.......... £ _____

Give details of:
(a) contracts and other work in hand _____
(b) any sums due for work done _____

☐ I have been unemployed for _____ years _____ months

☐ I am a pensioner

4 Bank account and savings

☐ I have a bank account

☐ The account is in credit by .... £ _____

☐ The account is overdrawn by.... £ _____

☐ I have a savings or building society account

The amount in the account is .... £ _____

5 Property

I live in ☐ my own property ☐ lodgings
☐ jointly owned property ☐ council property
☐ rented property

N9A Form of admission and statement of means to accompany Form N1 (Order 9, rule 2)

MCR 601494 11/93 C

6 Income

My usual take home pay *(including overtime, commission, bonuses etc)*	£	per
Income support	£	per
Child benefit(s)	£	per
Other state benefit(s)	£	per
My pension(s)	£	per
Others living in my home give me	£	per
Other income *(give details below)*		
	£	per
	£	per
	£	per
Total income	**£**	**per**

8 Priority debts *(This section is for arrears only. Do not include regular expenses listed in box 7.)*

Rent arrears	£	per
Mortgage arrears	£	per
Community charge arrears	£	per
Water charges arrears	£	per
Fuel debts: Gas	£	per
Electricity	£	per
Other	£	per
Maintenance arrears	£	per
Others *(give details below)*		
	£	per
	£	per
Total priority debts	**£**	**per**

7 Expenses

(Do not include any payments made by other members of the household out of their own income)

I have regular expenses as follows:

Mortgage *(including second mortgage)*	£	per
Rent	£	per
Community charge	£	per
Gas	£	per
Electricity	£	per
Water charges	£	per
TV rental and licence	£	per
HP repayments	£	per
Mail order	£	per
Housekeeping, food, school meals	£	per
Travelling expenses	£	per
Children's clothing	£	per
Maintenance payments	£	per
Others *(not court orders or credit debts listed in boxes 9 and 10)*		
	£	per
	£	per
	£	per
Total expenses	**£**	**per**

9 Court orders

Court	Case No.	£	per
Total court order instalments		**£**	**per**

Of the payments above, I am behind with payments to *(please list)*

10 Credit debts

Loans and credit card debts *(please list)*

	£	per
	£	per
	£	per

Of the payments above, I am behind with payments to *(please list)*

11 Do you wish to make an offer of payment?

- *If you take away the totals of boxes, 7, 8 and 9 and the payments you are making in box 10 from the total in box 6 you will get some idea of the sort of sum you should offer. The offer you make should be one you can afford.*

☐ I can pay the amount admitted on _____
or
☐ I can pay by monthly instalments of £ _____

12 Declaration   I declare that the details I have given above are true to the best of my knowledge

Signed _____   Dated _____

Position *(firm or company)* _____

Defence and Counterclaim

When to fill in this form
- Only fill in this form if you wish to dispute all or part of the claim **and/or** make a claim against the plaintiff (counterclaim).

How to fill in this form
- Please check that the correct case details are shown on this form. You must ensure that all the boxes at the top right of this form are completed. You can obtain the correct names and numbers from the summons. The court cannot trace your case without this information.
- Follow the instructions given in each section. Tick the correct boxes and give the other details asked for.
- If you wish only to make a claim against the plaintiff (counterclaim) go to section 5.
- Complete and sign section 6 before returning this form.

Where to send this form
- Send or take this form immediately to the court office at the address shown above.
- If you admit part of the claim and you are asking for time to pay, you will also need to fill in the blue admission form (N9A) and send **both** reply forms to the court.
- Keep the summons and a copy of this defence; you may need them.

Legal Aid
- You may be entitled to legal aid. Ask about the legal aid scheme at any county court office, citizen's advice bureau, legal advice centre or firm of solicitors displaying this legal aid sign.

What happens next
- If you complete box 3 on this form, the court will ask the plaintiff to confirm that he has received payment. If he tells the court that you have not paid, the court will tell you what you should do.
- If you complete box 4 or 5, the court will tell you what you should do.
- If the summons is not from your local county court, it will automatically be transferred to your local court.

1 How much of the claim do you dispute?

☐ I dispute the full amount claimed *(go to section 2)*

or

☐ I admit the amount of £ _____ and I dispute the balance

If you dispute only part of the claim you must **either:**

- pay the amount admitted to the person named at the address for payment in box (2) on the front of the summons or if there is no address in box (2), send the money to the address in box (1) (see How to Pay on the back of the summons). Then send this defence to the court.

or

- complete the blue admission form and send it to the court with this defence.

Tick whichever applies

☐ I paid the amount admitted on _____

or

☐ I enclose the completed form of admission

(go to section 2)

In the

                                                      County Court

Case Number *Always quote this* _____

Plaintiff *(including ref.)*

Defendant

The court office is open from 10am to 4pm Monday to Friday

---

2 Arbitration under the small claims procedure
How the claim will be dealt with if defended

If the claim is for £1,000 or less it will be dealt with by arbitration (small claims procedure) unless the court decides the case is too difficult to be dealt with in this informal way. Costs and the grounds for setting aside an arbitration award are strictly limited. If the claim is for £1,000 or less and is not dealt with by arbitration, costs, including the costs of a legal representative, may be allowed.

If the claim is for over £1,000 it can still be dealt with by arbitration if either you or the plaintiff asks for it and the court approves. If the claim is dealt with by arbitration in these circumstances, costs may be allowed.

Please tick this box if the claim is worth over £1,000 and you would like it dealt with by arbitration. ☐
(go on to section 3)

3 Do you dispute this claim because you have already paid it? *Tick whichever applies*

☐ No *(go to section 4)*

☐ Yes I paid £ _____ to the plaintiff

on _____ *(before the summons was issued)*

Give details of where and how you paid it in the box below *(then go to section 6)*

Case No. [_____]

4 If you dispute the claim for reasons other than payment, what are your reasons?

Use the box below to give full details. *(If you need to continue on a separate sheet, put the case number in the top right hand corner.)*

5 If you wish to make a claim against the plaintiff (counterclaim)

If your claim is for a specific sum of money, how much are you claiming? £ [_____]

- If your claim against the plaintiff is for more than the plaintiff's claim against you, you may have to pay a fee. Ask at your local court office whether a fee is payable.

- You may not be able to make a counterclaim where the plaintiff is the Crown (e.g. a Government Department). Ask at your local county court office for further information.

What are your reasons for making the counterclaim?

- Use the box opposite to give full details. *(If you need to continue on a separate sheet, put the case number in the top right hand corner.)*

(go on to section 6)

6 Signed
(To be signed by you or by your solicitor)

Give an address to which notices about this case can be sent to you

Postcode [_____]

Position *(firm or company)*

Dated

D

Share certificate

Certificate Number
2368912

Transfer Number
0000192

Date of Registration
25OCT93

Number of Shares
------55------

ROLLS-ROYCE plc

(Incorporated under the Companies Acts 1948 to 1967   Company Number 1003142)

THIS IS TO CERTIFY that

is/are the

Registered Holder(s) of *FIFTY FIVE* *

ORDINARY SHARES OF 20p each,

fully paid in ROLLS-ROYCE plc

subject to its Memorandum and Articles of Association

GIVEN under the Securities Seal of the Company

The new Ordinary shares rank *pari passu* in all respects with the
existing Ordinary shares save that they do not rank for the interim
dividend of 2.00p (net) per Ordinary share in respect of the year
ending 31 December 1993, to be paid on 10 January 1994 to
shareholders on the register on 22 October 1993.

NOTE:

This is a valuable document. Keep it in a safe place.

No transfer of any of the shares comprised in this certificate will be registered unless accompanied by this certificate.

Registrars: National Westminster Bank Plc, Registrar's Department, PO Box 82, Caxton House, Redcliffe Way, Bristol BS99 7NH.

IC/419/N80

265

E

Standard consumer contract

PERRYS

USED VEHICLE PURCHASE AGREEMENT

Full Name and Address of Buyer _____

Post Code_____

Telephone Home:_____ Work:_____

VEHICLE PURCHASED (SCHEDULE A)

Make	Model	Delivery Date		Price	
Reg. No.	First Reg.	Finance Required YES / NO		Road Tax	
Mileage	Colour	Salesmen		Warranty	
Recorded mileage cannot be relied on as being accurate unless supported by Dealership confirmation.	Stock No.	Chassis No.		Delivery Pack	
ACCESSORIES					
OTHER ITEMS					
FUEL					
SPECIAL INSTRUCTIONS					
				SUB TOTAL	

PART EXCHANGE (SCHEDULE B)

Make	Model	Part Exchange Full Allowance	
Reg. No.	First Reg.	SUB TOTAL	
Mileage	Colour	O/S Finance with F.C. Finance Ref.	
R/F Tax Expiry Date	MOT Expiry Date	Add Settlement Figure of	
INITIAL DEPOSIT PAID BY CASH/CHEQUE/OTHER			

	TOTAL	

DECLARATION BY THE SELLER

1. The vehicle was/was not purchased by me new.

2. The vehicle was/was not used abroad before being registered in the United Kingdom.

3. The mileometer reading is .... and it is/is not correct.

   If not correct the approximate true mileage is ....

4. The vehicle has/has not been used for self-drive hire, hackney carriage or taxi work.

5. The vehicle has/has not been involved in any accident which resulted in a total loss claim.

6. A current MoT test certificate has/has not been handed over by me.

7. A current registration document VA has/has not been handed over by me.

8. The vehicle is free from any lien or any other encumbrance whether financial or otherwise other than as set out by me above.

"I declare that the information given above is to the best of my knowledge and belief correct".

Date _____ Signature _____

AMOUNT DUE FROM FINANCE COMPANY

NET FINAL BALANCE DUE FROM CUSTOMER	£	

The Buyer agrees to purchase the Vehicle(s) and other articles specified in Schedule "A" subject to the terms and conditions set out in Schedule "C" overleaf, and acknowledges having received a copy of this agreement.

Buyer's Signature _____

The Seller accepts and confirms this order subject to the terms and conditions of sale set out in Schedule "C" overleaf.

For and on behalf of the Seller _____

Approved by Business Manager _____

Approved by Sales Manager _____

CONSUMER TRANSACTION ACT

Nothing contained herein is intended to affect, nor will it affect, a consumer's statutory rights under the Sale of Goods Act 1979 or the Unfair Contract Terms Act 1977 or any amendment thereof.

Registered Office: Cambridge House, Bluecoats Avenue, Hertford, SG14 1PB

PP 2225 Group/91

Perrys' standard terms and conditions (schedule C)

The following standard terms and conditions are taken from the back of the PERRYS used vehicle purchase agreement reproduced on the opposite page.

1. **Interpretation**
   1.1 BUYER means the person whose order for the vehicle is accepted by the seller.

   SELLER means whichever of the Perry Group plc subsidiary companies is the contracting party in these conditions.

   VEHICLE means the vehicle or vehicles plus any accessories which the seller is to supply in accordance with these conditions.

   CONDITIONS means the terms and conditions of sale set out herein.

   FORCE MAJEURE means any circumstances beyond the reasonable control of the buyer or the seller (including without limitation, any strike, lockout or other form of industrial action).

2. **Basis of Sale**
   2.1 The seller shall sell and the buyer shall purchase the vehicle in accordance with the details overleaf and subject to these conditions. No variation to these conditions shall be binding unless agreed in writing between authorised representatives of the buyer and the seller.
   2.2 The seller's employees or agents are not authorised to make any representations concerning the vehicle unless confirmed by the seller in writing. In entering into the contract the buyer acknowledges that it does not rely on, and waives any claim for breach of, any such representations which are not so confirmed.

3. **Price**
   3.1 The price of the vehicle shall be as stated overleaf.
   3.2 A deposit shall be paid by the buyer upon the placing of this order.

4. **Delivery**
   4.1 Unless otherwise specified in writing, delivery is to be taken at the seller's place of business within 7 days of notification to the buyer that the vehicle is ready for delivery.
   4.2 The seller will use its best endeavours to secure delivery on the estimated delivery date but shall be under no liability whatsoever for loss occasioned by delay of delivery.
   4.3 If the seller shall fail to deliver the vehicle within three months of the estimated delivery date stated in the contract the buyer may by notice in writing to the seller require delivery of the vehicle within 21 days of receipt of such notice. If the vehicle shall not be delivered to the buyer within the 21 days the contract shall be cancelled, and the deposit shall be returned to the buyer with the seller being under no further liability.
   4.4 If the buyer shall fail to take and pay for the vehicle within 14 days of notification that the vehicle is ready for delivery, the seller shall be at liberty to treat the contract as repudiated by the buyer and thereupon the deposit shall be forfeited without prejudice to the seller's right to recover from the buyer by way of damages any loss or expense which the seller may suffer or incur by reason of the buyer's default.

5. **Risk and Property**
   5.1 Risk or damage to or loss of the vehicle shall pass to the buyer:
   5.1.1 In the case of a vehicle to be delivered at the seller's place of business at the time when the seller notifies the buyer that the vehicle is available for collection; or
   5.1.2 In the case of a vehicle to be delivered otherwise than at the seller's place of business, at the time of delivery or, if the buyer wrongfully fails to take

delivery of the vehicle, at the time when the seller has tendered delivery of the vehicle.

5.2 Notwithstanding delivery and the passing of risk in the vehicle, or any other provision of these conditions, the vehicle shall remain the sole and absolute property of the seller as legal and equitable owner until such time as the seller has received in cash or cleared funds payment in full of the price of the vehicle together with the full price of any other vehicle the subject of any other contract between the seller and the buyer.

5.3 Until such time as the property in the vehicle passes to the buyer:

5.3.1 The buyer shall hold the vehicle as the seller's fiduciary agent and bailee and shall keep the vehicle separate from others of the buyer and third parties and properly stored, protected and insured and identified as the seller's property.

5.3.2 The buyer shall not be entitled to resell the vehicle, unless the seller has given the buyer express written authority to do so.

5.3.3 The seller shall be entitled at any time to require the buyer to deliver up the vehicle to the seller and, if the buyer fails to do so forthwith, to enter upon any premises of the buyer or any third party where the vehicle is stored and repossess the vehicle.

5.3.4 The buyer shall not be entitled to pledge or in any way charge the vehicle by way of security for any indebtedness.

6. Part Exchange

6.1 Where the seller agrees to allow part of the price of the vehicle to be discharged by the buyer delivering a used motor vehicle to the seller, such allowance is hereby agreed subject to the following further conditions:

6.1.1 That such used vehicle is the absolute property of the buyer and is free from all encumbrances, or that such used vehicle is the subject of a hire purchase agreement or other encumbrance capable of cash settlement by the seller, in which case the allowance shall be reduced by the amounts required to be paid by the seller in settlement thereof.

6.1.2 That if the seller has examined the said vehicle prior to his confirmation and acceptance of the order, the said used vehicle shall be delivered to him in the same condition as at the date of such examination (fair wear and tear excepted).

6.1.3 That such used vehicle shall be delivered to the seller on or before delivery of the vehicle to the buyer.

6.2 In the event of the non-fulfilment of any of the foregoing conditions the seller shall be discharged from any obligation to accept the said used vehicle or to make any allowance in respect thereof, and the buyer shall discharge in cash the full price of the vehicle to be supplied by the seller.

7. Warranties

7.1 Where the vehicle is sold to another member of the motor trade the seller shall only be liable to the buyer in respect of defects in the condition of the vehicle insofar as such defects would not have been capable of being ascertained by inspection of the vehicle before or on delivery.

7.2 Notwithstanding the above sub-clause the vehicle is sold subject to and with the benefit of the USED VEHICLE WARRANTY, the terms of which are detailed in the used vehicle warranty booklet.

7.3 Where the vehicle is sold under a consumer transaction, the statutory rights of the buyer are not affected by these conditions nor by the used vehicle warranty.

8. Insolvency of Buyer

8.1 Without prejudice to any other right or remedy available to the seller, the seller shall be entitled to cancel the contract without any liability to the buyer, and if the vehicle has been delivered but ownership has not passed, the price shall become immediately due and payable notwithstanding any previous agreement or arrangement to the contrary, or the seller may elect to exercise its rights under clause 5.3.3 if:

8.1.1   The buyer makes any voluntary arrangement with its creditors or becomes subject to an administration order or (being an individual or firm) becomes bankrupt or (being a company) goes into liquidation (otherwise than for the purposes of a solvent amalgamation or reconstruction) or

8.1.2   An encumbrancer takes possession, or a receiver is appointed, of any of the property or assets of the buyer; or

8.1.3   The buyer ceases, or threatens to cease, to carry on business; or

8.1.4   The seller reasonably apprehends that any of the events mentioned above is about to occur in relation to the buyer and notifies the buyer accordingly.

9. Notice

9.1   Any notice given hereunder must by in writing and sent by post to the residence or place of business of the person to whom it is addressed and shall be deemed to have been received in due course of post.

10. Force Majeure

10.1   If either the buyer or the seller is affected by force majeure it shall forthwith notify the other of the nature and extent thereof, and neither party shall be deemed to be in breach of this agreement or otherwise be liable to the other by reason of any delay in performance or non-performance of any of its obligations hereunder to the extent that such delay or non-performance is due to any force majeure which has been notified to the other, and the time of performance of that obligation shall be extended accordingly.

10.2   If the force majeure in question prevails for a continuous period in excess of three months, the buyer and seller shall enter into bona fide discussions with a view to alleviating its effect or to agreeing upon such alternative arrangements as may be fair and reasonable.

F

Negotiated business contract

CENTRAL COLLEGE

OVERSEAS AGENCY AGREEMENT

This agreement is made between Central College, College Lane, Newton, Wessex, England WS11 2AA (telephone: [1234] 123456 Fax: [1234] 456789) hereinafter referred to as 'the College' and

Name:

Address:

Telephone:

Fax:

hereinafter referred to as 'the agent'.

This agreement provides for a non-exclusive agency arrangement for the following geographical territory:_____

The College is willing to pay commission of 13% of tuition fees to the agent for students recruited by the agent to take up courses with the College.

It is hereby agreed as follows:

1. The agent undertakes, as appropriate, to recruit students to courses offered by the College which are relevant to their needs and abilities.

2. The agent will provide the College on the official forms with written details of the students, including their name and address and the courses recommended by the agent, with the College course reference. These details must normally be received by the College at least two weeks before the start of the course.

   The majority of courses commence in the third week of September in each year.

3. The College will send to the agent confirmation of acceptance of a place on the course together with tuition fee details.

4. The College will confirm to the agent that recruited students have been enrolled once the course fees have been paid.

5. On notification of student enrolment and payment of course fees the agent will invoice the College for 13% of the tuition fees paid. By separate agreement and arrangements, a different payment method may be arranged.

6. The College undertakes to pay the commission due within 28 days of the receipt of an invoice.

7. In the event that the agent is able to recruit 16 or more students for one course the College will negotiate with the agent for a different commission rate.

8. The College undertakes to supply the agent with updated information on a regular basis.

9. The terms of this agreement may be amended from time to time by written agreement between the parties and will be subject to review at least once every two years.

10. The agent agrees not to assign or under-let any part of this agreement to a third party without the prior approval of the College.

11. Either party may terminate this agreement by three months written notice to the other party.

12. Nothing in this agreement infers that the College enters into a sole agency agreement for the defined territory.

13. This agreement is made between the College and the agent:

Signed on behalf of the College _____

Name: _____

Position: _____

Date: _____

Signed on behalf of the agent _____

Name: _____

Position: _____

Date: _____

G

Answers to review questions

Chapter 1

1. The existence of a company is not affected by the death of any, or all of its members. The company is said to have *'perpetual succession'*.

2. *Limited liability* means that the members' liability is limited to the amount they have agreed to pay for their shares. Creditors have no access to the private assets of members. The company's liability is not limited, it must pay its debts as long as it has assets to do so.

3. *Vicarious liability* means liability for the wrongful acts of other people and it arises because of an employer/employee relationship between the parties. The employer will normally be liable for the wrongful acts of employees committed within the course of their employment.

4. The company memorandum will state 'the liability of members is limited', no further details are needed. This means that liability is limited by shares. When such a company issues shares it will fix a price. Once this price has been paid, the member cannot be required to pay any more to the company even if it goes into insolvent liquidation. If the full amount has not been paid the member is liable for the amount unpaid on the shares, but no more.

5. The certificate of incorporation is conclusive evidence of the fact that the formalities of registration have been complied with. *'Conclusive evidence'* means that the registration cannot be challenged even if actual evidence is produced to show that the formalities were not complied with.

   The reason for this is that once the company has commenced business and entered into contracts it would be unreasonable for either side to be able to avoid the contract because of a procedural defect in the registration of the company.

6. The fact that the separate corporate personality of a company prevents outsiders from taking action against its members (even

though an outsider can find out who they are and how many shares they hold) has led to comparison with a veil. The corporate personality is the veil, and the members are shielded behind it. There are several situations when the law is prepared to lift the veil of incorporation. For example, if in the course of a winding up, it becomes apparent that the business has been carried on with intent to defraud creditors the court may order that the persons responsible, for example the directors, make a contribution to the company's assets.

7. A private company will usually restrict the right to transfer its shares by giving the directors an absolute power to refuse to register any transfer.

Chapter 2

1. The main changes are:

   i. Add the public limited company clause to the memorandum.

   ii. Change the name clause in the memorandum, so that is ends with 'public limited company'.

   iii. Remove any restriction on the right to transfer shares from the articles.

   It may also be necessary to increase the company's capital, because a public company must have a minimum capital of £50,000.

2. Every company must publish its name:

   i. Outside all its places of business.

   ii. On all letters, orders, invoices, notices, cheques and receipts.

   iii. On its seal, if it has a seal.

3. Passing off occurs when somebody represents their goods or business as those of someone else. Passing off is usually committed by imitating someone else's goods, or by selling goods under the same or a similar name.

4. The person who ordered the goods is liable to pay for them. The company did not exist when the contract was made. Therefore it cannot sue or be sued on contract.

5. The *company name* is the name appearing in the memorandum of association lodged with the Registrar of Companies. It must end

with 'limited' or 'public limited company'. There are certain restrictions on the choice of company name, in particular the name cannot be the same as that of an existing registered company.

A *business name* is a name chosen by a company, partnership or sole trader as the name under which they wish to trade. There is no requirement for the registration of business names, but there are various publicity requirements, contained in the Business Names Act 1985, for example that the business name must be stated clearly on all business letters, order forms, invoices, demands for payment and receipts.

6. When a new company is formed the following documents must be sent to the Registrar of Companies:

   a. Memorandum of Association

   b. Articles of Association

   c. Details of the first directors and secretary (Form 10)

   d. A statutory declaration stating that all the legal requirements relating to incorporation have been complied with

   e. A statement of capital

   The registration fee of £50 must also be paid.

7. a. Every company must have a *memorandum* which sets out its basic constitution and defines the relationship of the company with the outside world. It will contain the following six clauses (i) name, (ii) registered office, (iii) objects, (iv) limitation of liability, (v) capital, (vi) association (i.e. the signatures of the first members). In addition the memorandum of every public company will state that 'the company is to be a public company'.

   b. The *articles* are the internal regulations of the company. They deal with, for example, the issue and transfer of shares, directors' powers, procedure at meetings, the payment of dividends and the powers and duties of the secretary.

8. The main procedures at the first meeting are:

   a. Appoint new directors, secretary and auditors

   b. Fix the date of the financial year end

   c. Determine banking arrangements

d. Decide the address of the registered office

e. Make arrangements for keeping the statutory books, e.g. the register of members.

It may also be necessary to allot new shares.

9. A company does not need to list the names of its directors on its notepaper, but if it does wish to do so, it must show all names, not just some of them.

Chapter 3

1. A statement of the first directors will be delivered to the Registrar of Companies when the company is formed. Subsequent directors are normally *appointed by the company in general meeting* i.e. by an *ordinary resolution*. Directors can also be removed by ordinary resolution, whether or not they have a service contract. However such a removal may be a breach of contract for which the company would have to pay damages.

2. The basic duty of the auditors is to report to the members on the accounts laid before the company at the annual general meeting. 'Accounts' includes the balance sheet, profit and loss account and group accounts (if any). The report must state whether, in the opinion of the auditors, the accounts have been properly prepared and whether they give a *true and fair view* of the company's state of affairs. In order to form their opinion the auditors must carry out such investigations as are necessary. They have a right of access to the books, accounts and vouchers of the company. They may also require from the officers such information and explanations as they consider necessary.

3. The *register of members* will contain the name and address of each member and the number of shares held. It will also record the date of entry onto the register and the date of cessation of membership. The register may be computerised.

4. Employees have no right to insist that an employee representative is present at either company meetings or board meetings. An employee of a public company could of course purchase a few shares and thus gain entitlement to attend company meetings (but not board meetings).

5. Liquidation is the process by which the life of a company is brought to an end and its property administered for the benefit of its members and creditors. Liquidation often occurs when a company has run into financial difficulties. However this is not always the case, for example a successful company may be liquidated as part of a reconstruction of the companies in a group.

   A *receivership* will occur when a company fails to pay interest to debenture holders (lenders) and the debenture holders take steps to enforce their security. The receiver's basic duty is to collect in the assets charged and to exercise the debenture holders' powers of sale, paying the proceeds to them. It may then be possible to return control of the company to the directors, however in most cases the difficulties of the company will be such that liquidation will inevitably follow.

6. Lenders will consider numerous factors before agreeing to lend money to a company. The main factors are the company's track record, the value of any security for the loan, the level of finance provided by owners and managers, the viability of the company's business plan, the proposals for repayment of the loan and the personal skills and quality of the managers.

7. The main methods of creditor protection are:

   a. Publicity which enables creditors to find out basic information about the company before they grant credit.

   b. Protection of the capital fund of the company, for example by providing that dividends can only be paid out of profits and not out of capital.

   c. Increasing creditor's powers when the company goes into liquidation (although this may of course be too late to be of practical benefit).

Chapter 4

1. The main reason for liquidation is that the company is unable to pay its debts. In such a situation the creditors may petition for a *compulsory liquidation* (provided a demand for more than £750 has not been satisfied within three weeks) or they may persuade the directors to put the company into a *creditors' voluntary liquidation*.

2. The Official Receiver is appointed as liquidator by the court at the time the winding-up order is made. He will investigate the company's affairs and the causes of its failure. He will summon meetings of members and creditors. These meetings will appoint a liquidator in place of the Official Receiver.

3. A *members' voluntary liquidation* is a liquidation commenced by a resolution of the company (normally a special resolution) in circumstances where the directors are prepared to make a *'declaration of solvency'* i.e. a statement that, following inquiry, in their opinion, the company will be able to pay its debts within a stated period of not more than 12 months. A *creditors' voluntary liquidation* is a liquidation commenced by the company in circumstances when no declaration of solvency can be made. The company is likely to be insolvent i.e. unable to pay its debts as they fall due.

4. When a director of a company that has gone into insolvent liquidation carries on the business when he knows, or should have known, that the company could not avoid liquidation, he will be guilty of *wrongful trading*. The court may order the person to make a contribution to the company's assets, in order to meet the company's debts.

5. When a company cannot pay its debts it may make an agreement with its creditors that each of them will accept an equal proportion of what is owed to them. This is known as a *voluntary arrangement*.

6. The most likely reason to wind up a successful company is that following a take-over, the company is no longer required within the structure of the new group. In such a case all of its creditors will be paid and the remaining assets will be transferred to another company within the group.

7. The main consequences of Liquidation are:

   a. The company will cease business

   b. The directors' powers cease

   c. Shares cannot be transferred

   d. The liquidation is widely publicised.

Chapter 5

1. a.   The minimum number of members for a public company is two, and for a private company is one. The number for private companies was reduced from two to one by the Companies (Single Member Private Limited Companies) Regulations 1992. There is no maximum number of members for either public or private companies.

   b.   The minimum number of partners is two and the maximum is generally twenty. However in the case of certain professional partnerships such as solicitors, accountants and estate agents there is no maximum.

2.   A partnership is defined by the Partnership Act 1890 as 'a relation which subsists between persons carrying on a business in common with a view to profit'.

3.   No formalities are necessary to create a partnership. A partnership may therefore be made verbally, although for practical reasons writing is usually used.

4.   Partners and businessmen in general often prefer to resolve their disputes by arbitration rather than have them decided in court. The main advantages of arbitration are that the proceedings are in private and that the arbitrator will have special knowledge of the particular trade or business. Arbitration may also be faster and cheaper than court procedure. An arbitration clause in a partnership agreement is a contract. It is not possible to completely avoid court jurisdiction, but the court will not normally hear the dispute until the parties have first attempted to have it settled by an arbitrator.

5.   A *sleeping partner* is a partner who takes no active part in the business. A sleeping partner may have provided capital and may take a share of profits.

6.   The death of a partner will automatically dissolve the partnership unless the partnership agreement provides to the contrary.

Chapter 6

1.   A contract *uberrimae fidei* is a contract of utmost good faith. People entering into such contracts must disclose to the other party every material fact within their knowledge at the time the

contract is made. If they do not do so the other party can avoid the contract. Contracts of insurance are also contracts uberrimae fidei.

2. The admission of a new partner must be agreed by all existing partners.

3. The Partnership Act 1890 states that in the absence of agreement profits and losses will be divided equally. April and June are each therefore entitled to £2,750.

4. Partners may of course make any agreement that they wish. However in the absence of agreement, a partner must account for any profit made in a business which competes with the partnership business.

5. The firm is liable for the negligence of each partner if committed in the ordinary course of the firm's business or with the authority of the other partners.

6. A creditor may sue any partner for the full amount of any debt owed by the firm. Individual partners must then obtain a contribution from the others.

Chapter 7

1. A *'partnership at will'* is one that has been entered into for an unspecified period of time.

2. There is no one universally accepted definition of *goodwill*. Basically it is the benefit that arises from a firm's business connections or reputation. It is the value of every advantage that has been acquired by the old firm, in particular the fact that existing customers are likely to continue to resort to the business after it has been sold. A person who purchases goodwill will normally obtain the right to use the name of the old firm and the right to represent himself as the successor of the old firm.

3. Dissolution by agreement requires the agreement of all of the partners.

4. A contract in *restraint of trade* is one which restricts a person from freely exercising a trade or profession. When a business is sold the buyer will normally insist on a restraint of trade clause preventing the seller from running a competing business. Such a restraint is allowed provided it is no more than is necessary to

protect the particular business bought i.e. it must not cover an unreasonably wide area, nor run for an unreasonable length of time. What is reasonable will depend on the particular type of business.

5. Dissolution is implemented by collecting together and selling the firm's assets. The proceeds are used to pay creditors, repay loans and capital to partners and (if the assets are sufficient) distributing any surplus to the partners.

6. After dissolution the authority of each partner is limited to actions necessary to wind up the partnership and complete contracts entered into before dissolution, but unfinished when dissolution began.

Chapter 8

1. a. Directors will usually own company shares, but it is not a legal requirement that they do so.

   b. Directors often have service contracts, giving them the status of company employees as well as company directors. However this is not essential, and would not be the case for non-executive directors.

2. *Dividends* are payments made out of profits to the members of a company. Dividends paid to preference shareholders will be at a fixed rate, whereas dividends paid to ordinary shareholders will vary with the prosperity of the company. Shareholders do not have an automatic right to dividends even if profits are available, since directors may consider it better to retain profits within the company.

3 If A lends money to B and C promises to pay A if B does not, a contract of guarantee has been made between A and C. Since shareholders have limited liability, persons lending money to companies often require directors to enter into a contract of guarantee, which may be secured on their house, so that if the company does not repay the loan, the lender will recover the money from the director.

4. The company is liable to pay corporation tax, not the directors or shareholders

5.
Total Income	£30,000
Less personal allowance	£3,445
Taxable income	£26,555
Tax payable at 20% (20% of£3,000)	£600
Tax payable at 25% (25% of £20,699)	£5,174.75
Tax payable at 40% (40% of £2,855)	£1,142
Total tax payable	£6,916.75

Chapter 9

1. The Registrar of Companies' fee for registering a limited company is £50. Of course the total formation costs will be well in excess of this amount.

2. A ready-made company is one that has been formed for the specific purpose of being sold to a person who wishes to start a new business. The buyer purchases a name and constitution. The company will have no assets or liabilities and will not have traded.

3. A business will need to take out employers' liability insurance and (assuming the business uses a vehicle) third party motor insurance.

4. A *special resolution* is needed to change the name of a company. This is a $\frac{3}{4}$ majority of the members who chose to vote. It is not a $\frac{3}{4}$ majority of all of the members of the company. The change of name must be registered with the Registrar of Companies. This will cost £50.

5. PAYE stands for pay as your earn. It is tax deducted by the employer from the employee's salary or wages.

6. Value added tax is only charged if the goods in question are subject to value added tax (for example there is no VAT on books) and provided the business has a sufficient turnover (i.e. sales) per year. Currently a business with an annual turnover of less than £45,000 does not need to register for VAT and therefore need not charge VAT to its customers.

Chapter 10

1. *Franchising* is basically selling someone else's product or service in your own business. The franchisor allows the franchisee to use a particular name or to sell products in such a way that the franchisee operates a business that is legally separate from that of the franchisor.

2. A *workers' co-operative* is a business owned and democratically controlled by the members, who will be mainly or entirely employees. They operate under different principles form other businesses, in particular membership is open to all employees and members have one vote each, irrespective of their financial commitment.

3. Most companies *limited by guarantee* are educational or charitable organisations which raise their funds by subscription. The liability of members is limited to the amount that they have agreed to pay in the event of winding up. Provided the company does not go into liquidation they will not need to contribute anything. In a company limited by shares each member's duty is to pay for their shares in full. This will normally be required at the time the shares are issued.

4. There are a number of reasons why franchising may be less risky than starting a business from scratch, in particular the business idea and operating methods will have been tried and tested and the franchisee will receive start-up help, training and continuing support.

5. Supporters of workers' co-operatives claim that there is increased job satisfaction and reduced conflict since the workers and owners are the same people. There is a possibility of higher motivation and quality, since employees' benefits are more closely related to the quantity and quality of work done.

6. The main disadvantages of purchasing a franchise are:

   i. Lack of independence

   ii. Initial costs

   iii. Risk of failure of the franchisor

Chapter 11

1. 'Simple majority' means more than half. Sometimes students say that a simple majority is 51%. This is not the case, for example 51% of 1,000 is 510, whereas more than half of 1,000 is 501.

2. A *prospectus* is a document published by a public company when it wishes to obtain funds from an issue of shares or debentures to the public. It will contain detailed information about the company, the directors, the reasons for the share issue and so on. In contract terms the prospectus is an invitation to treat.

3. *Preference shares* are shares which give their holders certain preferential rights, for example a fixed rate of dividend, which must be paid before the ordinary shareholders are entitled to any dividend. Preference shareholders also have priority over ordinary shareholders for the return of capital if the company goes into liquidation. On the other hand preference shareholders do not normally have the same voting rights as ordinary shareholders.

4. Two types of company meetings are *annual general meetings and extraordinary general meetings*. Any company meeting which is not an AGM will be an EGM.

5. S.459 Companies Act 1985 states that any member may petition the court for an order on the ground that the affairs of the company are being, or have been, conducted in a manner which is unfairly prejudicial to the interests of its members generally or some part of the members, or that any proposed act or omission is or would be unfairly prejudicial.

6. There are four types of company resolution:

    a. An *ordinary resolution* is a simple majority of members who chose to vote. An ordinary resolution is used whenever the Companies Acts or the company's constitution does not require a special or an extraordinary resolution.

    b. A *special resolution* is a $\frac{3}{4}$ majority of members as above.

        Special resolutions are required for certain important company decisions, for example to change the company name. Members must be given 21 days notice of a special resolution.

    c. An *extraordinary resolution* is a $\frac{3}{4}$ majority of members as above.

However only 14 days notice is required. Extraordinary resolutions are used to commence the voluntary winding up of an insolvent company.

d. *Written resolutions.* These only apply to private companies. The unanimous agreement of all members can be substituted for any resolution at a general meeting (except a resolution to remove a director or auditor before the end of their period of office).

Chapter 12

1. If some members wish to remove the managing director they should consider:

   a. Whether they have sufficient support to pass an ordinary resolution removing the person from his position as director.

   b. Whether the managing director has been in breach of a service contract. If so would the breach justify termination of his contract as managing director without the need to pay damages for breach of contract? If there is not a breach, removal as director will be valid, but damages will nevertheless be payable for breach of the service contract as managing director.

2. The original *ultra vires rule* stated that contracts which were beyond the objects stated in a company's memorandum would be void. Since 1989 if a person deals with a company in good faith, the power of the directors to bind the company, or authorise others to do so, is free of any limitation under the company's constitution. Thus the ultra vires rule will not apply to any completed act, so the contract will be enforceable by both the company and the other party. Members may still however seek an injunction to prevent an intended ultra vires act, or seek compensation from directors who have made an ultra vires contract which has caused the company to lose money.

3. There is no requirement to pass any examinations to become a company director.

4. The main duties of the company secretary are to ensure that the company's documentation is in order and that returns are made to the Registrar of Companies. The secretary will also take

minutes of meetings and send notices to members. The duties will of course vary depending on whether the secretary is a full time employee of the company, or a part time contractor, for example the company solicitor or accountant, who is engaged as and when needed.

5. Standard company articles will provide for the directors to appoint one of their number as the managing director.

6. The secretary is an agent of the company. Like any agent he will bind the principal if he acts within the scope of the express authority given to him by the directors. In addition the secretary has apparent authority to bind the company on contracts concerned with office administration, for example hiring office staff and purchasing office equipment. However the secretary cannot, for example, bind the company on a trading contract, nor can he borrow money on behalf of the company.

Chapter 13

1. An *independent contractor* is a person who is taken on to produce an agreed result and who in the actual execution of the work is not under the control of the person for whom it is done. It is important to distinguish independent contractors from employees, since an employer will not be liable for the negligence of an independent contractor, but will be liable for the negligence of an employee if the employee is acting within the course of employment.

2. There is no requirement for a contract of employment to be in writing. However once the contract has been agreed, the employer must provide the employee with a written statement of the main terms of employment, not later than two months after starting work. This is not however the contract and employees are not required to sign anything in connection these written particulars.

3. An *express term* of a contract is a term that has been specifically agreed between the parties. Often express terms will be agreed in writing. *Implied terms* are terms that have not been specifically agreed by the parties, but are nevertheless part of the contract either because an Act of Parliament has inserted the term in the contract or because the courts, in the course of making decisions,

have defined particular implied terms. For example an employment contract need not expressly state that the employee must not allow people outside the employer's control to perform his tasks, since this term will be implied.

There are a number of implied terms both on the part of the employer and employee in a contract of employment. It will be seen later that there are also implied terms in, for example, contracts for the sale of goods.

4. There is no general duty to provide work. However there are some exceptions, for example where work is essential to provide a reputation for future employment or where remuneration depends on the provision of work, for example sales commission.

5. It is an implied condition in a contract of employment that the employee will show good faith and loyalty to the employer. Therefore an employee must declare any profit over and above the agreed pay and may only keep it with the agreement of the employer.

6. The statement of terms and conditions of employment given to an employee is not a contract. However it may be taken into account by a court or industrial tribunal as evidence of the terms of the contract of employment.

Chapter 14

1. The remedies for *unfair dismissal* are:

   a. *Reinstatement* i.e. the employee is treated as if dismissal had not occurred.

   b. *Re-engagement* i.e. the employee is re-employed, but not necessarily in the same job or on the same terms and conditions.

   c. *Compensation*, which consists of a basic award calculated by reference to the period of employment, the age of the employee and the employee's weekly pay. An employee may also be eligible for a compensatory award, an additional award or a special award.

2. *Redundancy* occurs when an employee is dismissed because either:

a. The employer has ceased, or intends to cease, either to carry on the business, or to carry on the business in a place where the employee was employed, or

b. The requirements of the employer's business for employees to carry out work of a particular kind have ceased or diminished, or are expected to cease or diminish.

3. An employer must give an employee at least one weeks notice after one months employment, two weeks notice after two years employment, three weeks notice after three years employment and so on, up to twelve weeks notice after employment lasting twelve years or more. If a contract of employment specifies a longer period, this longer period will apply.

4. *Industrial tribunals* are independent judicial bodies. They deal with the full range of employment related disputes, for example unfair dismissal, redundancy, equal pay, maternity rights, race discrimination, sex discrimination, trade union membership rights and occupational pension schemes.

5. *Constructive dismissal* occurs when an employer has made such a serious breach of the contract of employment that the employee is entitled to regard the contract of employment as at an end. Although the employer will not have formally terminated the contract, the employee will be able to claim for unfair dismissal.

6. ACAS promotes good industrial relations by advising employers on a wide range of industrial relations and employment matters and by providing conciliation officers to help settle disputes. It also publishes a code of practice called 'Disciplinary Practice and Procedures in Employment'. This gives practical advice on how to draw up disciplinary rules and procedures and how to operate them effectively.

Chapter 15

1. Companies have a contractual obligation to pay debenture interest (loan interest) to debenture holders. They must pay debenture interest so long as they have funds to do so, whether or not profits have been earned. Dividends are payments made to shareholders. A company has no contractual obligation to pay dividends. Dividends may only be paid out of profits, not out of capital. A company may however pay dividends out of the accu-

mulated profits of previous years, if it has made no profit in the current year.

2. A *floating charge* is a type of security. It gives as security some or all of the present and future assets of the company, for example the company's stock-in-trade. The company can still deal with the assets in the ordinary course of business. As stock is sold it will be released from the charge. Similarly new stock will automatically become subject to the charge.

3. A floating charge will convert to a fixed charge (this is known as crystallisation) when either:

   a. The company fails to pay interest to debenture holders, and the debenture holders either appoint a receiver, or apply to the court to do so, or

   b. Winding up commences, or

   c. Business ceases, or

   d. An event occurs which is specified in the document creating the charge as causing it to crystallise.

4. From the lender's point of view a floating charge is less secure than a fixed charge, since the value of the assets subject to the charge will fluctuate. It is likely that when the charge is needed i.e. when the company has failed to pay debenture interest because it is in difficulty, the value of the assets subject to the charge will be low. A second disadvantage is that if a seller of goods has 'reserved title' until payment, a floating charge will not, on crystallisation, attach to those goods (see Chapter 25.3).

5. A person is said to have *constructive notice* of something, if the law regards them as having knowledge of the 'thing' whatever the state of their actual knowledge. Once a charge has been registered with the Registrar of Companies, everyone is regarded as knowing of its existence. A later chargeholder cannot therefore claim priority over a registered charge by claiming that they did not know of its existence.

6. A *receiver* is a person appointed by the debenture holders when debenture interest has not been paid. The receiver will collect together and sell the assets subject to the charge and pay the debenture holders out of the sale proceeds. Any surplus will be returned to the company.

7. The main remedies of debenture holders are:

a. To sue as creditors for interest owed.

b. To petition as creditors to wind up the company on the ground that it is unable to pay its debts.

c. To apply to the court to appoint a receiver.

d. To appoint a receiver themselves if this right is given in the document creating the debentures and setting out their rights.

8. It is important to register a charge with the Registrar of Companies since it will enable other potential lenders to find out whether the assets offered by the company as security are already subject to charges. If a charge is not registered within 21 days it will not be an effective security.

Chapter 16

1. A binding contract may be made by anyone who has express, or implied authority to contract on behalf of a company. This will include directors, the company secretary and company employees. The extent of implied authority will depend on the person's position. For example the company secretary does not have implied authority to enter into trading contracts. Someone who knew they were dealing with the company secretary for such a contract would not therefore be able to hold the company liable. Similarly a junior employee, employed as a salesman, could bind the company on a contract for the routine sale of its products, but clearly would not have implied authority to sign a lease or employ staff.

2. The *objects clause* sets out the activities that the company may engage in. Originally it was intended to tell potential members the kind of business they were investing in. Prior to 1989 an act outside the objects clause was ultra vires and void and could not be enforced by the company or by the other party to the contract. Neither companies nor outsiders favoured this inconvenient limitation on company powers, so companies would seek to avoid the ultra vires rule by having very long and widely drafted objects clauses.

    Following the Companies Act 1989 it is sufficient for the memorandum to state that the object of the company is to carry on business as a general commercial company. This will allow it to carry on any trade or business whatsoever and to do anything incidental to any trade or business carried on by it.

Furthermore a contract cannot now be called into question on the ground of lack of capacity by reason of anything in the company's memorandum. It is probably therefore true to say that the objects clause no longer serves any useful purpose.

3. The *ultra vires rule* limits the contractual capacity of corporate persons (and other bodies such as local authorities, who have defined powers). It does not apply to natural persons and therefore does not apply to partnerships, which have no legal existence separate from that of the partners.

4. Six examples of such contracts are given in paragraph 4.b, for example borrowing money, signing cheques, and buying and selling goods.

Chapter 17

1. There are a number of different torts. In each case they involve the breach of a duty owed to persons generally, such duty being fixed by the law. The law of torts deals with a wide variety of wrongs, for example:

   a. Intentionally or negligently causing physical injury (trespass to the person and negligence).

   b. Interfering with the enjoyment of another person's land (nuisance and trespass to land).

   c. Defamation (libel and slander).

   A *tort* must be distinguished from:

   i. A *breach of contract*, where the obligation arises from an agreement between the parties, and

   ii. A *crime*, where although the duty is fixed by the law, the object of proceedings is to punish the offender rather than compensate the victim.

2. The main remedy available to the victim of a tort is damages. This is a payment of money designed to put the injured party in the position he would have been in if the tort had not been committed. In some cases an injunction, for example ordering a person to stop committing a nuisance would be an appropriate remedy. Some specific torts have their own particular remedies,

for example reasonable force may be used to remove a tres-
passer.

3. Although it can only act through human agents it is possible for
    a company to be found guilty of committing a criminal offence,
    provided the statute creating the offence makes it clear that the
    company is primarily liable. The Companies Acts of 1985 and
    1989 create many such offences, for example both the company
    and the individual responsible will be guilty of an offence if the
    company fails to submit an annual return.

4. There is no general duty for companies to act in a socially
    responsible way. However the general law, and a number of
    statutes impose social duties on employers. For example every
    employer who employs 20 or more persons is obliged to give
    employment to a quota of registered disabled persons. The stan-
    dard percentage is 3%, although in reality there are insufficient
    registered disabled persons for all employers to comply with this
    requirement. This provision also answers question 3. above,
    since if it is not complied with both the individual responsible
    and the company commit a criminal offence. However the most
    recent conviction was in 1975.

5. *Defamation* is the publication of a false statement that would tend
    to injure a person's reputation or cause them to shunned by ordi-
    nary members of society. If the statement is written or in perma-
    nent form it is libel. If the statement is spoken it is slander.
    Slander is a civil wrong, whereas libel is also a criminal offence.

6. An employer who has been held vicariously liable for the negli-
    gence of one of their employees can seek an indemnity (i.e.
    compensation) from the employee. In practice they are unlikely
    to do so since they would be insured. The employee is also
    unlikely to have the funds to provide such compensation.

Chapter 18

1. It is not necessary for the vast majority of contracts to be written.
    Even contracts of employment and partnerships need not be in
    writing. Contracts which must be in writing include sales of
    land, consumer credit agreements, cheques, share transfers and
    contracts of insurance.

2. An *implied term* is a contract term that has not been expressly agreed by the parties, but which has been included either as a result of judicial decisions, or by an Act of Parliament.

3. The element of value in a contract is known as *consideration*. It is not right to think of consideration as money, since each party to a contract must give consideration. For example in a contract for the sale of goods the buyer's consideration is a payment of money and the seller's consideration is the handing over of goods.

4. Persons under 18 (minors) have restricted capacity. They will be bound by contracts to purchase necessary goods and services or by contracts of employment, unless they are clearly not beneficial to the minor. In theory the capacity of corporations is also limited by reference to their objects clause. It has however already been noted that since 1989 this has no real practical importance.

5. If a person is judged by an *objective test* they are judged according to the inferences that a reasonable person would draw from their words or conduct. Thus if they looked as if they intended to make a contract, they cannot later claim that they did not actually intend to make a contract. Clearly it is more practical to judge contractual matters by reference to an objective test than the alternative *subjective test*. If a subjective test is applied the court must decide the case by reference to the individual's actual state of mind, so far as it can be ascertained. A subjective test is therefore applied to determine whether a person is guilty of murder, since in order to commit this crime a person must both kill another person and intend to kill or harm them.

6. *Damages* are a payment of money to the victim of a breach of contract or a tort. Contract damages are normally unliquidated. This means that they are fixed by the court rather than stated in the contract. If the contract does state an amount to be paid in the event of a breach these are known as liquidated damages. Tort damages are always unliquidated, since there cannot be any agreement that a tort is about to be committed.

Chapter 19

1. In contract the existence of an agreement is determined by asking whether there has been an *offer* and an *acceptance*. In this example there are two identical offers, but no acceptance. Thus although it might appear that there is an agreement, there is no valid contract.

2. An offer may be terminated by:

    a. Revocation i.e. withdrawal of the offer, provided the revocation is communicated to the offeree.

    b. Refusal or counter-offer i.e. an offer of a lower amount.

    c. Lapse of time, either at the end of a fixed period or after a reasonable time.

    d. Failure of a condition subject to which the offer was made.

3. *Consideration* is the element of value in a contract. There must be *'something for something'*. A person cannot sue if they receive something for nothing. Consideration may be executory or executed, but it may not be past. Executory consideration is the price promised by one party in return for another party's promise. Executed consideration is the price paid by one party for the other party's promise. For example where there is a credit sale the buyer has provided executory consideration, but in a sale for cash the buyer's consideration is executed. Past consideration occurs when the act put forward as consideration was completed before any return promise was made.

4. An *invitation to treat* is an invitation to another person to make a contractual offer. Examples include goods on display in a shop (even if priced), goods in catalogues, an auctioneer's call for bids, a prospectus issued by a company for the sale of shares and general advertising of goods. Since an invitation to treat is not a contractual offer, it can not be converted into a contract by acceptance.

    In FISHER v BELL (1961) the distinction between an offer and an invitation to treat was relevant to determine whether or not a criminal offence had been committed. A shopkeeper who displayed flick-knives in his window was accused of 'offering for sale' these weapons in contravention of an Act of Parliament. He was found not guilty, since although he had displayed the goods, accepted buyers' offers and sold the goods, he had not offered them for sale, because goods on display are not an offer to sell, they are an invitation to treat.

5. Unless the offeror has specified a time then the offer will terminate, an offer will cease to exist after a reasonable period of time has passed. What is reasonable will depend on the goods. Clearly an offer to sell perishable goods will lapse more quickly.

6. Two issues are raised by this problem. Firstly have Martin and Nigel impliedly agreed to share the prize money? Secondly, if they have, was their agreement intended to create legal relations? If a term is to be included in the contract it must be expressly stated or be included by implication. The term Nigel is seeking to rely on will only be implied if it is so obvious that it goes without saying.

Intention to create legal relations would only be relevant if the court were prepared to imply such a term. Intention is determined by an objective test of the parties' words and conduct. In domestic or social arrangements there is a presumption that legal relations are not intended, but this presumption may be set aside by evidence of actual intention.

The case of SIMKINS v PAYS (1955) is in some respects similar to Martin's case. Three ladies who shared a house entered a competition run by a newspaper. They sent in three entries on one coupon and agreed to share the prize money which any entry might win. This was held to be a legally binding agreement. The important difference between this case and Martin's case is that in Martin's case there is no express agreement to share the prize money.

It seems likely that no promise to share the prize money could be implied merely because Nigel paid the entry fee. Even if such a promise were to be implied, there does not appear to be sufficient evidence to disturb the presumption that in social and domestic arrangements legal relations are not intended.

Chapter 20

1. A *misrepresentation* is an untrue statement of fact which plays a part in inducing the contract. A *fraudulent misrepresentation* is a statement which is known to be false, or made without belief in its truth, or made recklessly, not caring whether it is true or false.

2. The victim of an *innocent misrepresentation* will lose the right to rescind the contract i.e. the right to be restored to the pre-contract state of affairs if:

   a. With knowledge of his rights, he affirms the contract i.e. continues to regard the contract as in existence.

   b. If it is impossible to restore the parties to the pre-contract state of affairs.

   c. If someone else has acquired rights over the subject matter.

   d. If too much time has elapsed.

3. Andrew's advertisement is an invitation to treat i.e. an invitation to make an offer. Brian's offer of £4,500 is a valid offer, which is then terminated by Andrew's counter-offer of £4,800. Andrew's sale to Charles for £4,500 is a revocation by conduct of his offer to sell to Brian for £4.800. However revocation must be communicated and received if it is to be effective and there has been no communication to Brian. Therefore if Brian 'accepts' before he knows (or should know) of Andrew's sale to Charles, Andrew will be in breach when he fails to deliver to Brian. It does not make any difference that Andrew would not expect Brian to accept without a test drive. Brian's remedy is damages, he cannot recover the car from Charles.

4. If the contract between Carol and Denise was void for mistake then no title to the jewellery would pass to Denise. Consequently Denise could not pass title to Eileen. Therefore Carol would be able to recover the jewellery from Eileen.

   If the contract between Carol and Denise was merely voidable for fraud then Denise would be able to pass title to Eileen if she sold to Eileen before Carol avoided the contract with Denise. Avoidance would be achieved by informing Denise, or if she cannot be found (as is probable) by doing everything possible to recover the goods, such as informing the police.

   The case is similar to PHILLIPS v BROOKS (1919) when a crook obtained possession of a ring worth £450 in return for a cheque by claiming he was Sir George Bullough. The seller checked the purchaser's credentials by comparing the address given by the crook with Sir George Bullough's address in the telephone directory. The cheque was dishonoured and the crook disappeared with the £450, having pawned the ring. It was held that there was no mistake as to identity since the parties had dealt face to face. The pawnbroker therefore obtained title to the ring.

Thus the contract is merely voidable for fraud and, assuming Denise sold to Eileen before avoidance, Carol will not be able to recover the goods.

5. *Duress* is some form of pressure which influences a person to make a contract. *Economic duress* occurs when a party to a contract abuses a position of economic power, for example by refusing to enter into new contracts unless the other party agrees to a change of terms in an existing contract.

6. The main factors determining the reasonableness of a restraint of trade clause imposed on an ex-employee are:

    a. The *area* of the restraint. The larger the area covered, the less likely it is that the restraint is reasonable.

    b. The *duration* of the restraint. Similarly the longer the period, the less likely it is to be valid.

    The decision will depend on the type of business. In one case involving international armaments sales a worldwide restraint was upheld. In another case involving a solicitor's clerk a lifetime restraint was upheld, since solicitors' clients are likely to have lifelong loyalty to individuals working for the firm.

Chapter 21

1. a. A *condition* is a vital term, going to the root of the contract, breach of which normally entitles the innocent party to treat the contract as at an end and to claim damages.

    b. A *warranty* is a term which is subsidiary to the main purpose of the contract, breach of which only entitles the innocent party to damages.

    Conditions and warranties may be expressly agreed between the parties, or they may be implied, for example by the Sale of Goods Act 1979.

2. The title of the Unfair Contract Terms Act 1977 is rather misleading, since it is not concerned with fairness of contracts in general, only with certain types of contract term, primarily exemption clauses. Also it is not confined to contracts, since it applies to notices attempting to disclaim liability for negligence.

The Act provides that no-one acting in the course of a business can, either by contract, or by notice given or displayed, exclude liability for causing death or injury due to negligence. A person can exclude liability for other loss due to negligence, but only if he can prove that the exemption clause is reasonable.

3. *'Merchantable quality'* means that the goods must be as fit for their usual purpose as is reasonable to expect having regard to any description applied to them, the price and all other relevant circumstances.

4. An *exemption clause* excludes a person's liability for their own breach of contract. A *limitation clause* limits their liability to specified situations, or to a maximum award of damages. An *agreed damages clause* (also known as liquidated damages) specifies the amount of damages to be paid in the event of a breach. If a breach occurs this amount must be paid even if it differs from the actual loss. If however it is substantially in excess of the likely loss it will be regarded as a penalty and the clause will be void.

5. A person will be bound by an exemption clause if they sign a document containing the clause, unless its meaning had been misrepresented to them. An exemption clause may also be incorporated into a contract by notice. However the notice must be brought to the attention of the person concerned before the contract is made. A notice on the back of a ticket already purchased would therefore be ineffective.

6. The Supply of Goods and Services Act 1982 implies conditions that:

    a. Where the supplier is acting in the course of a business he will carry out the service with reasonable care and skill.

    b. Where the supplier is acting in the course of a business, he will carry out the service within a reasonable time.

    c. Where the price is not determined by the contract, the person dealing with the supplier will pay a reasonable price.

Chapter 22

1. A contract will be discharged by *frustration* if an event occurs which:

a. Was not contemplated by the parties when the contract was made.

b. Makes the contract fundamentally different from the original contract.

c. Which neither party was responsible for, and

d. Which results in a situation to which the parties did not intend to be bound.

For example a contract will be frustrated if it is dependent on the continued existence of a specific thing which is destroyed.

2. A contract is not frustrated if it becomes unexpectedly more expensive or unprofitable for one of the parties. If a person terminates in this situation they would be in breach of contract.

3. *Anticipatory breach* occurs when one of the parties to a contract, before the date fixed for performance, says that he will not perform on the agreed date. The innocent party may chose to keep the contract alive and press for performance, or 'accept' the breach and sue for damages immediately.

4. In order to discharge a contract by performance, a person must precisely fulfil the contractual obligations. For example in Re: MOORE AND LANDAUER (1921) a supplier of tinned fruit agreed to supply the goods in cases containing 30 tins each. When he delivered the goods about one half were packed in cases of 24 tins each. The correct total amount of tins were delivered and the market value of the goods was unaffected. However the seller was held to be in breach of contract and the buyer was entitled to reject the whole consignment. Jack is therefore in breach and Arnold will be entitled to reject the consignment of golfballs.

5. A *warranty* is a subsidiary contract term. If a warranty is broken the innocent party is entitled to damages, but does not have the right to treat the contract as at an end.

6. A contract may be discharged by frustration although it is not literally impossible to perform, provided events destroy some basic assumption on which the parties have contracted. In KRELL v HENRY (1903) Henry hired a flat in Pall Mall to view the coronation procession of Edward VII. The procession was cancelled due to the King's ill health. Because the rent was very high and the letting was for only one day, it was clear that the

purpose of the contract was to view the procession and the contract was held to be frustrated when the procession was cancelled. However this case is most unusual. Normally a person cannot rely on frustration merely because supervening events prevent him using the subject matter in the way that he originally contemplated. Thus in AMALGAMATED INVESTMENT AND PROPERTY CO. v JOHN WALKER (1977) a person who contracted to buy property for re-development could not rely on frustration when, between contract and completion, the buildings were listed as being of special architectural and historic interest, thus preventing development. It is therefore clear that Eric will not be able to cancel his reservation without committing a breach of contract.

Chapter 23

1. Damage is not too remote if it:

   a. Arises naturally from the breach itself, or

   b. If it was foreseeable as the probable result of the breach.

   For example Jenny purchases a new pair of shoes. Later the same day whilst running to catch a bus the heel breaks and she falls twisting her ankle and tearing her skirt. She also misses the bus and fails to arrive at a important job interview. The job is given to someone else.

   The cost of repair or replacement of the shoes is 'loss naturally arising'. The court is likely to regard the twisted ankle and torn skirt as foreseeable as probable, so Jenny would receive compensation. However she would not receive compensation related to her failure to arrive at the job interview, since such loss is not foreseeable as probable.

2. *Liquidated damages* are damages agreed in a contract as payable in the event of a breach. The courts will enforce such a term provided it is a genuine estimate of the loss, even if the actual loss is a greater or lesser sum.

3. An *injunction* is an order of the court directing a person not to break a contract. An injunction may be used to prevent a defendant from:

   a. Breaking a promise not to disclose trade secrets.

   b. Implementing an unjustified threat to terminate a contract.

c. Entering into contracts with other persons which are inconsistent with the contractual duties to the plaintiff.

4. False. An award of damages for breach of contract is designed to place the innocent party in the position he would have been in if the contract had been performed, not the position he was in before the contract was made.

5. The plaintiff has a duty to *mitigate* the damage. This means that he must minimise the loss arising from the defendant's breach of contract or negligence. For example if Dave's car is worth £500 and it suffers £1,000 worth of damage in an accident caused by Fred, Dave cannot get the car repaired and sue Fred for £1,000. He should mitigate the loss by buying a similar car on the open market for £500.

6. *Specific performance* is not normally awarded if damages would be an adequate remedy. It will therefore apply to contracts for the sale of unique items, for example a sale of land or an original work of art.

Chapter 24

1. An agent will have express authority to perform any act specifically covered by the agency agreement (whether written or oral). The agent will also have implied authority to do:

a. Anything which is necessary to perform the express functions, and

b. Anything which is customary in the trade or profession in question.

A principal may restrict the authority of the agent by giving appropriate instructions, but the instructions will not restrict implied authority unless the principal also informs persons dealing with the agent that the authority has been reduced to less than normal.

If a person's words or conduct lead another to believe that an agent has been appointed and has authority, he will not be able to deny the authority of the agent, even though no agency was agreed. The agent is said to have *apparent authority*.

Agency may be terminated by:

a. Agreement between the parties.

b. Revocation of the agent's authority by the principal, although this may constitute a breach of the agency agreement, or a breach of a contract of employment.

c. Death or insanity of principal or agent.

d. Bankruptcy of the principal.

e. If a fixed term agreement comes to an end.

f. Accomplishment of purpose.

g. Illegality or frustration of either the subject matter or the operation of the agency agreement.

2. Agency may be created by:

a. Express agreement.

b. Implication i.e. implied from the conduct of the parties.

c. Ratification i.e. where the principal adopts a contract made on his behalf by someone who had no authority to make the contract.

d. Necessity, when a person faced with an emergency cannot get instructions from the owner of goods and, acting in good faith, disposes of them or incurs some expense in relation to them.

3. The agent is entitled to agreed commission or other remuneration. The principal must also indemnify the agent for any losses incurred in the course of the agency. An agent is not entitled to retain any additional profit made as a result of his position, unless this has been disclosed to and agreed by the principal.

4. A *cheque is crossed* by placing two parallel lines across the face of the cheque. These are usually printed on the cheque by the bank, but there is no requirement that they are pre-printed. The effect of a crossing is that the cheque must be paid into a bank account and may not be paid as cash over the counter. If the bank pays cash over the counter to someone other than the true owner, it remains liable to the true owner.

5. *Insurable interest* means that the insured must be so related to the subject matter of the insurance as to benefit by its existence or suffer from its destruction. A person therefore has an insurable interest in their property or in their own life or in the life of their

husband or wife. A person does not have an insurable interest in property belonging to someone else.

6. The customer must:
   a. Indemnify his bank (the paying bank) when it makes authorised payments on his behalf.
   b. Take reasonable care when writing cheques to prevent alteration of the amount.
   c. Inform the bank if his cheque book is stolen or if he is aware of any forgeries.

7. If an insurance contract is a contract of indemnity (e.g. fire insurance) and an event occurs which is covered by the policy, the insured person will be compensated for their actual loss, so far as it does not exceed the sum stated in the policy. Insurance contracts which specify a fixed sum to be paid if the event occurs are not contracts of indemnity.

Chapter 25

1. A *sale* is a binding contract for the immediate transfer of title. An *agreement to sell* is a binding contract to transfer title at a future time or subject to some condition yet to be fulfilled. An agreement to sell becomes a sale when the time elapses or when the conditions are fulfilled.

2. The main implied terms in the Sale of Goods Act 1979 are:
   a. By S.12(1) there is an implied condition that the seller has a *right to sell* and pass title to the goods.
   b. By S.13 there is an implied condition that the goods will correspond with the *description*.
   c. By S.14 where goods are sold in the course of a business and the buyer makes known to the seller the purpose for which the goods are being bought there are implied conditions that:
      i. The goods are of *merchantable quality* unless the defects are brought to the buyer's attention before the contract is made, or as regards defects which the buyer's examination ought to have revealed.
      ii. The goods are reasonably *fit for their purpose*, except where the circumstances show that the buyer does not

rely, or it is unreasonable for him to rely, on the skill and judgment of the seller.

d. By S.15 in a sale by *sample* there are implied conditions that the bulk will correspond with the sample and that there are no defects which would not be apparent on a reasonable examination of the sample.

3. A *reservation of title clause* in a contract will state that the property (ownership) in the goods will not pass to the buyer until the goods have been paid for, or some other contract conditions have been satisfied. This will protect the seller should the buyer go into liquidation, since the seller will be able to recover the goods. This is preferable to joining trade creditors in their claims against the assets of the company.

4. To succeed in a negligence claim the plaintiff will have to establish a number of facts, in particular they will need to prove that the defendant was at fault i.e. that the defendant did not act as a reasonable person would have acted in the particular situation. In a product liability claim against a manufacturer there is no need for the plaintiff to prove that the manufacturer was at fault or was unreasonable in any way. The plaintiff will need to show that:

a. The product contained a defect.
b. That he suffered damage.
c. That the damage was caused by the product, and
d. That the defendant was a producer, 'own brander' or importer of the product.

5. There are several reasons why it is important to know the time at which the property in goods (i.e. the title) passes. The main reason is that risk passes with the property. Thus if the goods are damaged it is the owner who must bear the loss. Another reason is that once the property has passed to the buyer, the seller can sue for the price.

6. A *lien* is the right to retain possession of goods (but not to re-sell them) until the contract price has been paid. The unpaid seller's lien is for the price only, it does not enable the seller to retain possession for any other purpose, for example to recover the cost of storing the goods during the exercise of the lien.

Chapter 26

1. When a person buys goods on *hire purchase* the shopkeeper will sell the goods to a finance company, not the consumer. The finance company will then hire out the goods to the consumer in return for hire purchase payments. When the consumer has paid all the instalments he will exercise an option to purchase the goods, usually for £1. Until this has been done the goods belong to the finance company, so if the consumer attempts to sell the goods no title will pass.

2. The consumer may *terminate* a consumer credit agreement at any time by giving written notice to the person authorised to receive payments. The consumer must pay amounts already due, plus the amount, if any by which one half of the total price exceeds the total money already paid, or such lesser amount as may be specified in the agreement. If the agreement attempts to impose additional liability on the consumer the term will be void.

3. A consumer credit agreement is *cancellable* if it was signed by the consumer at a place other than the place of business of the owner, creditor or any person acting on their behalf. It is basically intended to give people who are pressured into signing agreements at their own home, a 'cooling off' period during which time they may reconsider their purchase.

4. Goods purchased on hire purchase become *protected goods* once one third or more of the total price has been paid. The creditor cannot recover possession of such goods except by order of the court.

5. If a consumer fails to make the agreed payments under a consumer credit agreement, the owner may apply to the court to recover possession of those goods. The court may make a number of orders, including a time order giving the consumer more time to pay.

6. To the nearest whole number the APR is 36%. If John had borrowed £1,000 on 1st January 1994 and made one repayment of £1,200 on 1st January 1995 the rate of interest would have been 20%, but it must be remembered that in this example John begins his repayments one month after he has taken out the loan. The APR calculation must therefore take into account the monthly reduction in the amount outstanding.

Chapter 27

1. The Data Protection Act applies to *automatically processed information*, i.e. information processed by a computer. It does not apply to information which is held and processed manually in ordinary paper files. The Act does not cover all computerised information, only that which relates to living individuals. There are also specific exemptions, for example personal data used for calculating and paying wages and pensions.

2. A data user's register entry will contain the data user's name and address plus:

    a. The personal data which the data user holds.

    b. The purposes for which it is used.

    c. The sources from which the data user intends to obtain the information, and

    d. The people to whom the data user may wish to disclose the information.

3. The Act gives various rights to individuals concerning personal data held about them. They have a right to compensation if damage has been caused by the loss, unauthorised destruction or unauthorised disclosure of personal data. They may insist that inaccurate data is corrected or deleted. They have a right of subject access i.e. a right to be supplied with a copy of any personal data held about them. In certain situations an individual may also complain to the Registrar.

4. The Data Protection Tribunal considers appeals by data users against the Registrar's decisions, for example his refusal to register an application or the service by the Registrar of an enforcement or de-registration notice.

5. A data user who fails to register as required by the Act commits a criminal offence. The maximum penalty is an unlimited fine.

6. If a data user fails to comply with the Data Protection Principles or other relevant legislation the Registrar may serve an enforcement notice requiring the data user to take specified action to comply with the particular principle. Failure to comply with an enforcement notice is a criminal offence.

Chapter 28

1. The *Office of Fair Trading* was set up in 1973 by the Fair Trading Act. Its main aim is to protect consumers by looking out for unfair and uncompetitive business practices and taking steps to correct them. The OFT has negotiated codes of practice with a number of trades. These codes set out consumer rights and what action to take in the event of disputes. The OFT does not have local offices and cannot deal directly with individual shopping problems.

   The OFT will keep a watch on trading practices and suggest changes to the law if it is unsatisfactory. The Director General of Fair Trading can take action against traders who commit offences or break obligations to consumers. The Director General can also refuse to licence anyone who is considered unfit to operate a consumer credit business. He also has powers to ban people from acting as estate agents and he can apply to the High Court to seek to ban misleading advertisements. Finally the OFT keeps a watch on monopolies, mergers and restrictive or anti-competitive trade practices. In some cases issues may be referred to the Monopolies and Mergers Commission for detailed investigation.

2. *Environmental health officers* normally work for local borough councils. Their job is to deal with food safety as well as to protect and improve the environment. They will inspect the places where food is handled, including markets, shops and restaurants to ensure that food is safe and prepared in hygienic surroundings. They also have power to deal with bad quality housing, air pollution, noise, pest control, working conditions and a number of other matters, for example mortuaries.

3. *The Consumers' Association* is funded through the subscriptions of its 800,000 members. Currently the subscription is £59 per year.

4. The *kite mark* is awarded by the British Standards Institute to indicate that a product has been tested and has complied with standards to do with safety, quality or performance.

5. The electricity industry is regulated by the Office of Electricity Regulations (OFFER). The gas industry is regulated by the Office of Gas Supply (OFGAS). The water industry is regulated by the Office of Water Supply (OFWAT) and the telecommunications industry is regulated by the Office of Telecommunications (OFTEL). Each is these bodies are independent of Government,

but were set up by Acts of Parliament in the 1980s. Their functions vary, but will generally cover matters of pricing, supply, quality of service and complaints.

6. The Parliamentary Commissioner for Administration (the Ombudsman) investigates complaints relating to the administrative acts of Government Departments, where the allegation is that an incorrect procedure has taken place. The Ombudsman will only act where there has been a complaint, there is no power to initiate investigations.

Chapter 29

1. A *monopoly* is deemed to exist if a company or group of companies controls at least one quarter of the national or local market for the supply of particular goods or services.

2. The *Monopolies and Mergers Commission* is an independent advisory body with no executive power. When a matter has been referred to the Monopolies and Mergers Commission by the Director General of Fair Trading or the Secretary of State for Trade and Industry, the Commission will report to the Government whether the monopoly or merger situation operates against the public interest and it will make recommendations. The public interest is defined by reference to a number of factors, but the emphasis is placed on the need to promote competition.

3. Restrictive trading agreements are agreements by which producers, suppliers or exporters restrict the manufacture, supply or distribution of goods by, for example, setting minimum selling prices or agreeing to regulate the supply of goods or services. The general rule is that a restrictive trade agreement is presumed to be invalid, as contrary to the public interest, unless the parties can justify the restriction before the Restrictive Practices Court.

4. Manufacturers can recommend minimum selling prices for their goods, but they cannot require their goods to be sold at a certain price.

5. There are eight 'gateways' in the Restrictive Trade Practices Act 1976. If an agreement falls within one of these gateways it will not be void. Three examples are given in paragraph 2.b. Two further examples are:

a. Agreements expressly authorised by statute.

b. Agreements between two parties for the use of patents, registered designs or trademarks.

6. A *merger* occurs when two companies join together under the name of one of them, or as a new company formed for the purpose. A merger may also be called an amalgamation. Mergers generally only take place where there is agreement between the directors of both companies.

A *take-over* is the acquisition by one company of sufficient shares in another company (sometimes referred to as the target company) to enable the purchaser to control the target company. Sometimes take-over bids are contested by the board of the target company and on some occasions rival bids are made for the control of the same company. A take-over differs from a merger in that both companies will remain in existence, unless at some future time the acquiring company decides to wind up the target company.

Chapter 30

1. The main aim of the European Union is to establish a common market where there can be free movement of goods, services, persons and capital between Member States. This should lead to development and expansion of economic activity and a general rise in standards of living.

2. In the early 1980s there was concern that the movement towards a common market was not progressing with sufficient speed. The EU Heads of Government therefore committed themselves to establishing a single market over a period expiring 31st December 1992. This commitment was enacted in the UK in the Single European Act 1986. This Act defines a single market as 'an area without internal frontiers in which the free movement of goods, persons, services and capital is ensured'.

The Act is intended to assist the free movement of goods by breaking down technical barriers (for example differing national product standards), national restrictions, subsidy policies and so on.

3. *Article 85* sets out in broad terms a prohibition on agreements which have as their object or effect the prevention, restriction or

distortion of competition within the Common Market. Four examples are given in paragraph 3.a.

4. *Article 86* prohibits any abuse of a dominant position within the Common Market, or within a substantial part of it, if such abuse may affect trade between Member States. Four examples of potential abuses are set out in paragraph 4.c.

5. The jurisdiction of EU legislation is limited to agreements affecting trade between two or more Member States. If a merger or restrictive trade practice affects only the UK market, it may only be dealt with by the UK courts.

6. A number of examples are given in both Chapter 29 and Chapter 30. These include for example:

   a. Abusing a monopoly position by selling at too high a price.

   b. Seeking to eliminate competition by selling at too low a price.

   c. Agreements to share markets or sources of supply.

Chapter 31

1. £1,000.

2. The High Court.

3. County court cases will be heard either by *Circuit Judges*, or by assistant judges known as *District Judges*. If the case is dealt with under the small claims procedure it will be heard by a District Judge.

4. If a small claim is disputed by the defendant, the District Judge may decide that a *preliminary appointment* to see the plaintiff and defendant is necessary. At the preliminary appointment the District Judge will read the claim and the defence and ask questions to see whether there is any possibility of settling the dispute. If it cannot be settled the District Judge will decide how the case should be dealt with and what documents or other evidence the plaintiff must provide for the arbitration hearing. The preliminary appointment will take place in private in the Judge's Chambers.

5. A defendant has 14 days to reply to a summons. If the defendant does not reply the plaintiff should ask the court to send the defendant an order to pay the money that is owed. This is called

'*entering judgment by default*'. The plaintiff makes the request by filling in the form attached to the notice of issue (form N205A).

6. If the Judge is undecided about the evidence, the defendant will win the case. In all court actions there is an obligation on the person bringing the action to prove their case. In a civil action the plaintiff must prove the case on the balance of probabilities. In a criminal case the burden of proof is much higher and the prosecution must prove their case beyond reasonable doubt.

Index

GNVQ Advanced Business

S Danks

Based on the author's very well received A Level/GNVQ text published in October 1993, this text is aimed solely at GNVQ Advanced Level. It is organised by the eight mandatory units, and takes account of the constuctive comments made by over 100 business studies lecturers in a recent survey of their requirements.

Contents: Business in the economy; Business systems; Marketing; Human resources; Employment in the market economy; Financial transactions and monitoring; Financial resources; Business planning; Core skills; Test papers.

1st edition • 400 pp (approx) • 275 x 215 mm
ISBN 1 85805 083 9

Business within Europe
For GNVQ Advanced Business

J Cordell

Written specifically for the GNVQ option, this new course text meets the requirements of all the awarding bodies (BTEC, RSA and C & G). It provides students with the basic knowledge content of the course and with the research and analysis skills necessary to discover the further information for their assignments.

Contents: Why Europe; Finding out about Europe; European society and business; Comparing markets; Some markets compared; Euro-pean marketing and the law; Move or stay? Future prospects; The thumbnail guide to Europe.

1st edition • 200 pp (approx) • 215 x 145 mm
ISBN 1 85805 084 7